LEMON-AID

'77 EDITION

Distributed exclusively in Canada by

MUSSON BOOK COMPANY,
30 Lesmill Road,
Don Mills, Ontario

Copyright, Ottawa 1976, held by Les Editions Edmonston Ltée

Bibliothèque Nationale du Québec
Dépôt légal - 4th trimestre 1976

LEMON-AID

Phil   Edmonston

TABLE OF CONTENTS

ACKNOWLEDGMENTS

I wish to thank all those persons who helped make this book possible. Special thanks is given to the Automobile Protection Association for allowing me to use much of its material.

Phil Edmonston
Montreal,
July 1976

PREFACE

Why a book on cars? Consider the following facts.

More cars are born in Canada every year than people - in some senses, it is probably a blessing that they do not last any longer than they do.

More people between the ages of 1 and 33 die in or because of automobile collisions than for any other reason.

In fact, traffic fatalities constitute the largest cause of violent death to people of any age. It is said that the automobile has been responsible, directly or indirectly, for the deaths of more than 25 million people since its invention, a toll exceeding the population of this country.

Except for a home, the automobile is likely to be the largest single purchase any Canadian will make... and, because of the motor vehicle's short life span, the probability is that most Canadians will buy more than one. Not only do cars not survive long but they are also replete with defects, both of a safety and a performance nature. A staggering percentage of cars built or sold in Canada and in the United States over the last decade have been recalled.

Furthermore, the automobile industry is one of the largest advertisers in North America. In the United States alone, it is estimated that "The Big Three" spent $350 million in the media in 1974.

Canadians are bombarded by commercials and advertising messages emanating from both sides of the border. To know that their contents could be believed would be comforting but the relation to reality is slim.

We were told about the tests the Firenza was put through at GM's tough "Punishment Park" and we all know how it fared on less gruelling Canadian highways. After the release of internal Ford company documents mentioning that its cars were suffering rust problems one to two years earlier than their competitors, Ford engaged in an anti-corrosion emphasis advertising campaign without having assisted the owners of earlier Ford vehicles suffering corrosion problems. To top that off, owners of some 1975 and 1976 vehicles manufactured by Ford were already undergoing corrosion problems despite the advertising.

What about the recent spate of m.p.g. advertising which stresses fuel savings? The industry-wide campaign is terribly misleading to consumers who can scarcely hope to achieve results which remotely approximate those used in most of the advertising.

The Department of Consumer and Corporate Affairs itself has pointed out the following criticisms of the program:

1. No consideration is given to factors of wind, weather, road construction, use of radial tires, drivers' good or bad driving habits, etc.

2. The "highway" test average speed is only 49 mph.

3. The tests are made in a laboratory, not on the road.

4. The test fuel used is lead free 100 Octane Super Premium, a brand not generally available to motorists.

5. It may be possible for manufacturers to tune their test cars to perform better on the dynamometer than in actual driving conditions.

6. The EPA uses a complex chemical computation based on an analysis of the exhaust to calculate fuel economy... (which) may produce fuel economy results up to 5% higher than other methods. Where this discrepancy does exist, it is magnified when converted from the small U.S. gallon to Canadian imperial gallon.

To all of these criticisms we could add the fact that, whatever value the EPA figures may have is confined to their presentation as a total list so that the consumer may refer to the results on a comparative basis. When they are used in isolated fashion, as they generally are by Canadian advertisers, they cease to have any meaning at all. They merely mislead.

The automobile is also the source of more frustration than any other single consumer commodity. Almost any consumer protection office or consumer association which takes complaints from the public, has the automobile at the top of its list. In fact, as a general rule, these consumer complaints demonstrate a heightened sense of frustration, even an agonizing desperation on the part of the writer, who generally does not know where to turn.

And the reason for the frustration is real. Most car manufacturers want to have as little to do with the consumer as possible after he has bought the product. Oh, they profess otherwise, but generally do nothing.

The frustration results, in small part, from the fact that the purchaser knows so little about the technical aspects of the automobile (which has, in any case, become so much more complicated a machine over the course of this century).

In larger part, the frustration results from the stonewalling the owner receives from his manufacturer and dealer who take advantage of him at every turn. They disclaim responsibility for defects, blaming them on consumer misuse. They hide their own errors, refusing to disclose those having nothing to do with safety **since no law obliges them** to order a recall for **performance-related** defects.

Ten years ago, the consumer would have been at a dead end. No was no.

What we have come to learn through the work of Ralph Nader, Phil Edmonston and others is that the problem or defect is as likely to be found at the doorstep of the manufacturer as not and that it is possible to fight City Hall or General Bullmoose. That is, after all, what they have done, as have thousands of consumer complainers and litigants. You can do it as well.

That is the point of the book. Its author advises you on how to avoid the problems in the first place and what to do when you can't. His first piece of advice is probably the soundest; namely, don't buy a car if you can help it, since, when you do, the sticker price does not begin to represent the cost, both to you and to society, of your decision.

If you must, then Phil Edmonston recommends that you buy a used one. The theory of recycling is as useful here as anywhere. In any case, whether you buy new or used, you can rest assured that you will have problems sooner or later and Phil is the expert on the art of complaining. He coined the term "corporate ju-jitsu" and certainly wears the black belt in the art. He can tell you which consumer pressure tactics are likeliest to work, and when and where they should be applied. His roadside manner is unequalled.

The book will also provide insights into the confidential documents which companies are so unwilling to disclose and the practically unknown warranty extensions for Datsun, Toyota, Honda, Volvo, Volkswagen, Audi, Mazda and others, as well as the list of recommended and non-recommended dealers from coast to coast culled from the files of thousands of Rusty Ford Owners and others.

Finally, when all else fails and you have to go to court, Phil will tell you how, from a layman's point of view. And Phil has been in the courts on a regular basis for the last six years — as a catalyst, as an expert witness, and yes, as a defendant! Phil's efforts have obviously made some headway for he has been sued by automobile manufacturers, dealers, companies in related fields, and even by an insurance company - the Good Hands people.

But, the best of the plaintiffs is Nissan (Datsun), which has sued Phil twice for a total of $4 million, thereby fulfilling in Canada for consumer advocacy the role which General Motors played in the United States for Ralph Nader in keeping consumer advocates in the public eye. And, in this case, Datsun's folly is the public's benefit.

If, like Phil, you begin this book with the idea and knowledge that every car has a little lemon in it, then, by the time you finish it, you may learn how to squeeze back!

RONALD I. COHEN
APPEL GOLFMAN COHEN & COOPER

MONTREAL, JULY 7, 1976

INTRODUCTION

WHAT IS THE APA?

The Automobile Protection Association is a non-profit, public-interest, consumer corporation founded 7 years ago to bring the powers of honest lawyers, mechanics, and journalists to the aid of motorists victimized by fraud or mechanic incompetency.

Corporate Ju-Jitsu to Make the Seller Beware
Every motorist's complaint goes through a committee of mechanics for verification, a publicity committee that exposes the dishonesty as a warning to the public, and a legal committee that uses ordinary laws in extraordinary ways to resolve the dispute.

If fraud or incompetency has been proven to exist, in a franchised gas station or within a well-known new car dealership, the APA takes the complaint through its three regular committees. If the garage or car dealer ignores the APA's demands for justice, a from of consumer corporate Ju-Jitsu is used by the Association. The APA may organize a boycott, press conference, picketing, or bring legal action all at once or spread the activities over several days.

APA Financing
The Automobile Protection Association is a non-profit, public-interest corporation financed in the following ways:

1. Selling of APA Publications *(Justice for the Exploited Motorist,* and *Lemon-Aid),*
2. Lecture, radio and television appearances.
3. $10 membership fees.
4. Government research grants.

Because the APA is independently financed, it is also independently controlled. No donations are accepted from private interests such as oil, automobile manufacturers or automobile insurance companies.

APA Membership

Motorists may join the Automobile Protection Association for a yearly membership fee of $10 and an annual renewal fee of $5.

For this membership fee, motorists receive the following services:

1. A list of recommended and dishonest garages across Canada.
2. Membership card.
3. Window sticker showing APA membership.
4. Legal assistance from APA lawyers or before the small claims court.
5. Association support in settling claims.
6. Automobile repair inspections and price verification.
7. Counselling from honest mechanics.
8. New car purchase counselling on price, warranty and defects.
9. Used car purchase counselling on list prices and repair costs.
10. Insurance counselling on best and worst firms.
11. APA consumer bulletins.

APA Accomplishments

Over the past 7 years, the APA has been involved in numerous successful skirmishes with giant corporations and government bureaucrats.

1. Exposed Esso diagnostic clinics.
2. Investigated license bureau bribery and incompetence.
3. Picketed many auto dealers.
4. Probed worthless gasoline and oil additives.
5. Pushed for increased school bus safety.
6. Demanded the recall of millions of defective cars.
7. Exposed up-dating import car fraud (old cars sold as new).
8. Recovered millions of dollars for cheated consumers.
9. Prosecuted thousands of auto dealers.
10. Lobbied for stronger consumer protection laws.

In the past 7 years, the APA has grown to over 5,000 members. More than $7 million has been recovered in helping some 100,000 motorists.

During the fiscal year 1974-1975 the APA was very active in expanding its membership, securing additional funding from the government, and lobbying both the federal and provincial governments for more effective consumer legislation. As a result of the APA's efforts the federal government has established a special automobile complaints unit in Ottawa, and the Quebec Provincial government has just tabled Bill #7 that replaces the old consumer protection laws that were enacted just 5 years ago.

The APA itself has undergone a maturing process. Personnel are now hired on a full-time basis, para-legal expert witnesses are better prepared by the APA professionals, and the Association has linked up with other consumer groups across Canada. This aspect alone has given the APA a national voice and increased its own credibility.

In the future, the Association will expand its para-legal representations to the small claims courts of other provinces, fight to establish either *de jure* or *de facto* class actions throughout Canada, and organize all Canadian consumers to fight for compensation collectively, whether it be for the premature rusting of Ford's products, the defective motors of GM's Vega/Astre, or the national updating fraud perpetrated by many imported car companies operating in Canada.

AUTOMOBILE PROTECTION ASSOCIATION
292 St. Joseph Blvd. West - H2V 2N7 - P.O. Box 117,
Station "E", Montreal
Tel: 273-2477 - 273-5318

Enclosed please find:
(   ) $10.00 first year membership fee
(   ) $5.00 annual renewal membership fee

Payable to APA. Do not send cash by mail.
(   ) cheque   (   ) money order

Information: (   ) in French   (   ) in English

IN BLOCK LETTERS:

NAME:..

ADDRESS:..

.... TEL:...................

AUTOMOBILE: Make ....

.... Model Year..............

....

....

....

....

....

THE INFERNAL COMBUSTION MACHINE

I bought a car from G.M.C.,
An Envoy sixty-nine.
The biggest pile of mobile junk
That e'er came off the "line."

I swear that it was conjured up
As some nightmarish dream.
No self-respecting engineer
Would want to take the blame

For putting so much shoddy trash
Into one single car,
Then marketing the ghoulish thing,
Some client's life to mar.

The generator was the first
To herald troubles on.
It left it's moorings on the block
Down Highway 401.

The windscreen washer pump packed up
Likewise the wiper too.
The signal lights were faulty, and
The gear shift stiffer grew.

Front wheels were loose, their studs replaced,
A tie-rod broke as well.
This could have caused a speedy trip
To heav'n or e'en to hell.

Within the first nine months that I
This car did drive around,
A plague of oil leaks pestered me
And numerous faults were found.

The valves were readjusted twice,
Two gaskets were replaced,
The dowell pin was modified,
Before leaks were erased.

The carburetor was at fault
Right from the very start,
And finally they had to put
A new 'kit' in this part.

An oft' repeated problem is
The lack of any heat.
It seems, to rectify this flaw,
Will be a major feat.

Accelerator sticking is
A fault yet to be quelled.
Just when I think I'm slowing down
I find I'm jet-propelled.

And two months after purchase there
Were leaks in the exhaust,
And then again at five months old
Another breach was closed.

Then noxious trouble hit the scene —
'Twas fumes in the inside.
They tried to tell me it was paint —
'Twas carbon monoxide.

Eight months went by before I knew
The nature of this gas.
I've never met such ignorance
Or negligence so crass,

As that displayed in Ottawa
By educated men.
'Twas I who had the trouble checked
And it was only then

That remedies to right the wrong
Were tried - e'en though they failed.
It took six months and new exhaust,
Before success was hailed.

Another gasket's been replaced,
Ignition coil besides;
Down in the steering column still,
A faulty bearing hides.

And if you tell those G.M. boys
You're sickened with their gear,
A nauseating stream of bilge
Will penetrate your ear.

If Madam has lost confidence
In G.M.'s pile of rubble,
There's nothing they can do to help
Alleviate the trouble.

They've got her cash, that's all they care;
Spare parts are cheap as dirt;
Replaced ad infinitum by
Some brain-washed G.M. squirt,

Whilst Madam's car is getting old,
A lemon all it's life;
A source of sheer frustration and
Of never ending strife.

Since she has not the gall to sell
And can't afford to keep,
This aggravating box of tricks,
This contumacious heap;

The 'thing' is for disposal now
To anyone who thinks,
He has the time and cash in hand,
To juggle with a jinx.

The present problems might have been
Designed for Winter kicks;
The heating system's on the blink,
Accelerator sticks.

The water pump has ceased to work,
The thermostat's no more:
And your guess is as good as mine
'Bout what may be in store.

Elizabeth N. Cook

CHAPTER I

THE GOOD, THE BAD
AND THE UGLY

CHAPTER I

NEW CARS: THE GOOD,
THE BAD AND THE UGLY

In the wheel-and-deal jungle of new car shopping, practically everyone who has ever bought a new car has been at least partially cheated. For example; a dealer may refuse to sell a new car for anything less than a few dollars under the "sticker" price and then turn right around and sell the same car a few minutes later to somebody else for hundreds of dollars less. It all seems very mysterious and illogical to most consumers. Imagine walking into a major department store and bargaining over the sales price of a new stove in the same manner as is done by most new car dealerships with new car purchasers. Chances are that the department store would throw you out.

But, the automobile business is different; it is still a maverick industry where honesty and full disclosure of essential consumer information has come only through very recent federal legislation in the United States. And, in Canada, the federal government, through its blind reliance upon the automobile industry's promises of voluntary regulation, has abandoned its consumer protection mandate and become a handmaiden to industry. So, with inadequate legislation for protection, the average new car buyer can only arm himself with solid facts, patience, and the suspicious nature of a Sherlock Holmes. This chapter will deal with the basic facts needed to buy a new car.

WHERE TO BUY?

When buying a new car, the most important factor in the purchase of an automobile is to select a reliable dealer. Try to purchase the car from a franchised auto dealer, since this gives the protection of somewhere else to complain to if there is no action on the dealership level.

Beware of automobile brokers that promise to sell a new car for less than the dealer's cost. Such a thing is impossible, although some legitimate companies such as Car-Puter Inc. can sell certain new cars for about $125 over dealer cost, plus shipping.

A dealer's reliability can be checked out through a variety of ways. A few calls placed with the local consumer protection agency or the clerk of the regional small claims court will usually turn up some leads. It is also a good idea to talk with old customers driving vehicles identified by the dealer nameplate on the rear trunk. If these customers have been treated fairly by their dealer, they will be glad to recommend him.

Generally, franchised new car dealers located in small suburban and rural communities are less prone to engage in all the nefarious tricks of the trade found elsewhere. Prices may be lower too, since overhead expenses are often much lower than in metropolitain areas. This may not be true, though, if the surburban or rural dealership has a low volume of sales and must make the maximum profit on each sale.

New car dealers selling more than one make of car can present special problems. Overhead expenses can be quite high and franchise cancellation by the manufacturer in favor of an exclusive franchise elsewhere is an ever-present threat. Parts availability may also be a problem since a dealer with two separate franchises must split his parts inventory and may have an inadequate supply of replacements parts on hand.

SELECTING THE RIGHT CAR

The new 1977 car models are definitely smaller, lighter, and more economical than previous post-1971 models. Prices, however, are generally $250 - $300 higher this year. Along with this price increase comes the disturbing realization that a deterioration of product quality has also become widespread. For example, the new Chevrolet Monza with the optional V-8 engine is so poorly designed that its spark plugs cannot be changed unless the motor is lifted part way out of its compartment. Because of this engineering goof, Monza owners may spend much more for their tune-ups than other motorists.

Consumers are spending more money for less car in 1977. The

industry is committed to reducing the size of its cars to reduce gas consumption. As a result, its standard models are returning back to the same size and weight they had in the early 1950's.

Criteria for Selection

Before visiting any dealerships, draw up a list showing those features most desired in the new car. This chart should prevent the salesman from loading down the car with useless and expensive optional equipment. Ideally, the following features should be stressed:

1. Vehicle should be in the compact or intermediate size category to allow for some fuel economy, comfort and collision protection.

2. Parts should be easily available at reasonable cost.

3. The dealership network must be widespread, well-trained, and experienced.

4. The vehicle should have a history of average or low depreciation with few exterior model changes each year.

5. Repairs should be easy to make at any independent service station.

6. Rusting should not have been a problem with previous models.

7. Eight cylinder engines should be avoided unless you plan to tow a trailer.

Vehicles equipped with catalytic converters may cause problems because they require that only unleaded gasoline be used. In addition, there have been reports of fires caused by the excessive heat produced by the converter. In fact, the U.S. Air Force now requires that cars equipped with catalytic converters be prohibited from airfields while planes are being fueled. And if that were not enough, John Moran, a U.S. Environmental Protection Agency spokesman, has admitted that a recent $3.5 million study shows that the converters will give off .05 grams of sulphuric acid per mile in a fine mist, and thereby could create a serious health hazard.

Tire selection is also a very important part of new car buying. Be suspicious of the factory installed tires that are standard with each new car. Consumers have complained that some car manufacturers install tires that are no more than over-sized rubber bands that may not last more than the first 5,000 miles. Consider paying the extra money for radial tires since they should make up their extra cost through a longer tread life, generally between 20,000 to 30,000 miles more than regular tires, increased gas economy, and better high speed performance. Before leaving the dealership, make sure there is a spare tire in the trunk that has not been used. Check the tread wear by inserting a quarter in the tread of the spare and comparing the depth of penetration with the tread on the remaining four tires. Please read page 23 before buying radial tires, however.

If a new car is purchased during the first few months of its official introduction, select the vehicle from those cars already in stock. This provides the opportunity to really examine the vehicle closely for transport damage and also to verify if all options are included. This verification should never be done on a rainy day or at night since many mechanical flaws such as oil leakage or premature rusting may be missed. Usually, the dealer will sell the cars in stock for a bit less than those cars that have to be specially ordered. Also, if the vehicle is ordered, there is a good chance the factory will goof on at least 10 percent of the options that were ordered. Sometimes, too, the vehicle may not arrive for 3-6 months after ordering and any subsequent price increases (usually about 3 percent) will have to be paid by the purchaser.

New cars purchased late in the model year should be specially ordered from the factory so as to minimize premature rusting and insure that the car is as "new" as possible.

The Perimeter of Protection
With the introduction in 1927 of front and rear bumper, side running boards, and simple fenders, a protective perimeter was formed to protect the car and its occupants. These basic parts did not readily relay damage from impacts to the adjacent area of the auto body and frame. Since then, however, the auto body proper has crept constantly outward toward the protective perimeter, and either diminished what protection there was, or done away with it entirely. The designers are creative enough to meet this challenge, but it has not been in the manufacturers' interest to cut down on the high profits realized from repairs to cars that are easily damaged.

Now we come to the art of dangerous designing. If an automobile engineer set out to design an automobile with intentional built-in factors that would contribute to accident involvement and expensive repairs, here is what he would do in nine simple steps:

1. Give a large expensive expanse of glass but neglect to give wipers large enough to clean a safe portion of the glass in hazardous conditions.

2. Place all lights at such low levels on the car body that they are easily damaged by minor accidents and easily obscured by road dirt and spray.

3. Put the headlights in cavelike recesses so at night, or when there is limited visibility, they cannot be seen from the side by

other drivers. This will aid in snow collection around the lights and force the car owner to pay for side running lights also.

4. Complicate the headlight problem by installing concealling covers that are expensive to repair and can freeze closed tight under freezing conditions.

5. Put rear-view outside mirrors far enough away from the driver so that his field of vision is reduced, and no adjustment can be made from the driver's seat without expensive remote control options.

6. "Protect" the car with ornamental bumpers that only absorb 1 percent of the impact.

7. Give minimal or no protection to side door panels so that they are easily chipped when the door is opened or when another car touches them.

8. Construct "hidden" windshield wipers that get frozen into their cave-like compartments in winter, and get stuck up by leaves and other foreign matter in fall.

9. Construct "hidden" gas tanks that form part of the rear trunk compartment and may act as a "bomb" in rear-end collisions.

PAYING THE RIGHT PRICE

Don't place too much confidence in suggested retail prices. In the U.S., the federal government forces car dealers to display the suggested price on a sticker that is affixed to the window of new cars. In Canada, a more relaxed situation exists. However, no matter where you buy a car, remember that if the sticker says you pay $3,500, you can begin at that figure and reduce it, by bargaining, at least several hundred dollars.

Most new car salesmen are reluctant to give you the information on the amount of profit each car brings. It will be easy to find the dealer's profit, though, if you remember that the following percentages usually apply:

Luxury (fully equipped) Models	27 percent above cost
Standard	25 percent above cost
Compact	21 percent above cost
Subcompact	10-15 percent above cost

In purchasing a compact, for example, the sticker price may be $4,000 complete. Count on one-fifth, or about $800 going to the dealer. With this information, it should not be too difficult to arrive at a fair price that makes both **parties happy**.

15

Before going to the dealer, be sure to find out how much insurance and financing charges would cost from an independent agency. Many times the dealer gets a special extra 2-4 percent kickback when he has the customer insure or finance his car through the dealership.

Percentage of Accident-Involved Vehicles in which the most serious injury was fatal or serious

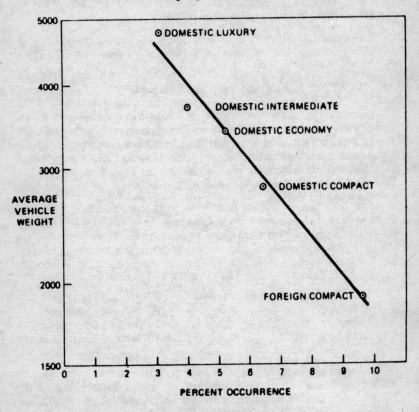

Source: New York State Highway Department Study Conducted For DOT

Customers who are on guard against paying too much for a new car often fall prey to the habit of selling their trade-in for not enough. So, consult one of the many used car guides that give used car values before agreeing to any trade-in deals.

Usually these books are difficult to acquire and car dealers seldom turn them loose. Some banks and insurance companies, though, keep copies on hand and allow consumers quick access to them.

New car prices are lowest during the first three months of winter. And, if the weather has been especially bad, the prices will be even lower. It's best to visit the dealership late at night since the salesmen will be more flexible in negotiating prices and more prone to be worn down by the slightest sales resistance.

Try to visit the dealership near the end of the month. During this period the salesmen must achieve their monthly quotas to be eligible for special sales bonuses. Even if there are no bonuses, most salesmen will want the extra sale posted just to show the boss a better monthly performance.

SIGNING THE CONTRACT

If there ever is a single most important rule with contracts, it should be never to sign a contract lacking in any details or one which is blank. Check the contract to see if the financing is being done by the company you have chosen, and for the monthly payments agreed upon. If the salesman offers to meet your demands, pencils your demands into the contract, then says he will get the boss's approval **after** you sign, you had better be careful. Get the approval **before** signing the contract.

Another rule to remember before signing the sales contract, is never take any verbal promises from the salesman concerning the car. This is especially true of your car's trade-in value. Many salesmen may quote a fantastic price for Old Nellie, but after signing, you may discover that "the boss refused to approve" the salesman's high quote for the car. Is the contract invalid after a trick like this? Very seldom. Any agency using this trick will have all the legal right to enforce the contract signed. Read the entire contract and force the salesman to list completely in the contract all the obligations of both parties.

Perhaps it would be best to make clear at this point that not all new car dealers are crooks, or shady operators. Many new car dealers are active, respected members of the business and social community. The salesmen working for them may own their homes and have been working successfully for many years. Practically every salesman has had extensive training in the correct sales techniques to apply with most customers and legitimate sales techniques are good for the industry.

A line must be drawn, though, against those sales tricks that just waltz on the borderline of fraud. For your assistance, here is a list of the most popular and objectionable sales tricks used by most new car dealers.

Highballing — the dealer quotes a low price no other dealer can match, then after you sign, he "discovers" he has made a mistake.

Easy Credit — credit is never "easy." If the payments are small, the interest is high, or else you will have a big last payment.

Selling Below Cost — no dealer will sell below cost. He can always sell to a used car dealer for a $25-$50 profit.

Buy at Once — don't let the salesman convince you that you must buy right away. Always compare several dealers' prices.

No Cash Deals — if the dealer is pushing credit that is not needed, chances are he is aiming at making a double profit; one on the car sale, and the other on the financing charges.

Bait Advertising — this trick is used to advertise a phoney deal to lure customers into the showroom so they can be sold on the regular car models.

Miscellaneous — stay away from salesmen who slip a note under the wiper blade of your car quoting an irresistible price for your car. Many times these salesmen act as private parties just to fool you into trusting them. This type also loves to make use of phrases as "wholesale," "demonstrator," or "repossessed." Demand proof for every important claim made.

CANADIAN

DEALERS AFTER SALE SERVICE

Makes	Quality of service	Adequacy of Repairs	Availability of parts	Fairness of charge	Courtesy of dealer
AMC	+	A	—	+	+
AUDI	—	—	—	—	A
BMW	++	++	A	A	++
BUICK	+	A	A	A	A
CADILLAC	++	A	A	A	A
CHEVROLET	--	--	A	--	—
CHRYSLER	—	--	—	--	—
CITROEN	A	A	—	—	—
DATSUN	A	—	A	—	A
DODGE	--	--	A	--	—
FIAT	--	--	--	--	--
FORD	—	—	A	—	—
GMC	A	A	A	A	A
HONDA	++	++	A	++	++
INTERNATIONAL	—	—	—	A	A
JEEP	—	—	—	+	+
LINCOLN	+	+	+	A	A
MAZDA	--	--	—	--	A
MERCEDES BENZ	—	—	A	—	A
MERCURY	—	—	A	—	A
OLDSMOBILE	A	A	+	—	A
OPEL	A	A	A	A	A
PEUGEOT	A	—	A	A	A
PLYMOUTH	A	A	A	A	A
PONTIAC	A	A	A	A	A
PORSCHE	A	A	—	—	A
RENAULT	—	A	+	—	—
TOYOTA	--	--	+	--	A
VOLKSWAGEN	—	--	--	—	+
VOLVO	--	--	A	—	A
BRITISH LEYLAND*	--	--	—	—	A

*British Leyland products included the Austin, Rover, Triumph, MG, Jaguar.

++Much better than average
+ Better than average
A Average
—Worse than average
--Much worse than average

THE PSEUDO-EXPERTS

Consumers looking for objective, useful information to help them choose a new or used car will find that the automobile industry has a strangle-hold on the media, with few exceptions.

Car Columnists

Take car columnists, for example. Many major newspapers across North America offer their readers information of special appeal to automobile enthusiasts by employing an automobile columnist. Theoretically, this idea is a good one, and the stated purpose of informing the motoring public is to be encouraged.

However, in practice, most North American car columnists do nothing more than re-write and publish the constant stream of biased and misleading press releases emanating from the automobile industry. Very little investigative reporting is carried out because that type of public interest journalism does not sell advertising, takes considerable effort, and will result in the drying up of information sources within the industry.

It is important to note that car columnists do not carry much respect within their own profession. They generally rank a little below travel columnists and barely above the daily horoscope in importance. One of the few times a car columnist is noticed is usually around late September or in the spring when new models are being introduced and newspaper publishers fall over themselves trying to get a piece of the advertising pie.

Automotive executives find car columnists useful for giving the automobile industry a respectable image and for defending the industry from attacks by public-interest consumer groups. In this context the columnists do their jobs well.

For example, what automobile columnists have criticized GM for its failure to provide Vega owners with adequate compensation to cover constant motor and fender replacements on its 1971-1974 models? Or, why did **Automotive News** run a front page story quoting GM executives who admitted the 350 and 400 series automatic transmissions were defect-prone and would be guaranteed for 50,000 miles and then refused to follow up on the story when GM officials later denied the claims and consumers were forced to seek compensation before the small claims courts? The Ford Motor Company has been particularly adept at using the press to "stonewall" inquiries, and mislead the American public. Henry Ford II recently summed up his own personal opinion of the public's right to be informed in the following dispatch from the Associated Press:

Ford's Idea:
Keep Quiet

"Never complain, never explain," Ford Motor Co. chairman Henry Ford II says of his weekend arrest and subsequent fine for drunken driving in California.

With that short comment, the auto chief chuckled and headed for an industry banquet last night in Detroit where he received a 30-second standing ovation from nearly 3,000 beginners.

Ford was charged in Santa Barbara, Calif., with drunken driving after his arrest in a car Saturday night with a companion, Kathleen Duross, a shapely 35-year-old Detroit model and interior decorator.

Municipal court judge Arnold Gowann's sentence was a fine of $375, the amount Ford posted as bond after his arrest, a suspended 35-day jail sentence and two years probation."

This policy of stonewalling public inquiries has been used often by the Ford Motor Company in the cover-up of its premature rusting problems with its 1969-1973 models. In the political context, investigative reporting would blow open Ford's rust cover-up, but in the automotive trade journals and among most car columnists the dictum "Never complain, never explain," becomes the golden rule.

Car columnists are also great moochers. They are given all the latest new models to test drive and continue to get these free cars as long as their reports are favourable. It's not surprising to see how car columnists quickly learn the art of superlative description for mediocre models, and become masters of the understatement when describing "lemons."

Travel junkets are another fringe benefit most automobile columnists receive from the industry. Although, many of the more reputable national newspapers have made rules prohibiting industry-paid junket traveling, most newspapers still allow the practice. This is one reason why the major automobile manufacturers choose exotic vacation spots to wine and dine the car columnists at the annual press preview of new models.

Published Car Tests
A lot of popular car magazine and so-called car experts make use of some pretty effective gimmicks like the "Car of the Year" ploy, or extensive articles describing the driving advantages and disadvantages of the new cars marketed each year. These reports are usually written around September or October of each year so as to coincide with the lucrative advertising that most companies place in their favorite journals. Actually these supposedly independent car tests are a lot of baloney.

Automobile testing done by most popular car magazines is carried out over the period of a week or two. The car is supplied by the manufacturer and tuned to just the right specifications. Of course, the dealer's servicing of the vehicle will be impeccable. Finally, the manufacturer will probably load the car with an assortment of expensive options to compensate for any of the vehicle's obvious faults.

With this rigged test, the car maker cannot lose. And especially if the tester wants other free courtesy cars to test, the published report had better gloss over the more obvious vehicle defects, and treat in the superlative some of the car's more mediocre features. Also, if the magazine or newspaper receives advertising from the manufacturer, any criticism that gets through the driver's own self-censorship will be muted by the editor. Another very important reason for discounting these tests is that they cannot predict a car's vulnerability to rust and poor servicing.

The "Car of the Year"
This has been used so often that it has started to get out of hand. Just this year, **Motor Trend** decided to choose 10 cars of the year as a special bonus to its subscribers. Even the automobile industry's trade paper **Automotive News** had to step in with an editorial blasting the whole concept of choosing a car of the year. In essence the criticism of the practice centred on the fact that different drivers have different needs and appreciate cars on a purely subjective basis. Therefore, every car ever produced could be the car of the year for somebody. In conclusion, the best place to look for new and used car ratings is the April edition of **Consumer Reports** or **Lemon-Aid.**

NO "NEW" CARS

There is no guarantee a vehicle is really "new", since the dealer may have disconnected the odometer and used the car for several thousand miles as a "demonstrator" for his customers' or staff's private use. Even if the car has not been used, it may have been left out-of-doors for a considerable length of time. New cars left outdoors often deteriorate as rapidly as a used car driven on a daily basis. In fact, most new car dealers have to keep their cars running periodically to prevent the rusting of internal mechanical components. Nevertheless, rust will attack any new car that is left outside for more than a few weeks. Often gas lines will be clogged by particulates formed by the rusting of the gas tank interior. This can lead to complicated motor problems.

SAFETY-RELATED DEFECTS

Since 1966, more than 47 million automobiles have been recalled by both federal governments for the correction of safety-related mechanical defects. Statistics show that most recall campaigns only succeed in reaching about 70 percent of those vehicles needing correction. Therefore, it is a safe bet that many of the used cars offered for sale both privately and by dealers are potential time bombs if their hazardous defects have not been repaired.

Once a car is recalled, the manufacturer is obliged to repair that vehicle regardless of the number of prior owners, or mileage, or time in service. Remember, automobile repairs are expensive enough without paying for repairs that are the manufacturer's responsibility.

Anyone wishing to check out whether or not a used car has been recalled should write **The Director, Road and Motor Vehicle Traffic Safety, Ministry of Transport, Ottawa, Ontario, K1A 0N5.**

Radial Tire Alert
Radial tires are a good investment for new car buyers expecting to keep their car a minimum of 5 years with an annual mileage of 10,000 miles or more. Nevertheless, some radial tires presently on the market may be hazardous and should therefore be checked carefully before being put in service. The best method for verifying the safety and reliability of a radial tire is to write **The Director, Road and Motor Vehicle Traffic Safety, Ministry of Transport, Ottawa, Ontario, K1A 0N5.**

Because of their proven incidence of tread separation and defective construction certain Firestone, Goodyear, and Uniroyal radial tires should be carefully examined before being driven at high speeds. In many tire tests carried out by both private and public agencies Michelin tires have performed exceptionally well. However, these tires may be especially vulnerable to sidewall damage from side impacts on curbs, etc.

TIRE COMPLAINTS

Transport Canada received and investigated 162 complaints about automobile tires for the twelve month period ending March 31, 1976.

The investigations led to the recall of 102 cars by Ford and 14,666 cars by General Motors.

During the same period, a further seven recalls involving 4,700 vehicles were initiated by tire manufacturers.

Transport Canada inspectors took 44 samplings involving a total of 1,716 tires and subjected them to high speed laboratory testing. Failures were recorded in two samples.

With the recent high volume sales of steel belted radial tires, much of the testing involved this type of tire. The department confirmed that this type of tire offers better traction and durability than standard tires, and can increase gas mileage.

The Motor Vehicle Tire Safety Act, requiring replacement tires to comply with the same safety standards as tires on new cars, is expected to take effect later this year. Transport Canada says it will continue to monitor tire manufacturers through public complaint investigation and a program of tire testing.

Tires manufactured according to the Canada Motor Vehicle Safety standards are safe only if they are properly installed and maintrained according to the vehicle owner's manual.

All the tires on a car should be the same size and construction. Mixing different sizes and types of tires (bias ply, bias belted and radial) can make the vehicle dangerously unstable, particularly at high speeds.

Tire pressures should be checked at least once a month and during extreme fluctuations in weather temperatures. Inflation pressure should be measured when the tires are cold. An accurate pocket tire pressure gauge used first thing in the morning before setting out will indicate if adjustment is necessary.

Additional pressure, as specified in the vehicle owner's manual (usually four pounds), is essential for full-load and high-speed driving. Incorrect tire pressure will adversely affect the handling of a car and can lead to increased tire wear and possible premature tire failure.

Tires should be checked regularly for road wear and damage. Insufficient tread depth is both illegal and highly dangerous since it greatly reduces the tire's grip in wet or slippery conditions. Uneven tread wear indicates that repairs or adjustments to the car's suspension system may necessary.

Vibration or shaking is usually an indication of a tire problem. Wheels should be balanced and tires examined for damage, including tread separation, cracks, or bulges in the side wall, and losses of chunks of rubber from the tread. If damage is suspected, tires should be replaced or examined by an independent expert. Don't take defective tires back to the manufacturer. They may never be seen again.

The most demanding situation for tires is holiday driving, often at full load and for long distances at high speeds in hot weather. Tires should be checked carefully before setting out, and during the trip.

Motorists or other interested persons are requested to advise Transport Canada, the tire manufacturers, and the Automobile Protection Association of any tire safety problems.

If a tire manufaturer refuses to replace for free a defective tire or disclaims responsibility for damages caused by the tire, contact the Automobile Protection Association, the clerk of your local small claims court, or a lawyer.

TIRE COMPLAINTS, TESTING RESULTS AND RECALLS BY TIRE MANUFACTURERS

	Public Complaints	Compliance Test Samples (39 tires per sample)	Test Failures	Tires Recalls	Number of Vehicles Recalled
BRIDGESTONE		2			
DAYTON	1				
DUNLOP	2	3			
FIRESTONE	30	10		3	4,130
GENERAL	5	5		1	61
GOODRICH	5	3		1	500
GOODYEAR	69	16	2	3	14,774
MICHELIN	3	1			
TOYO	1				
UNIROYAL	27	4			
UNKNOWN	18				
TOTAL	161	44	2	8	19,465

CHRYSLER INTER COMPANY CORRESPONDENCE

TO: ALL DISTRICT SERVICE MANAGERS

SUBJECT: CORDOBA/CHARGER SMOOTH
ROAD RIDE COMPLAINTS

Goodyear and Chrysler Engineering are co-operating in an indepth investigation of the subject condition. It is to the advantage of all concerned to persevere for a short time when a field service procedure will be made available.

Until the full procedure is released, most of the complaints can be resolved by what will be Step #1 of that procedure, namely the tire/wheel runout and balance correction procedure outlined in the attached Newsletter, No. 133.

These steps should be carefully followed by dealers that you select, where properly trained personnel and equipment are available.

After following this procedure, if tire(s) are isolated as a primary cause, the dealer should make contact with his tire manufacturer's store for additional assistance.

If after their assistance a problem still exists, your personnel should become involved.

KNG/bm   K.N. Gilboe
Attach.

1976-1977
PRODUCT CRITICISM

GENERAL MOTORS

With its 1977 models, General Motors is still the largest United States automobile manufacturer with the largest number of different models on the world market. The company's cars and dealers can be found in almost every country in the world. In Canada, GM has captured almost 60 percent of the new car market.

GM makes better 1970-1977 model cars in the intermediate, full-sized, and luxury range than any other American car manufacturer. It also has a reputation for making the self-destructing 4-cylinder sub-compact cars such as the Monza, Vega, Astre, etc. GM's compact cars, such as the Nova and Acadian have an average frequency of repair history up to the 1977 models.

1977 Model Defects
The most serious re-occuring defects found in the 1976 and 1977 intermediate, full-sized, and luxury GM models concern the premature rusting of the doors and fenders on Cadillacs, Oldsmobiles, and Buicks, and defective automatic transmissions affecting the 350 and 400 transmission series on the 1975 models. Almost all new GM cars have severe paint problems. The paint just lifts off the metal and gives the car an acne appearance.

For 1975 and 1976, GM's 4-cylinder sub-compacts generally suffer from a chronic lack of quality control affecting the motor, transmission, body, interior, suspension, and other mechanical components. The Vega and Astre, for instance, have been afflicted with premature rusting, and motor overheating from 1971 up to the 1975 model year. It's not surprising that many owners refer to their Vega as a "monster" and their Astre as a "disastre".

27

Warranty Performance

General Motors has been far from generous with consumers claiming repairs under its 12,000 mile/12 month warranty, and its defunct 5 year/50,000 mile warranty has been a cruel joke used to sell cars, not repair them. For 1976, General Motors has offered an extended warranty of 60,000 miles on its Vega and other 140 CID engines. Already some consumers have complained that this guarantee is not effective because General Motors has not improved the quality of its 1976 models.

"Secret" Warranties

Because of the large number of consumers complaining about their defective cars, GM has extended the warranty up to 5 years on motors of 1971-1974 Vegas and Astres and will also replace free of charge fenders which have rusted prematurely. The company has also secretly extended up to 50,000 miles the guarantee on its 350 and 400 series automatic transmissions covering the 1973-1975 model years. Unfortunately, GM does not guarantee the gas mileage advertised for its 1976 cars in the media. Thus, many consumers have complained of getting 30 percent less gas mileage due to the catalytic converter.

One of the most common problems associated with GM's 1976 models is the insufficiency of the interior ventilation in many of the large sized models such as the Monte Carlo and Le Mans. The ventilation problem may be caused by three design deficiencies; the fan used to recirculate interior air is too weak, the catalytic converter produces an excess of heat from the manifold through the entire exhaust system (this heat transfer is particularly felt along the front passenger side of the 1976 models) and the absence of side window vents to propel fresh air into the interior at low speeds.

Anyone buying a new 1976 General Motors intermediate or large model would be wise to test the interior ventilation before buying that particular model. Air conditioning is recommended for businessmen using GM's intermediate or large cars for business trips during the summer months. The air conditioning option is recommended only for businessmen, since the 20 percent increase in fuel consumption caused by the air conditioner can be deducted as a non-taxable expense.

Another common problem reported by consumers on the 1975 and 1976 General Motors models is the inadequacy of the "hidden" windshield wiper design on most General Motors cars this year. These windshield wipers are enclosed in cave-like recesses that serve as collectors for leaves, dirt, and snow that impair the functioning of the wipers and may cause the wiper motor to burn out completely. Also, a number of motorists have complained that the 1975 and 1976 model with the "hidden" wiper design does not permit the wipers to clean the windshield on the driver's left side, thus, leaving a foot wide band of snow and ice that creates a hazardous blind spot for the driver.

Many of the new 1977 models manufactured in September and October may be damaged in transit because of General Motors' rapid delivery of these models for their Canadian introduction. This problem of transit damage affects all models, however, the Ventura model appears to the most frequently affected with reports of water seepage occuring in the rear trunk areas. With the 1977 General Motors models, consumers should check the date of manufacture plate found on the door frame of the driver's door. This government-required plate will tell you how "fresh" your new '77 car really is in the same way as smart food shoppers will squeeze bread to determine its freshness. Any new intermediate or large model manufactured by General Motors is not recommended if its date of manufacture is before March.

Many General Motors customers have filed small claims lawsuits against the company due to the paint peeling of GM's Buick Century (1973-1976 models), Oldsmobile Cutlass (1973-1976), Cadillac (1973-1974), and Vega/Astres (1971-1974). More than 90 percent of the lawsuits filed in the Small Claims Courts in Canada have resulted in the customers receiving from $200-$300 compensation from the courts. General Motors has admitted that a special agreement has been reached between its dealers to give compensation for paint defects on those models already listed if those owners affected make a special request to the dealer. This "goodwill" warranty extension is completely up to the selling dealer and has been granted because of the poor quality paint and inadequate preparation of the affected automobiles.

GM's dealer network has been caught in a price-cutting squeeze. Dealers are getting smaller discounts when buying their new '77 models wholesale from the manufacturers. By trimming the dealer discount, General Motors has forced its dealers to push the sale of optional equipment, extra guarantees, financing, and insurance.

The dealer discount has been cut an average of 3.3 percent, and may average about $70 per car. For consumers, this means new car price bargaining will be tougher and will be played for smaller stakes, depending upon the model purchased.

'77 GM DEALER DISCOUNT CHART

MODELS	DISCOUNT
Small Cars	15 percent
Intermediates	19 percent
Standards	22-24 percent
Luxury cars	25 percent

Remember, the dealer's wholesale discount is a good indication of that dealer's profit, and when dealing with new car dealers, a smart consumer will try to bargain down the retail price by at least 10 percent on the intermediate, standard, and luxury-sized model cars. For small cars, most consumers can reduce the retail price by 5 percent excluding the optional equipment purchased.

Optional equipment is generally priced 50 percent above dealer cost, therefore you should offer to pay the suggested price less 20 percent. Be careful, however, that the optional equipment you order is the same kind that is actually installed in your car. It has been reported that some General Motors dealers have been selling car radios that were supposedly manufactured by Delco, but were actually inferior brands that were manufactured in Japan. This practice has become so prevalent that Delco has taken full-page ads in **Automotive News** to warn the public of this practice.

Nova

The Nova has received very few complaints from owners with its 1976 model except for heat problems with the catalytic converter. Because its exterior appearance has changed little during the past 3 years, the 1976 Nova depreciates very slowly. Service is easily obtained and parts are available at a reasonable cost through General Motors' extensive dealer network or from local junkyards. The interior space is adequate for small families, but the rear trunk space may not be adequate for the luggage of an entire family.

Monte Carlo

General Motors' 1976-1977 Monte Carlo is one of the best medium-sized cars available in America. Apart from some minor problems such as poor interior ventilation and inadequate windshield wipers, the Monte Carlo's frequency of repair record is better than other GM models. Depreciation is so slow that a "black market" has developed where some consumers are willing to pay exaggerated prices for a new or used Monte Carlo. However, some consumers have complained that the rear side windows are too small and thus create a hazardous "blind" spot for drivers using their rear-view mirror.

Chevrolet Corvette

As with the Monte Carlo, the Chevrolet Corvette will always remain a popular special interest sports car in North America. For this reason alone, the Corvette's annual depreciation rate is lower than that for other '77 models.

Corvette ownership has 3 serious disadvantages, however. Insurance is difficult to find at reasonable rates, specialized Corvette mechanics are difficult to find, and gas mileage is a nightmare. Because of these disadvantages, the Corvette is a recommended best buy only for businessmen able to deduct its high operating costs from their annual taxes.

Chevrolet Chevette

General Motor's Chevette for 1976-1977 is not recommended because of a number of consumer complaints concerning its poor gas mileage, erratic braking performance, and inadequate after sales service. The Chevette's metric calibration has also begun to create problems for mechanics at independant garages that do not have the required metric tools.

In Canada, both the Chevette and its sister model the Acadian sell for about $3,400 without the optional rear seat and about $100 more with the rear seat included. For this price, the Chevette is not as good a buy as competing Japanese and European models such as the front-wheel drive Honda and Renault 5.

Chevrolet Vega, Astre, Starfire, Monza and Skyhawk

These mini-compacts from General Motors all have the same things in common — a high retail selling price, inadequate interiors and trunk space, and persistent mechanical defects. The Vega and Astre models now have a 60,000 mile warranty covering motor defects. However, General Motor's failure to honor prior Vega warranties indicates that 1976-1977 Vega/Astre warranty extension may just be nothing more than a cruel publicity gimmick used to sell more cars.

GM's Monza, Starfire, and Skyhawk may also have problems with excessive gas consumption, suspension defects, braking difficulties, and a small engine compartment that can make routine motor repairs incredibly expensive unless you know a mechanic who is a midget.

FORD MOTOR COMPANY

The Ford Motor Company is the second largest American automobile company with approximately 25 percent of the domestic automobile market in North America. Ford's philosophy as stated by its founder, Henry Ford, was to provide cheap, efficient, and dependable transportation that the average worker could afford to buy. This philosophy resulted in the production of such automotive classics as the Model T and the Model A.

While Ford was selling its mass-produced, cheap and efficient vehicles, General Motors decided to compete by adopting bold annual styling techniques that made their cars radically different from one model to another and from one year to another. This marketing plan known as "Sloanism," after GM's president at the time, caught Ford by surprise and succeeded in making GM the largest selling car manufacturer in North America. In Canada, Ford has slipped to third place behind Chrysler, perhaps because of rusting defects.

Ford Defects
Recent Ford models have had serious defects affecting their transmissions (C-4 especially), 351 CID motors (premature wear of the valve guides), and the quality of paints used on their luxury cars.

Luxury cars such as the Thunderbird, Mark IV and Lincoln Continental have been especially affected by numerous defects affecting the electrical system, doors, body sealing, locks, suspension, etc. In fact, Ford's luxury cars have been so defect-prone, that they have often been called Ford's "luxury lemons." Ford's 1976 vehicles have been the subject of a misleading advertising investigation into consumer complaints about premature rusting.

Most Ford dealers and consumers will agree, however, that Ford's pre-1971 models were excellent buys. Models such as the Galaxie, Falcon, and Mustang were well-known for the quality of their engineering and the dependability of their performance. Unfortunately since that time, the quality of many of Ford's models has sharply declined. Presently, the Maverick and Mercury Comet are the best quality cars (except for severe rusting problems) one can buy.

Ford Rusting
Ford vehicles manufactured between 1969 and 1973 will rust one to two years earlier than cars made by its competitors. The rusting is severe and usually results in large perforations occuring along the doors, front fenders, hood, and rear end. After 3 or 4 years the rusting may make the car resemble a

giant Swiss cheese. Some consumers have joked that Ford's rusting problems are so severe that their cars are actually "biodegradable," that is, that they disappear a little bit each day. A U.S. Department of Transportation investigation has been initiated into catastrophic failures of the suspension system caused by the premature rusting which may affect the idler arm components. So far no defect has been found, however.

Warranty Performance
Next to Chrysler, Ford's warranty has the worst track record of all the American car manufacturers. This conclusion is reached as a result of the thousands of North American consumers who have been refused compensation for premature rusting, defective transmissions, and defective motors.

Actually, though, it has not just been Ford's refusal to compensate consumers that has provoked so much consumer anger and distrust. Ford's warranty credibility has been mostly harmed by its misleading statements dealing with the rust problem, its deceptive marketing of 1970 Cortinas as 1971 models (see **King** vs **Paddy Shannahan Ford,** or **Helene Brosseau** vs **Lewis Motors),** and Ford's misleading statements regarding the mileage performance of its new cars.

Ford Hidden Warranty Extensions
Because of Ford's numerous mechanical defects, since 1969 at least 33 "secret" warranty extensions have been carried out on its 1969-1973 cars and light trucks.

CHRYSLER

The third largest domestic automaker, Chrysler has just come out of a sales nose dive that almost destroyed the company. Chrysler vehicles are infamous for water leaks, premature rusting of the front fenders, braking defects, and a poor front suspension. Some owners of Chrysler's luxury models also report that the heating and air conditioning system is failure-prone.

Chrysler makes the best compact cars that can be found on the American market with its Volare and Aspen models (formerly Valiant and Dart). These two best selling models along with the new Cordoba have succeeded in saving the company from bankruptcy.

Warranty Performance
Chrysler has adopted a new 1976 model warranty which allows unlimited mileage during the 12 months that the car is guaranteed. This warranty would be really spectacular - if Chrysler did not have such a poor warranty record in Canada. Some of

Chrysler's dealers have had to be condemned before the small claims courts before they allowed certain repairs under Chrysler's new car warranty. Of the four American car manufacturers, Chrysler has had the most serious (Ford rusting excepted) warranty problems with its customers.

Cordoba

The Chrysler Cordoba is not recommended for 1976 or 1977. Customers have already begun to complain about poor paint quality and uneven paint application. Severe road vibrations are said to occur at speeds from 40 to 60 miles an hour. It has been reported that water seepage can appear in some of the 1976 Cordoba models manufactured in early September. And topping off the list of Cordoba problems are reports that the brakes may wear out prematurely and need replacement after little more than 5,000 miles. Before buying a Cordoba, it would be wise to try a 1976 Valiant Brougham demonstrator for much less, or a new Volare or Aspen.

Aspen/Volare

Consumers will not find many major changes in the 1977 Chrysler-Plymouth models except for the addition of a few minor body changes on the new Dodge Aspen and the Plymouth Volare. Both of these new models are relatively free from serious defects with the exception of some reports of rear brake lock-ups and motor stalling. Nevertheless, since this is only the second year these models have been presented to the public, it would be wise to test-drive your choice and make a detailed list of defects to be corrected before accepting delivery.

Dart/Valiant (Demonstrators)

Fortunately, Chrysler dealers may still have some 6 cylinder Dodge Darts and Plymouth Valiants. Both of these models get up to 24 miles to the gallon. There have been some reports of starting difficulties with the 1976 Dart and Valiant, but this problem does not appear to be widespread. Because the Dart and Valiant have changed their exterior appearance very little in 1976, body and mechanical parts are easily available and inexpensive.

Since the 1975-1976 Dart and Valiant models also have a solid reputation for durability, their rate of depreciation in 1977 is far less than similar cars of competing manufacturers. As a result, the Dart and Valiant are recommended best buys for consumers wishing mechanical dependability combined with interior spaciousness and good gasoline economy.

Colt/Cricket/Plymouth Arrow

Another excellent car buy is the 1976-77 Dodge Colt, Cricket, and Arrow brought over from Japan. These cars are extremely economical with low gasoline consumption and have been the object of few consumer complaints. The interior is spacious and the cars are easily handled in city traffic. There have been a few reported instances of parts shortages on the 1976 models, but this is not unusual for Japanese cars during the first few months of their introduction. Despite these minor shortcomings, these cars are considered excellent buys.

AMERICAN MOTORS

Since the launching of its Buyer Protection Plan in 1971, American Motors has eliminated most of the quality control problems found in its early models. In fact, all of its 1976 models are relatively defect free, except for some complaints concerning the Gremlin's drum brakes, excessive gasoline consumption, minor paint discoloration, rusting, poor interior finish and water leaks around the doors.

The quality of its dealer network, however, is American Motors' most vulnerable area. Because the Buyer Protection Plan gives extended protection from factory defects to all 1977 models, it is crucial that the selling dealer carries out the required pre-delivery inspection (P.D.I.) and subsequent warranty repairs in an honest, competent, and conscientious manner. Unfortunately, American Motors has been forced to sign up some dealers who have been rejected by other auto manufacturers. Therefore, it's not surprising to find consumers still complaining about defects caused by poor servicing or irresponsible dealership practices. Generally speaking, though, American Motors offers a better than average new car warranty for factory defects and another good warranty on dealership repairs.

Generally, the Matador and Hornet look to be the best buys for 1977 because of their parts availability, durability, and easy servicing. Both vehicles have adequate interior space. The Hornet interior does offer a bit more room, however.

The 1977 Pacer cannot be recommended as a good buy. Ziebart Limited has circulated a confidential warranty guide showing that the Pacer may be rust-prone because of certain design deficiencies. It is not known whether the 1977 Pacers will have similar design problems. It may be wiser to wait for next year's Pacer before taking a chance with the 1977 models. If a Pacer is purchased, demand a guarantee against premature rusting from the dealer. Other problems with the Pacer include sloppy interior finish, poor low-speed maneuverability and poor gas mileage.

RECOMMENDED MODELS 1976-1977

SUBCOMPACTS

Honda Civic
One of the least expensive subcompacts, the Civic has an excellent warranty, good dealership support, and very sophisticated engineering. Depreciation is slow. Parts availability is excellent. Check the date of manufacture on the driver's door; should be August 1975 or later. Some paint, motor, and starting problems reported. The Honda Civic is still an excellent urban car.

Dodge Colt, Cricket, Arrow
A subcompact with lots of interior room and baggage space. Very few major repairs have been reported. Parts availability and prices are reasonable. Gas mileage is excellent. Some rusting reported. Depreciation is slow. Dealership network and warranty performance by Chrysler is inadequate.

American Motors Gremlin
A car that looks like it was cut in half, the Gremlin is a good subcompact that is reliable and very durable. Gas mileage is not spectacular, though, and rear passengers may have insufficient space. The American Motors Buyer Protection Plan is better than the average warranty offered by the automobile industry. The dealer network needs improving. Parts are inexpensive, but may be rare because of recent strikes at American Motors.

Toyota Corolla
Good gas economy, low depreciation and excellent parts availability are the main characteristics of the Toyota Corolla. Motor and transmission parts may be expensive and failure-prone. Watch for premature rusting on the front fenders. Also check the date of manufacture.

Renault 5, Renault 12
The Renault 5 and 12 are two of the best performing and engineered subcompacts to be found on the market. With their front-wheel drive and radial tires they are virtual snow machines. Unfortunately, the cars' quality and reliability is almost wholly dependent upon the dealership's honesty and competency. Any bit of negligence in normal maintenance will quickly change these cars into "lemons." Depreciation is severe. Parts availability is good but some motor parts may be expensive. The dealership network across Canada is weak. Warranty performance is very mediocre. Be careful of premature rusting on doors, hood, and fenders as well as premature failure of the suspension system. Retail prices are too high. Renault will learn someday.

NON-RECOMMENDED MODELS
SUBCOMPACTS

General Motors Vega-Astre
Two of the worst cars on the market. Catastrophic motor failures, severe generalized rusting, and numerous safety-related defects are its best features. General Motors has not improved the motor or chassis for these 1976 models to the extent that these problems have been completely eliminated. Vega-Astre depreciation is very rapid, with some consumers only getting $500-$700 as a trade-in for the 1973 model. General Motors has refused to honor many rusting and motor claims under warranty. This is the perfect car for masochists or shy drivers wishing to meet people along the road.

Ford Pinto-Bobcat
Serious problems with corrosion and paint quality. Rapid depreciation. Gas mileage is not acceptable. Confidential Ford documents show the Pinto to be very trouble-prone from 1972-1974. There has been no confirmation that the 1975 to 1977 models have improved.

Fiat 124, 128 and 131
The Fiat is a great car. . . for Italy. But, in Canada, it has caused a considerable number of consumers much grief. the 1971, 1972 and 1973 128 models were recalled for premature rusting that could cause major suspension components to simply fall away. Dealership servicing and warranty claims are a nightmare. Depreciation is high. Parts availability is poor. Until proof of improvement is shown, the 1976-1977 models are not recommended.

Skyhawk/Starfire and Monza
Once again, GM plays its nasty little styling game of making three cars out of one. Only the most naive styling freaks would fall for this marketing gambit since both the Skyhawk and Starfire are copies of the Monza body style. With these models, General Motors continues its tradition of marketing subcompact "monsters" that are failure-prone, costly to maintain, and depreciate in value like last year's IOS stock.

Skyhawk owners report defects affecting brake wear, engine performance, gas economy, and severe front suspension vibrations between 30 and 50 miles per hour that makes steering difficult. Monza owners also complain of similar problems, but face the added problems of poor exterior finish (trim) and excessive engine noise. The Monza has also inherited the Vega engine, and this alone is reason enough to suspect the car's future reliability.

37

Capri 2

Touted by Ford as its "sexy European," traditionally, the reality of Capri ownership has been about as sexy as Robert Stanfield, for owners of earlier models. Interior space is inadequate, poor paint quality and premature rusting have been reported, service is costly, parts availability has been a chronic problem in the past and the same problem may loom ahead for the future. It appears that many Ford dealers prefer to stock up on the fast moving parts of the other Ford models that sell in greater numbers. The Capri's deficiencies are unfortunate because it is one of the few European models imported by Ford that looked promising. Should the rusting and servicing problems get sorted out, the Capri could become a great urban transportation vehicle.

Subaru

Plagued by a weak dealer network and inadequate parts supply, Subaru offers few exceptional features apart from its four-wheel drive model that is also offered by the competition at more competitive prices.

Datsun B-210

Datsuns have had a poor record for brakes and general rust resistance. Depreciation is average. Dealer network is inadequate. The B-210 has shown excellent gas economy. Unfortunately, parts availability and cost leave much to be desired and may continue to be a problem. Warranty performance also leaves much to be desired. No warranty improvements have been confirmed for the 1976-1977 models. The new F10 model is unimpressive.

Audi Fox/VW Rabbit, Scirocco, Dasher

Although these cars are not identical, their problems are. They are well-engineered cars that are not adequately maintained at the dealership level. Parts cost and availability may continue to be a problem with 1977 models. Depreciation is rapid. Volkswagen dealers gave much better service with the Beetle. The Rabbit should have been put in the pot a long time ago.

RECOMMENDED MODELS
COMPACTS

Plymouth Volare, Dodge Aspen, Valiant and Dart

The best compact cars on the market. Excellent quality, reliable, and inexpensive to service. Parts availability and cost is very reasonable. Don't depend too much on Chrysler's warranty; the warranty is seldom extended. Beware of Goodyear tire defects.

Ford Maverick and Mercury Comet

Two excellent Ford models that are essentially identical. They combine fair gas mileage with an excellent depreciation rate.

Parts cost is reasonable, with parts available at most dealerships. Some minor problems have been reported with the carburetor and brakes. Rusting is a serious problem and affects the whole car. These cars are not recommended for use in areas where corrosion is a problem in Ontario, Quebec, Nova Scotia and New Brunswick.

American Motors Hornet

An average car that has a better than average warranty. Periodic maintenance is inexpensive with good parts availability and low parts cost. Does not depreciate quickly. Choose the optional warranty extension. Dealer network a bit weak. Some paint and bumper defects reported.

NON-RECOMMENDED MODELS
COMPACTS

Ford Mustang II

Promoted as Ford's answer to the 1965 Mustang, the Mustang II has serious motor and suspension problems. Consumers have reported severe vibrations and poor gas mileage. No confirmation that premature rusting problems have been corrected.

Pontiac Ventura

Although similar to the Nova, the Ventura has had problems with paint quality, premature rusting, and poor body fits that allow water seepage. Poor gas economy is also a problem. As with most cars that use unleaded gas, the motor may be very noisy and subject to premature valve wear.

Volvo

Many complaints concerning motor, body, brakes, and suspension. No confirmation that the manufacturer has isolated and corrected these troubles. Volvo has extended its warranty to 36,000 miles. See Chapter V for a copy of the document.

RECOMMENDED MODELS
STANDARD

American Motors Matador

Good quality control and gas economy highlight this model. Small for a standard model. Passenger seating may be inadequate.

Buick LeSabre

The LeSabre has severe paint problems as do all new GM products. Avoid the catalytic convertor. Nevertheless, the LeSabre has an average frequency of repair record with most of the problems occurring with the transmission and motor.

NON-RECOMMENDED MODELS
STANDARD

Oldsmobile Delta
Transmission, rust-prone doors and front fenders, and severe paint problems are the main problems. General Motors has not extended guarantee for premature rusting. Transmission guarantee has been extended.

RECOMMENDED MODELS
LUXURY

Buick Riviera and Oldsmobile Toronado
Good quality control combined with a highly rust resistant body give added durability to these models. Toronado's front-wheel drive is very effective for driving in the snow. The chronic GM paint problem occurs in Toronados too.

Mercedes Benz
One of the best engineered cars around. However, the exhaust system is rust-prone and expensive to repair. Diesel models have more durable motors than other models. Depreciation is low.

NON-RECOMMENDED MODELS
LUXURY

Cadillac Seville, Eldorado, and De Ville
Since 1970, Cadillac's quality has declined due to inflation and mandatory emission control devices. Now, there are much better cars around in the $13,000 - $15,000 price range. The Cadillac has paint problems too.

Ford Thunderbird and Lincoln Continental
Ford's luxury lemons. Even Ford's own dealers complain about the traditionally poor quality of these two models.

RECOMMENDED MODELS
SPORTS CARS

General Motors Corvette
A reliable and very durable sports car. Depreciation is below average with an ever increasing number of used Corvettes being sold at high black market prices. A good new car investment. No paint problems.

NON-RECOMMENDED MODELS
SPORTS CARS

Triumph, Jaguar, MG
British Leyland may be on the brink of disaster. Poor warranty performance, unavailable parts, and expensive repairs are the most common problems.

CHAPTER II

USED CARS:
A FLIGHT TO FANTASY LAND

CHAPTER II

USED CARS:
A FLIGHT TO FANTASY LAND

WHY BUY A USED CAR?

A good used car should cost approximately $2,000, be no more than 2-4 years old, and give economical, reliable performance for at least 3 years.

The type of car referred to above is really not difficult to find. Depreciation is the primary factor for the low price of a two to four-year-old used car. Look at the following example of a typical new car purchase order and you will notice the enormous amount of money wasted when buying a new car.

Example 1: New Car Expenses
$4,000 Purchase price
$ 320 Sales tax
$ 730 Interest 16.8% (over 36 months on $3,000)
$ 125 Rustproofing
$5,175 Total cost

There are only two reasons for buying a new car; the manufacturer's guarantee and the prestige of possessing a new car. Unfortunately these two reasons do not stand up under close scrutiny.

Worthless Guarantees

New car guarantees seem to be intended to sell cars, not service them. In testimony before the United States Senate Subcommittee on Antitrust and Monopoly, auto industry spokesmen have repeatedly admitted that warranty work is refused by dealers because manufacturers fail to pay adequately for warranty repairs.

In one well-documented case presented before the Senate Sub-Committee on Anti-Trust and Monopoly, General Motors actually sent a confidential memo to all its dealers advising them to discourage warranty repairs unless the defects were safety-related.

Any consumer still not convinced that auto warranties are worthless should speak with any Vega or Astre owner. General Motors did nothing about the Vega and Astre's engine failures and front fender rusting until three years after the vehicles were purchased. Even now, owners are frequently turned away by dealers who refuse to fix these cars under warranty.

A used car purchase can be very economical. The following example shows why:

Example 2*: Used Car Expenses
$2,000 Purchase price
$ 160 Sales tax
$ 244 Interest 16.1 percent (over 36 months on $1,000)
$2,404 Total cost

Example 3: Comparison
$5,175 New Car
$2,404 Used car (2 years later)
$2,771 Total savings

It is evident that the average car buyer can save more than 50% by switching from a new car to a used car two years older. Of course, annual repairs will be necessary, but that would also be the case with a new car too. So, even by adding $200—$400 a year for repairs, considerable savings will still be realized.

Although used car prices are directly affected by the mileage a car has travelled, the importance of mileage in determining a used car's quality is overrated. Most car dealers figure 15,000 miles per year as average mileage for used cars, or a total life expectancy of only 100,000 miles for the car, before major repairs make selling the car unprofitable for the dealer.

---

*The $2,000 selling price is based upon a two-year-old vehicle that sold for $4,000 when new (see Example 1). Approximate mileage is 30,000 miles. Condition is average.

WHEN TO BUY

The best time to buy a used car is in the winter around January and February. It is also a good idea to visit the dealership just before closing. Since the dealer has very few customers this time of year, prices are very low. Also, when a customer arrives late at night, the dealer will want to make that one last sale to put him over the top of his quota if the day has been good. If the day has been terrible, with few customers coming in, the used cars failing to start, and snow covering most of the cars, the dealer will accept the lowest reasonable price just to encourage his salesmen to come back the next morning.

If no privately-owned cars are available, the next place to look is the franchised new car dealership. Many used cars are taken in as trade on a new car so there is a constant turnover of used cars available. Generally, a good new car dealership will not sell unsafe or poor quality used cars, prefering instead, to sell these cars at wholesale prices at different automobile auctions.

WHERE TO BUY

The most reliable and inexpensive used cars are sold mainly by private owners through newspaper classified ads. Prices are lower because the car's owner does not sell used cars as an occupation and does not expect to make a profit on the transaction.

If a used car is defective, and a limited guarantee has been given to the customer, the new car dealer has at least the garage facilities to honor whatever warranty was given. Just as with new cars, though, there is no guarantee that the warranty will be applied. However, a dealer without repair facilities cannot under any condition honor his warranty.

Buying a used car from a franchised new car dealer can cost from $200—$500 more than the same car bought from a private individual. For a good used car that has been completely reconditioned, though, this profit is not excessive.

Probably the worst place to buy a used car is at a corner used car lot. These places often specialize in inflated finance charges, rolling back odometers, and selling police cars and taxis as "executive" cars. These dealers have to deal in "junk" cars because their operating capital is insufficient to invest in good cars. There are some small used car lots that are an exception and do not sell junk, however, they are rare.

Repossessed cars are not a bargain either. Often finance companies or investment companies will offer repossessed cars for sale at prices even lower than those prices demanded by private owners. Unfortunately, repossessed cars are rarely well-maintained and they have often been abused.

Leased cars and cars put up for sale by car rental agencies are not good buys. A car with a mileage reading of 50,000 miles has most certainly gone over 100,000 miles. Furthermore, a rented car is driven by a variety of different drivers who have no obligation whatsoever to drive the vehicle correctly.

A final word should be said about used car dealers selling cars from their homes. First of all, this practice contravenes numerous zoning regulations, and is, therefore, illegal. Also these "Gypsy" dealers buy many of the cars they sell from automobile auctions where the quality is poor. Finally it is not a good idea to buy a used car from these dealers because one can never be sure that the car is not stolen or is not still owned by a finance company.

WHAT TO BUY

Four-Door Sedan: This is probably the most reliable used car model available. There is usually plenty of rear seat room, less road noise and body rattles, and a cheaper list price than other models. Also, the addition of side pillars increases the chances of surviving a rollover accident.

Two-Door Sedan: This model has all the advantages of the four-door sedan, except that the rear seat passengers have less room to enter or leave the rear interior.

Four-Door Hardtop: This model may cost more than the other used car models, and this type of car has a more streamlined appearance because of the absence of side pillars. As a result, road noise and dirt enter the interior more easily. This model is very popular because of its appearance, but chassis durability is not very great, with squeaks and rattles a common complaint.

Two-Door Hardtop: This model has essentially the same characteristics as the four-door hardtop, but offers less back seat space than other models. It is usually priced higher than the sedan.

Convertible: Any salesman selling a convertible in Canada automatically receives the P.T. Barnum award for salesmanship. Any consumer buying a used convertible should have his head examined. Because of Canada's extreme climatic conditions, the use of salt for road de-icing, and lack of rollover protection provided by convertibles, the purchase of a used convertible is not a good idea.

Convertibles are also expensive to maintain, particularly if the top needs replacing. It is also very uncomfortable to sit in seats heated by the direct rays of the sun. In fact, it is possible to be burned by some vinyl seats heated in this manner.

Station Wagons: If passenger and cargo space is a prime consideration, then a used station wagon is the answer. Station wagons still command high prices on the used car market, though, so don't expect to pay less than $2,000.

One of the most serious disadvantages of this model is the difficulty in keeping the interior heated in the winter. Exterior road noise is also a frequent problem because the interior has a tendency to echo normal road noise with added resonance.

To the insurance underwriter, cars more than five years old are not good risks. It is difficult to get comprehensive (material damage) coverage on such cars unless the car has been insured by the same company all along, or, unless an inspection has shown that the car has been kept in exceptionally good condition.

Things are even worse for liability coverage. Companies are afraid to insure these cars because of the high risks they present. It is well known that cars over five years old have many hidden defects (which don't necessarily show in most state and private vehicle inspections) such as defective steering linkage, worn wheel bearings, bad wiring, worn shock absorbers, and brake system leaks. Defects such as these endanger the lives of drivers, passengers, and the public in general.

When buying a used car, try to find the name and address of the previous owner. Since he no longer has an interest in the car, you may find out many of the defects that even the dealer does not know. Don't depend too much on the odometer reading. It is possible that a car driven 30,000 miles will be in better mechanical shape than another driven only 10,000 miles.

In choosing a used car, keep in mind that a recent, medium-priced car is a better buy than an older, more luxurious model. With an average sized family, the best buy is a recent compact, intermediate, or low-priced, full-sized line. The four-door sedan is the best body style because other styles tend to fall prey to drafts, rattles, knocks, and noises as they get older. Be careful of used convertibles since tops are expensive and hard to find for used cars.

Used Car Buyer Examination:
1. Make sure the doors close tightly and windows operate smoothly.

2. Check tire wear for balancing, aligning, steering, or frame problems.

3. Road test the car for gear shifting and power. Watch for black exhaust.

4. Check car underside for frame damage from an accident.

5. Look to see if the clutch or brake pedals are too old or too new for the mileage.

6. The car mats will also tell you how hard the car has been used.

7. Test the car's headlights at night to find their effectiveness.

8. Watch for small holes on the roof that may have held a taxi sign.

9. Check all Canadian cars for rust. Tap all metal surfaces for solidity.

10. Don't fall for a "private" car sale. Many dealers pose as private parties.

11. Check the motor for leaks.

12. Let the car stand idle for a few hours and look underneath it for leaks.

13. Listen for engine noises at idle and full throttle.

14. Compare the car's serial number with the motor serial number.

15. Push down on one end and see if the car comes up quickly, or, inches up. This checks the shocks. If the car comes up quickly, the shocks need replacing.

In conclusion, when buying a used car, don't expect to get new car performance. If the car was that good, it would have been sold long before you arrived on the scene.

CHOOSING A DEALER

For over 7 years the Automobile Protection Association has been receiving complaints against used car dealers. In fact, the majority of the complaints received by the Association concern used cars. As a result of these consumer complaints, hundreds of dealers have been brought before the courts by the APA.

It should be made clear at this point that the APA does not consider all used car dealers crooks. However, since many dealers do cheat the public, the APA has established its own guide listing recommended and non-recommended garages, and car dealers across Canada. This guide is used by the APA to direct motorists to dealers and garages that provide outstanding services to consumers.

Garages recommended by the APA are chosen because of the few complaints received against them at the APA's offices. Often APA volunteers will inspect a dealer's establishment posing as a customer. If the dealer's sales and service practices are acceptable, he is then referred a few clients during a short probationary period. Should no complaints be received during this period, the dealer is put on the APA's master referral list.

Any recommended garage or car dealer that changes ownership, gives unsatisfactory service, or, is condemned in a serious legal lawsuit is automatically dropped from the APA's recommended list.

RECOMMENDED GARAGES AND DEALERS

Many garages and car dealers are not recommended by the APA. These companies engage in business practices the APA finds unacceptable. Many of these garages and dealers have been successfully sued by APA members for false representations, false advertising and generally deceptive sales practices. Others are on this list chiefly because of the number of discontented customers they have registering complaints with the APA.

Of course, every dealer has some discontented customers. However, once a consumer group establishes that a customer's complaint is valid, that garage or dealer is obligated to set matters straight. Business functions by public consent, and its basic purpose is to serve constructively the needs of society — to the satisfaction of society. Consequently dealers insensitive to legitimate customer complaints are never recommended by the APA.

RECOMMENDED AND NON-RECOMMENDED DEALERS

The following dealers have been rated by the Automobile Protection Association on the basis of consumer complaints, lawsuits, and the degree of cooperation extended in settling valid consumer complaints. **NO DEALER CAN BUY HIS WAY ON OR OFF THIS LIST.**

Non-Recommended Dealers
and Car Salesmen
Guilty of False Advertising
(Section 33 C, Federal Combines Act)

J. Clark and Son Limited .... False Advertising
Fredericton, New Brunswick

Moncton Chrysler... " "
Moncton, New Brunswick

Robert Shaw.. " "
Montreal, P.Q.

Onward Motors... " "
Kitchener, Ontario

Don Robertson Chrysler Dodge .... " "
Brampton, Ontario

Surgener Motors... " "
Ottawa, Ontario

Birchwood Motors... " "
Winnipeg, Manitoba

Midway Chrysler Plymouth Ltd. .... " "
Winnipeg, Manitoba

Simon Kagan.. " "
Winnipeg, Manitoba

Wiley-Mercury Sales.. " "
Winnipeg, Manitoba

Pados Volkswagen Ltd. .... " "
Calgary, Alberta

Westtown Ford Sales.. " "
Edmonton, Alberta

Ralph Williams Motors Ltd. .... " "
Burnaby, B.C.

Bowell McLean Motors Co. Ltd. .... " "
Vancouver, B.C.

Harvac Investments Ltd... " "
Vancouver, B.C.

Harvey Soloway... " "
Vancouver, B.C.

Don Wheaton Ltd. .... " "
Toronto, Ont.

Delisle Auto Ltd... " "
Montreal, P.Q.

Lanthier and Lalonde .... " "
Montreal, P.Q.

Non-Recommended Dealers
and Car Salesmen
Guilty of Odometer Tampering
Under the Weights and Measures Act
Section 27 (1) - Odometers

Nature of Offence

Crown Auto Sales Inc. ....Odometer Tampering
Charlottetown, PEI

Walter F. Kupka... ”   ”
Vancouver, B.C.

Lorne Alvin Krochak... ”   ”
Regina, Saskatchewan

Barry Peter Hassler... ”   ”
Regina, Saskatchewan

P & E Enterprises... ”   ”
Saskatoon, Saskatchewan

Robert George Marston... ”   ”
Waterloo, Ontario

Reid Richardson... ”   ”
Stratford, Ontario

Bert Steele Motors Ltd.. ”   ”
Souris, PEI

David H. Applebaum .... ”   ”
Toronto, Ontario

Mic-Lor Holdings Ltd.. ”   ”
Edmonton, Alberta

Richard Cautley.. ”   ”
Edmonton, Alberta

William Lozaway... ”   ”
Saskatoon, Saskatchewan

Yvon Cretes... ”   ”
Pte. Gatineau, P.Q.

Steve Auto Ltd.. ”   ”
Chibougamau, P.Q.

Viens Chev Olds Inc.. ”   ”
Waterloo, P.Q.

Leclerc Auto Parts.. ”   ”
St. Elie d'Orford, P.Q.

L'Toyota Inc... ”   ”
Athabaska, P.Q.

Dennis Aubertin .... ”   ”
Calgary, Alta.

The following garages have been rated by local residents of their community who have had dealings with them. These ratings are by no means complete or all-inclusive. It is quite possible that there are some honest garages that have not been listed, just as there may be a few crooks who have also escaped detection.

Always confirm a garage or car dealer rating with a local consumer group or regional officer who handles complaints for the Minister of Consumer and Corporate Affairs.

If all else fails, check with the Better Business Bureau. But, remember, the BBB is ill-equipped to deal with auto complaints, so much of its information may not be current.

MONTREAL
Highly Recommended Dealers and Garages

The following agencies are highly recommanded because they have shown constant good faith and business honesty in settling complaints. Some of the dealers and garages have sent their own staff to act as expert witnesses, in the courts for consumers against other garages or dealers. The ( ) indicates the number of years the agency has been recommended.

Transmission Repairs:
AAMCO AUTOMATIC TRANSMISSION (4)
5464 Iberville — 482-8422

CANADIAN AUTO TRANSMISSION (6)
145 Bates Road, Mount Royal — 738-4794

General Repairs:
AMHERST AUTO REPAIR (6)
2014 Amherst — 522-1623

GARAGE DESNOYERS LTEE (6)
9922 Lajeunesse — 381-8585

GARAGE GABELIER EUROPEAN CARS (6)
226 Du Parc, Laval, P.Q. — 669-1365

GARAGE RIOUX (4)
2024 Holmes, St-Hubert — 678-6900

GULF SERVICE STATION (6)
4680 Ave du Parc — 276-9825

JEAN MURPHY STATION CALEX (5)
8745 Pie IX — 376-1963

MARCEL DUHAMEL (2)
Joseph & Atwater, Verdun — 768-5582

MONTREAL-NORD TEXACO (2)
3820 Henri-Bourassa E., Montreal — 321-2841

NELSON GARAGE (6)
1000 Decarie — 481-0155

OUTREMONT AUTO REPAIRS (6)
215 Van Horne — 272-3366

ROBIDOUX AUTOMOBILE (6)
675 Hauterive, Duvernay — 381-3343

TRANSATLANTIC AUTO REPAIRS (6)
1923 Wolfe — 525-7811

Auto Dealers:
AUTO HECK AM (3)
10,300 Pie IX — 323-4330

AUTO FORUM AM, (2)
2134 West, Ste-Catherine, Montreal —932-6151

BEAUGRAND AUTO AM, (2)
7871 est, Notre-Dame, Montreal — 354-2110

CONCORDIA AUTO Renault (4)
4440 Boul. Levesque, Laval — 661-0660

DUVERNAY TOYOTA (2)
1615 est, Boul. St-Martin, Laval — 387-6481

HOULE AUTO Toyota (4)
9080 Hochelaga — 351-5010

LONGUE POINTE CHRYSLER (5)
7150 Boul. Langelier, Montreal — 256-5092

PAQUIN ESSO Renault (6)
171 Blainville, Ste-Therese — 430-2233

RICHELIEU FORD (6)
3175 Victoria, Lachine — 637-5861

SIGI MOTORS Honda, BMW, (6)
1124 Bleury — 879-1550

Specialized Services:
EONIZER INC. ANTI-ROUILLE (6)
1095 St-Andre, Montreal — 844-3475

DELPLACE & ASSOCIES INGENIEURS (2)
4892 Ave Victoria, Montreal — 481-8887

HENRI SIGNORI RADIATEUR (6)
1051 Amherst, Montreal — 525-2571

M. MUFFLER (6)
1295 est, Bellechasse — 323-6420

Body Repairs:
HOULE AUTO BODY (2)
5377 Delormier, Montreal — 522-2560

Recommended Dealers and Garages

Transmission Repairs:
CENTRAL AUTO TRANSMISSION (5)
1255 Boul. Taschereau — 679-2730
TRANSMISSIONS AUTOMATIQUES DELISLES (2)
22 Boul. Industriel, St-Eustache — 472-1749

General Repairs:
DES PINS SERVICE (1)
3760 St-Denis, Montreal — 844-3445

DICK GARAGE (2)
6707 Clark — 276-6536

F. & H. GARAGE (2)
415 Michel-Jasmin, Dorval — 631-0462

FINA STATION SERVICE (1)
6920 Sherbrooke & Haig — 254-6009

FITAIRE AUTO Fiat, Citroen, Datsun, Peugeot, (2)
954 rue Champagneur, Outremont — 272-2160

GARAGE GILLES BATES (2)
5827 Beaulieu, Ville Emard — 766-4141

GARAGE KARNAS (1)
2232 rue L.O. David, Montreal — 722-2065

GARAGE NORBERT BMW, Mercedes, (1)
5329 Rivard, Montreal — 279-7219

GARAGE QUEBEC Citroen (2)
339 Gilford, Montreal — 843-4154

HUBERT GIRARD (3)
5350 Boul. Pie IX — 729-3013

INTER AUTO REPAIRS Fiat (1)
5465 De Maisonneuve, ouest, Montreal — 488-5747

JACQUES AUTO SERVICE (2)
5370 York, Montreal — 761-5891-2

JACQUES AUTO SPORT Volvo (1)
7085 St-Laurent, Montreal — 276-1488

JOE'S AUTO SERVICE (6)
5008 Decarie — 487-1722

MONTREAL 4 CYLINDRES Renault (1)
6695 Wilfrid Laurier, St-Hubert — 678-0971

RENE JULIEN (2)
11,015 St-Vital, Montreal-Nord — 322-2040

RONALD STATION SERVICE (2)
515 Lafleur, Lasalle — 366-8918

RUDI & WINNER'S GARAGE Volks, (1)
6965 St-Jacques, ouest — 482-0124

STATION SERVICE (2)
63 Boul. Anjou, Chateauguay, Centre — 692-0541

STATION SERVICE (2)
451 Broadway, Montréal-est — 645-1932

STATION SERVICE (2)
303 Victoria, Westmount — 486-0077

STATION SERVICE (2)
61 St-Jean-Baptiste, Chateauguay — 691-5880

METZ GARAGE Mercedes, (1)
33 Mozart — 273-4284

Auto Dealers:
BARNABE AUTO CENTRE, Chrysler, Dodge, (1)
Napierville — 245-3674 - Montreal — 861-8722

JAC AUTO Mazda (2)
14,200 ouest, Boul. Gouin, Pierrefonds — 626-6161

MILLE-ISLES AUTO Buick, Pontiac, (2)
381 Boul. Sauve, St-Eustache — 473-4624

TOUCHETTE GARAGE, Chrysler, Plymouth (1)
8065 Boul. Lajeunesse — 276-8583

UPTOWN Volvo (6)
400 Decarie, Ville-St-Laurent — 748-8807

Specialized Services:
LEBEAU AUTO GLASS (1)
5940 Papineau — 273-8861

SOUTHWARD TIRE (1)
5909 Upper Lachine Road — 489-7561

IDEAL ALIGNEMENT (3)
10,866 Place Moisan, Montreal — 325-0325

LECUYER TIRE (6)
750 St-Gregoire, Montreal — 271-2456

PICHE J. serrurier (5)
5564 St-Laurent, Montreal — 935-2261

GAGNON BATTERIES (2)
702 est, Jarry, Montreal — 274-7561

ZIEBART ANTI-ROUILLE (2)
201 Cure Poirier, Longueuil — 679-2776

Auto Parts:
LECAVALIER AUTO PARTS (6)
8864 St-Laurent, Montreal — 382-4334

Body Repairs:

ARTO AUTO BODY BMW (1)
6895 rue Marconi, Montreal — 277-3408

FRITZ BRENDEL AUTO BODY (1)
9450 Lalande, Pierrefonds — 684-8500

LAUZON AUTO BODY PARTS (1)
10551 Lamoureux, Montreal — 321-1511

QUEBEC & ONTARIO
Recommended Dealers and Garages

ST-JEAN
LE HOUX AND SIMARD (1)
450 Jacques-Cartier Sud — 347-6555

DENAULT LORRAIN LTEE Chrysler, (3)
361 St-Jacques, St-Jean — 658-8202

FORTIN AUTO British Leyland, Volvo, (1)
320 St-Jacques, St-Jean — 346-6263

MAGOG
BEAUDOIN STATION SERVICE (2)
1095 Main ouest, Magog — 843-7272

QUEBEC
MONTCALM AUTO Ford, (6)
901, 1ère Ave, Quebec — 529-3131

GOSSELIN AUTO Honda (1)
185 St-Sacrement, Quebec — 681-0525

DRUMMONDVILLE
LEMOYNE & FRERES Ford (6)
1144 Boul. St-Joseph, Drummondville — 478-4213

VALOIS & FRERES AUTO INC. Peugeot, (1)
200 Boul. Lemire, Drummondville — 478-3456

BEAULIEU TRANSMISSION AUTOMATIQUE (1)
1570 Boul. St-Charles, Drummondville — 478-4476

ACTON VALE
GARAGE DORES FONTAINE Renault (1)
1013 rue Daigneault, Acton Vale — 546-2313

ST-HYACINTHE
LOUIS A. GARIEPY (2)
R.R. # 2, St-Hyacinthe — 796-5043

MONTEBELLO
R. DUPUIS CHRYSLER
Montebello, Quebec

DORION
SHELL STATION SERVICE
73 Harwood, Dorion — 455-4142

TORONTO
DELPLACE ENGINEERS
603 Evans Ave., — 255-3925

FOUR SEASON AUTO BODY
1 Wicksteed Ave. — 421-7664

GEORGE'S AUTO SERVICE
27 Laidlaw, St-Markham — 294-1180

CITY WIDE TRANSMISSION
2781 Dufferin St. — 787-1754

CAR ALIGN SERVICES
736 Warden Ave. — 757-3552

BRITISH AUTO SPORT
Rear 407 Huron St. — 922-0855

PAUL's B.P.
3069 Lakeshore Rd. Oakville — 827-0612

HAWKESBURY
ALLEN MOTOR SALES Chrysler
185 Main St. — 453-9500

HOTTE VOLKSWAGEN
Cheneville, P.Q. —

OTTAWA
B.P. STATION SERVICE
227 Cumberland, Ottawa — 232-8558

Non-Recommended Dealers and Garages

ALIX AUTOMOBILE INC.
Montreal, P.Q.

AU GRAND SALON (1968) LTEE.
Montreal, P.Q.

AU PAVILLON DE L'AUTO MONTREAL INC.
Montreal, P.Q.

BELLEMARE DATSUN LTEE.
Montreal, P.Q.

BONAVENTURE CHEV.-OLDS. LTD.
Montreal, P.Q.

BOUL. DODGE-CHRYSLER (1963) LTD.
Montreal, P.Q.

CANBEC AUTOMOBILE INC.
Montreal, P.Q.

CHAMBLY AUTOMOBILE INC.
Chambly, P.Q.

CHAMPLAIN MOTORS LTD.
Montreal, P.Q.

CHARLESBOURG TOYOTA
Charlesbourg, Quebec

COITEUX AUTOS LTEE.
Montreal, P.Q.

COMETT AUTO INC.
Montreal, P.Q.

REAL CROTEAU AUTOMOBILE LTEE.
Longueuil, P.Q.

HAROLD CUMMINGS LTD.
Montreal, P.Q.

D.K. AUTOMOBILE INC.
Montreal, P.Q.

KAWASAKI MOTORS
Montreal, P.Q.

KEATING FORD SALES LTD.
Verdun, P.Q.

LACORDAIRE AUTO LTEE.
Montreal, P.Q.

LATREILLE AUTOMOBILE (Montreal) LTD.
Montreal, P.Q.

LE RELAIS CHEVROLET LTEE.
Montreal, P.Q.

LEWIS MOTORS FORD
Ottawa, Ont.

LONGUEUIL AUTOMOBILE (1968) LTEE.
Longueuil, P.Q.

MONTREAL C.M.I. TOYOTA LTD.
Montreal, P.Q.

MONTREAL CHRYSLER-PLYMOUTH INC.
Montreal, P.Q.

MONTREAL MOTOR VEHICLE STORAGE INC.
(Norman Barmash alias Norman Barry)
Montreal, P.Q.

NITTOLO MOTORS
Lachine, P.Q.

PARK AVENUR CHEV. (1968) LTEE.
Montreal, P.Q.

PASQUALE FILLIPIS AMERICAN MOTORS
Montreal, P.Q.

A.L. ROBERT AUTOMOBILES INC.
Montreal, P.Q.

ROCHELEAU AUTOMOBILE LTEE.
Montreal, P.Q.

ROTARY AUTO SALES QUEBEC LTEE.
Montreal, P.Q.

SIGNAL FORD TRUCK SALES LTD.
Montreal, P.Q.

STE-FOY TOYOTA INC.
Ste-Foy, Quebec

J.C. TESSIER AUTOMOBILE INC.
Montreal, P.Q.

DUVAL CHEVROLET INC.
Longueuil, P.Q.

HARLAND AUTOMOBILE LTD.
Dorval, P.Q.

LAVIGUEUR AUTO INC.
Laval, P.Q.

NOVA SCOTIA

Recommended Garages and Dealers

AL VICKERS GULF (General Repairs)
Dartmouth

CHAISSON MOTORS (Chrysler-Plymouth)
Dartmouth

WOODSIDE MOTORS
Dartmouth

MacLEAREN's GULF (General Repairs)
Halifax

HALIFAX CHRYSLER-DODGE
Halifax

Non-Recommended Dealers

WOOD MOTORS (Ford)
Halifax

HARBOUR MOTORS (Ford)
Dartmouth

SPORTSMAN EQUIPMENT (Honda)
Lower Sackville

BEACON AMERICAN MOTORS LTD.
Halifax

NEW BRUNSWICK (Moncton)

Recommended Dealers and Garages

STEVE'S MOTORS (GM)

BOURGEOIS GARAGE (British Leyland and Volvo)

ACADIAN MOTORS (Toyota)

D&L MOTORS (Used cars)

IVERSON SALES (Used cars)

HAMILTON AUTO BODY

HILLCREST AUTO BODY

BOB WOOD'S RIVERVIEW ESSO (American cars)

JOHNNY WILSON TEXACO (American cars)

MURRAY'S NEW AND USED AUTO PARTS

SUPERIOR TRUCK RENTALS

Non-Recommended Garages and Car Dealers

BRUNSWICK FORD
(One consumer sent to jail for protesting service)

PRESTIGE AUTO SALE (Fiat)

DRYDEN MOTORS (Ford)

MANITOBA

Non-Recommended Dealer

PEMBINA DODGE CHRYSLER
Winnipeg

BRITISH COLUMBIA

Recommended Garages and Dealers

JACK DALEY SHELL (General Repairs)
Vancouver

DON DOCKSTEADER (Volvo)
Vancouver

Non-Recommended Garages and Dealers

CLARK SIMPKINS (Fiat)
Vancouver

BILL DOCKSTEADER (Toyota)
Vancouver

BRENTWOOD DODGE LTD.
Vancouver

PALM MOTORS
Victoria

BROWN BROTHERS (Ford)
Vancouver

BEYWOOD MOTORS
Vancouver

CHRYSLER CREDIT OF CANADA LTD.*
Vancouver

JOHN BARNES (Automobile Wholesaler)
Victoria

TRUDEAU AUTOMOBILE REPAIRS
Victoria

LO-COST AUTOMATIC TRANSMISSION REBUILDERS LTD.
Vancouver

PINTO ENTERPRISES LTD.
Vancouver

MOTOR LEASE CANADA LTD.
Vancouver

62

SINCLAIR DATSUN SALES LTD.
Richmond

DOLLAR RENT A CAR LTD.
Victoria

TEXACO CANADA LTD.*
Vancouver

KINGSWAY FIAT LTD.
Vancouver

KINGSWAY HONDA SALES AND SERVICE
Vancouver

MIDWAY DISTRIBUTORS (1974) Ltd. (Suzuki Motorcycles)
Kelowna

WESTMINSTER CHEVROLET-OLDSMOBILE LTD.
Vancouver

KINGSWAY PLYMOUTH CHRYSLER
Vancouver

VICTORIA AUTOMATIC TRANSMISSION SERVICE LTD.
Victoria

TUFFY MUFFLER LTD. (Formerly "Midas Muffler Shops")
Vancouver

GRAND PRIX MOTORS LTD.
Vancouver

CUMMINS DIESEL SALES OF B.C. LTD.
Victoria

METRO TOYOTA LIMITED
Victoria

BARNEY's AUTO SALES AND SERVICE LTD.
Penticton

RICHPORT FORD SALES
Richmond

DOMINION CITY
Vancouver

---

*Both the Chrysler Corporation and Texaco were charged with engaging in deceptive practices by the B.C. provincial government. Both companies to sign statements of "Acceptance of Voluntary Compliance".

MUSGROVE FORD
Vancouver

PLIMLEY (Chrysler)
Vancouver

CONROY LANCIA-FIAT
North Vancouver

PACIFIC HONDA
North Vancouver

CHAPTER III

LEGAL LARCENY
AND SELF-DEFENSE

CHAPTER III

LEGAL LARCENY
AND SELF-DEFENSE

The following fraudulent practices are employed by car dealers throughout Canada. Although this list of rackets is long, it does not cover all of the confidence schemes presently employed.

In addition to listing the different rackets employed by car dealers, we have also presented key judgements condemning dealers for engaging in these practices.

MODEL YEAR UPDATING

Many foreign car, motorcycle, and snowmobile manufacturers, as well as some domestic mobile home manufacturers engage in the practice whereby year-old models are sold as the latest model at current prices. Consumers buying updated merchandise pay too much initially, and when the merchandise is sold again, they lose an extra year's depreciation.

Datsun, Mazda, Toyota, Renault, Fiat, Ford, Chrysler, and Citroen update their cars and have been condemned by the courts for doing so.

Updated cars are easy to spot. The federally required compliance plate, attached to the door pillar on the driver's side, will usually show that the car was made 8-75 or 8-76. Most cars made before September are of the current year model. Generally, the import car model year begins in September and ends in August.

If you have unknowingly bought an updated car, the following documents and court judgements should be helpful if your case goes before the small claims court. Other legal remedies may be sought in other court jurisdictions, so consult a lawyer if you wish.

In one well-publicized updating case, **King vs Paddy Shannahan Ford,** heard before a Toronto Small Claims Court, the Honourable Judge George Davies made the following comments on Ford's updating or "redesignating" 1970 Cortinas as 1971 models.

THE COURT: The plantiff claims damages in the sum of $400.00 in respect to the purchase by her from the defendant of a Cortina motor vehicle manufactured by Ford Motor Company of either Britain or England.

The plaintiff and her husband attended at the business premises of the defendant company and met one Goldberg, a salesman for the defendant. The plaintiff expressed a desire to purchase of a 1971 Cortina. Goldberg offered a 1970 Cortina which the defendant had in stock with immediate delivery. The plaintiff declined the offer, insisting she did not want a 1970 Cortina but only a 1971 model. Goldberg agreed to deliver one in approximately two weeks. The buyer's order and the agreement appears in this action as Exhibit 1.

Sometime after the delivery of this vehicle on January 15, 1971 according to Exhibit 2, the plaintiff and her husband became suspicious and finally, at a time which is not certain, enlisted the aid of a Mr. Edmonston of a Montreal based organization called "The Automobile Protection Association." Edmonston testified on behalf of the plaintiff and produced certain documentary evidence, notably a metal plate, which he took from the vehicle indicating the vehicle number, which appears as Exhibit 3.

He also produced a Cortina Shop Manual, Exhibit 4, which discloses the serial number to indicate that the vehicle was manufactured in July, 1970.

The plaintiff also called an employee of the Ford Motor Company of Canada who produced a letter dated October 7, 1970 which said letter inter alia authorized the dealers to reclassify or redesignate all new and unlisted 1970 Cortinas in stock effective October 15, 1970, to be 1971 models. That attached page of the said letter also identified the plaintiff's vehicle and it was established through this witness that said car was manufactured in July, 1970 as a 1970 model.

If there was any doubt of the method of proof in respect to the plaintiff's assertion that this was a 1970 motor, that doubt was certainly removed by the evidence of the defense.

Goldberg testified that he knew that the 1970 models were being reclassified as 1971 models effective. January 1, 1971. The purchase took place January 9th according to Exhibit I. In addition to Goldberg's evidence, one Cummings, the sales manager of the defendant company was also called and when shown Exhibit 7, he stated that all salesmen had been aware of the contents of that letter shortly after receipt by the company, either by memorandum or by information given at a sales meeting. In the Court's respectful opinion, the defendant through Goldberg was guilty of representation inducing the plaintiff to enter into a contract at the time when such representation was false. The Court therefore, finds that this was a fraudulent misrepresentation. In order to succeed in fraud or deceit, however, it must be specifically pleaded. In the absence of such pleading, the Court can afford no relief for fraud or deceit. The plaintiff's claim was hand drawn, and, if the plaintiff had not been represented by counsel who had been called to the Bar, perhaps in the exercise of equity and good conscience, the Court could perhaps have exproprio motu granted such an amendment. However, in view of the fact that the plaintiff at trial was represented by a member of the Bar, the Court did not feel it could on its own initiative, grant such an amendment and certainly none was asked for by counsel for the plaintiff.

In Derry v. Peek 14 App. Ca. 337, Lord Herschell included in his speech the following: "First, in order to sustain an action of deceit there must be proof of fraud, and nothing short of that will suffice. Secondly, fraud is proved when it is shown that a false representation has been made, (1) knowingly, or (2) without belief in its truth, or (3) recklessly, careless whether it be true or false. Although I have treated the second and third as distinct cases, I think the third is but an instance of the second, for one who makes a statement under such circumstances can have no real relief in the truth of what he states."

The doubt only of awarding exemplary or punitive damages for breach of contract appears to be by authority of Addis v. Gramophone Co. Ltd. (1909) A.C. 488 where Lord Atkinson stated at 496: "In many other cases of breach of contract there may be circumstances of malice, fraud, defamation or violence, which would sustain an action of tort as an alternative remedy to an action for breach of contract. If one should select the former mode of redress, he may, no doubt, recover exemplary damages of what is sometimes styled vindictive damages; but if he should choose to seek redress in the form of an action for breach of contract, he lets in all the consequences of that form of action."

In Denison v. Fawcett, Schroeder, J.A. at 319, says: "Exemplary or aggravated damages are not, broadly speaking, awarded in actions for breach of contract, since damages for breach of contract are in the nature of compensation, and the motives and conduct of the defendant are not considered relevant to the assignment of damages. The action for breach of promise of marriage and an action upon a contract against a banker for wrongfully refusing to pay his customers' cheques constitute exceptions to this rule. Generally, however, such damages may be awarded in actions of tort such as assault, trespass, negligence, nuisance, libel, slander, seduction, malicious prosecution and false imprisonment. If, in addition to committing the wrongful act, the defendant's conduct is "high-handed, malicious, conduct showing a contempt of the plaintiff's rights, or disregarding every principle which actuates the conduct of a gentleman", (to quote a few examples taken from the authorities) his conduct is an element to be considered as a circumstance of aggravation which may, depending upon its extent or degree, justify an award to the injured plaintiff in addition to the actual pecuniary loss which he has sustained. I do not think that it can be stated with any precision what may be classed as aggravating circumstances but malice, wantonness, insult and persistent repetition have always been regarded as elements which might be taken into account."

While the plaintiff's claim is capable of being framed in breach of contract, in my respectful opinion, it is equally capable of being framed in tort. While the representations of Goldberg cannot grant relief on the grounds of fraudulent misrepresentation, fraud not having been pleaded, therefore, one relies upon the second or third classification of a false representation as stated by Lord Herschell in Derry v. Peek suppra.

It is clear law that the plaintiff would be entitled to recission of the contract pursuant to Derry v. Peek or rectification according to later authorities. Rescission is out of the question in the instant case due to the delay. Rectification is not available either for the uncontradicted evidence of the expert witnesses called for the defence were conclusive in that the vehicle in question upon a trade-in or resale would be treated as a 1971 model due to the registration that disclosed that fact, further, according to Exhibit 7 the price of the alleged 1971 models was not increased over the 1970 model.

There would appear to be one further problem the plaintiff must overcome and that is punitive damages were not claimed.

In two cases in the Ontario Court of Appeal, the Court unanimously held that punitive damages need not be claimed specifically. They are Glenn v. Brampton Poultry Co. 18 D.L.R. (2d) 9; and Starkman v. Delhi Court Ltd. 1961 28 D.L.R. (2d) 269.

The facts in this case are identical to an unreported decision of His Honour Judge Wilmot, former Chief Judge of the County Court, unreported in 1961, therefore, if I had any hesitation in respect to the propriety of awarding punitive damages, I am bound by his decision.

In the words of Mr. Justice Schroeder, paraphrased: "In the Court's respectful opinion, the conduct of the defendant's servant in the case at Bar was high-handed, conduct showing a contempt of the plaintiff's rights, and disregarding every principle which actuates the conduct of a gentleman."

I am therefore strongly of the opinion that this conduct merits censure by the Court, and the award of punitive damages in the sum of $400.00, costs and a counsel fee of $40.00.

Any consumer who feels he has been victimized by this updating racket should contact the Automobile Protection Association, 292 St-Joseph Blvd. West, Montreal, Canada.

DEFECTIVE USED CAR LEMONS

If every consumer had each used car verified by an independent mechanic before purchasing it, most used car lemons could be nipped in the bud. Unfortunately few consumers take this simple precaution.

Once a lemon is bought, however, all is not lost. If you have proof the car was misrepresented to you verbally by the dealer, or misleadingly advertised in the newspaper, the dealer can be sued.

It is also against the law for car dealers to sell vehicles that contain "hidden defects." Therefore, if an independent garage is prepared to state that a used car is unsafe, or has so many defects it is worthless, chances are the contract can be cancelled under the "hidden defects" sections of the law. A lawyer must always be consulted for cases of this type.

ODOMETER TAMPERING

It is against the law to turn back a car's odometer. Any dealer turning back the odometer is liable to prosecution, under criminal law.

USED CARS SOLD "AS IS"

No dealer is permitted to sell an unsafe car to the public. Even if the car is sold "As is," the dealer has the obligation to recondition the vehicle to the extent where it is safe to drive. "As is" provisions in contracts do not absolve the dealership of responsibility for the condition of each and every used car he sells.

WORTHLESS GUARANTEES

Sometimes a used car dealer will delay repairing a used car until after his guarantee runs out. To avoid this racket, send a registered letter to the dealer listing the defects needing repair. If the repairs are not done before the guarantee expires, take a copy of your letter to the small claims court and claim the estimated amount the repair should cost elsewhere.

Oil companies such as Wynns give good used car guarantees through different used car dealers. The dealer is required to guarantee his cars the first month, though. If the dealer does not guarantee the car, he has broken his agreement with the oil company and the guarantee becomes worthless. If this happens, you may cancel your purchase because the dealer has failed to honor his guarantee.

FAULTY MANUFACTURE

Often a new or used car may contain performance-related and safety-related defects caused by the manufacturer. Usually, these cars are recalled by the manufacturer and corrected at no charge. Some used cars, though, may have been defective and never repaired. To check if your car has been recalled write to the Director, Road and Motor Vehicle Traffic Safety, Ministry of Transport, Ottawa, Ontario, K1A 0N5.

Performance-related defects are not subject to recalls because safety is not affected. However, consumers have cancelled many contracts before the courts by listing such diverse defects as water leaks, transmission troubles, motor problems, etc. etc.

Fleury vs **Fiat (Québec Superior Court).**
Mr. Fleury won judgement forcing the Fiat company to take back his defective new car. This case is important because the consumer brought suit directly against the manufacturer instead of the dealer, as is the usual custom, and also because of the judge's **obiter dictum** (side remark) that Fiat's guarantee when compared with its actual service amounted to no more than "promises in the air".

Western Pacific Tank Lines Ltd. vs **Brentwood Dodge, (Supreme Court of British Columbia 30945/74, June 2, 1975, Vancouver, Justice Meredith).**
This company bought a new 1974 New Yorker Brougham for $8,258 and immediately thereafter discovered it had a lemon on its hands. According to court documents, the following defects were recorded: capricious doors that stuck open or closed; severe water leaks around windows; defective door handles and locks; gauges for the engine temperature and gas tank not working, except that the gas gauge worked correctly if the rear dome light was switched on; defective radio and turn signal lights; and a defective headlight switch that would activate the windshield wipers and vice versa. The company got its money back, as well as $400 special costs. Cases cited to support the plaintiff were: **Gibbon** vs **Trapp Motors** (1970) 9, D.L.R. (3d)742, and **Lightburn** vs **Belmont Sales** (1969) 6,D.L.R. 300.

It is interesting to note that Chrysler products have had a history of water leaks, braking difficulties, and premature rusting of the front fenders. The Western Pacific decision confirms a similar decision once handed down by the Supreme Court of Canada in **Pizzagalli** vs **Touchette** where a Quebec Chrysler owner was allowed to cancel his contract because of water leaks.

THE RUSTPROOFING RACKET

Rusting is a serious affair, especially the premature rusting of a motor vehicle. Not only does it cause a vehicle to lose a great deal of its resale value, it also may create a serious safety hazard. One eyewitness to a collision involving an internally rusted out 1966 MG hit by a Rover going 40 miles an hour gives this account:

> "The Rover was started up, and once again came thun-
> dering round the bend to plough into the MG just behind
> its front wheel at about 40 mph. The results were ap-
> palling. The entire front of the car parted company

with the passenger compartment at the bottom leading edge of the door sills and at the bottom of the wind screen pillars. With nothing to resist it at door pillar height, the Rover bonnet had pushed the driver's door deep into the car, the floor was forced up against the seats, and the fascia ripped away. Any driver would undoubtedly have been killed, even if he had been wearing a seat belt.

The whole front of the car proved to be completely rotten. It had been patched with filler, with cardboard and with newspaper. The wings were a latticework of rust held together with filler and fibreglass, and the box sections and bulkheads had crumbled away on the impact.

This was just the sort of car that a non-technical motorist might have bought as a second car for his wife, or even for a holiday if he did not need a car all the year round."

Effective rustproofing compounds applied by competent experts could help reduce the severity of accidents caused by vehicles that are rust-prone. Unfortunately, the industry is too busy selling franchises and offering phoney guaranties to be concerned with offering North American motorists quality corrosion protection.

Ziebart USA, the godfather of the entire rustproofing industry, admits that it can no longer guarantee certain model cars such as the Fiat and General Motor's Vega. The Dura-coat rustproofing company based in Niagara Falls has been chased out of Quebec leaving numerous unpaid small claims court judgements, while at the same time having to defend itself from a fraud investigation initiated by Vermont's Attorney General. No wonder rustproofing has a bad reputation.

Motorist Survey (Rustproofing)
The results of a recent survey indicate that a majority of Canadian consumers feel they were cheated by rustproofing firms. These consumers complained of worthless guarantees, ineffective products, and misleading advertising.

The rustproofing questionnaires were answered by 308 motorists selected randomly from across Canada. Of this sample, more than 60 percent of the motorists responding stated they were dissatisfied with the rustproofing product purchased.

Points of Dissatisfaction
The following consumer complaints are listed in order of their frequency:

1. Severe rusting despite rustproofing.
2. Unsatisfactory application of product.
3. Product sticky, stains clothing, slow drying, falls off.
4. Misleading advertising.
5. Warranty not respected.
6. Warranty conditions not explained.
7. Follow-up inspections not possible.
8. Variation of $80 for same rustproofing done elsewhere.

Rusting with Rustproofing

Rustproofing products appear to be completely ineffective on cars which have a tendency to rust due to design defects in construction and the harsh Canadian climate. The following cars were found to be very rust-prone:

Datsun 510 and 240Z.
General Motors Vega and Astre.
Renault 15.
Peugeot.
Volkswagen 411, 412, Beetle, and Super Beetle.
Fiat, 124, 128.
Ford Maverick, Mustang, and Cougar.
Toyota Corolla.
Audi Fox.
Mercury Capri.
Citroen.
Jaguar XKE.
Mercedes.
Porsche 911.

Misleading Advertising

Misleading advertising is a serious charge. In the rustproofing survey, however, irate consumers repeatedly complained of being victimized by misleading statements of a variety of rustproofing firms.

One Dartmouth, Nova Scotia food company president declared:

"We own a subsidiary company..., and back in 1971 we had a couple of 1971 Ford Cars Ziebarted. One car was satisfactory, the other car cost us over $300.00 to repair rusted out areas.
The franchised Ziebart dealer in Saint John refused to even refund our money, and it seems strange that they can continue to advertise giving the consumer the impression that their product is guaranteed for 10 years, when in reality, all they are obligated to do is refund the money, and when they refuse to do this, we think it is time that an organization, like yours, brought the problems to the attention of the many unsuspecting consumers."

Rustproofing Profits

Rustproofing in Canada is profitable, though just how profitable is hard to tell. Nevertheless, the APA has found some sales literature used to recruit undercoating dealers for Castrol Oils (Canada) Limited that promises potential dealers an 80 percent profit on each sale! The Castrol company makes the following statements:

Simplicity

"The undercoating of a vehicle is a simple operation which can be carried out in a relatively short time (less than 1 hr.) and can very quickly be mastered by any one in the Service Department or P.D.I. Department.

Profitability

Despite its simplicity, undercoating remains a highly profitable venture and one which ought not to be neglected by the aggressive car dealer.

The figures which we show below are averages, but, nevertheless, serve to indicate the degree of profitability attributable to undercoating a vehicle with Castrol Surecoat."

Undercoating of Average-Sized Car

10 lbs Castrol Surecoat at 29¢	$2.90
Labour — 1 hr. at $3.00 per hr.	$3.00
Allowance against overhead	$11.00
Cost of Job	$6.90
Retail price of completed work	$35.00
Profit	$28.10
Profit as percentage of Sales Value	80%

In their haste to sell rustproofing franchises, many rustproofing firms apparently underestimate the time, money, and skill required. In one humourous recruiting ad placed in **Automotive News,** Quaker State made the following pitch:

> **Drums of profit — if you'll just give'em the air.**
> "No new car you sell is completely rustproofed. So here's the Quaker State Rustproofing System with a money opportunity that's hard to overlook. And no investment to speak of, if you have a lift and an air compressor. Ask your distributor about Quaker Koat and Metal Gard — two quick, easy, inexpensive steps to higher gross on your new car sales".

All of the rustproofing firms surveyed stress their warranties. However, upon close inspection, the warranties contained clauses that rendered them void if the product was not applied correctly,

75

or repairs were not done by the selling agent, or mandatory inspection missed, or rusting was exterior and not interior, or rusting was caused by stone chipping, or because of abusive use of vehicle, or extreme conditions, or damage by collision. With such as variety of excuses for voiding the warranty, the rustproofer has very little difficulty in picking and choosing arbitrarily those warranties he wishes to honor.

ACROSS CANADA

RUSTPROOFING COMMENTS (1975)

Survey Breakdown

	Satisfied	Dissatisfied	Total
Ziebart*	55	95	150

Not recommended. There were too many complaints of sloppy workmanship, 24,000 mile check-up voided guarantee if missed, ineffective against rust, sloppy public relations, warranty unsupported by performance.

Dura-Coat	4	26	30

Not recommended. Consumer complaints include: slowness in responding to complaints, product ineffective against rust, warranty not valid, product soft and sticky, wears off, stains.

Tuff-Coat	6	17	23

Not recommended. Consumers complained that the product was ineffective, messy, and carelessly applied; that complaints were not acted upon, and that the warranty was not honored.

Vital Rustproofing (Vitalizing)	6	9	15

Not recommended. Consumers noted that the product was ineffective against rust, was improperly applied, started to peel away, also that the yearly inspections were poor and that the cost was too high for the job.

Miscellaneous	30	40	90

These companies had too small a sample of responses to evaluate. Companies involved are True-Guard, Superior, Rustop, Poly-Oleum, Quaker State, and Goodyear.

---

*Many of the Ziebart complaints were against one Ottawa Ziebart dealer, Ottawa Rustproofing Limited, believed to be operated by George Aliferis under the name of "Spartan Auto Care." As a result of these serious shortcomings, the APA cannot recommend Ziebart except in Quebec where the Dealer's Association agrees to let the APA arbitrate complaints. The Eonizer Rustproofing Company also has been recommended by the APA in Quebec for 6 years.

Legal Recourse

If you cannot get satisfaction from the company that rustproofed your car, you may seek redress in the small claims court. Consumers may cite **Jan Svoboda** vs **Lemenns Automobile** (Longueuil No. 32-000934-746) where Volvo was forced to pay $300 for a 1971 Volvo that had rusted in 1974 despite its Ziebart treatment.

Lawyers advise that if a dealer applied the rustproofing compound, send two registered letters to the dealer. The first letter should ask for reimbursement due to the ineffectiveness of the product, and the second letter should hold the dealer responsible for the rusting damages caused by the ineffective product. Remember, if you paid the dealer, he's responsible.

CONFIDENTIAL DOCUMENTS SHOWING PREMATURE RUSTING PUBLISHED BY ZIEBART RUSTPROOFING LTD. (1976)

MODEL:
AMC Pacer
PROBLEM:
Poor Access
LOCATION:
Front hood seam and lower rear quarters
CORRECTION:
Process hood lip per technical manual instructions (Page B1, Item No. 6 AMC). Process ¼ panels per Page B3, Item No. 1, but omit critical note. Process lower ¼ panels per Page B4, Item No. 3. Repeat at two year inspection.

*It is possible that this vehicle, due to continuing problems, may not be guaranteed in its entirety in future. This action if taken will not be retroactive on those vehicles already processed.

MODELS:
Volkswagen Rabbit, Dasher, Sirocco (Imported cars)
PROBLEM:
Poor or no access.
LOCATION:
Front hood lip and doors.
CORRECTION:
Hood, process per technical manual instructions (Page 28.01, Item No. 9, Rabbit) (Page 28.11, Item No. 7, Sirocco).
Hood not guaranteed on V.W. Rabbit or Sirocco.
Doors in addition to technical manual instructions door panels must be removed on all of the above mentioned models.

MODEL:
Citroen
PROBLEM:
Manufacturer
LOCATION:
Total body construction.
CORRECTION:
Nil.
NO GUARANTEE ISSUED ON THIS VEHICLE.

MODEL:
Datsun 510, 1200 Sedan and Coupe, Pick-up
PROBLEM:
No inner wheelhouses. Result, mud, dirt and salt build up at head-light eyebrows, fender reinforcement, pocket areas at fender support.
LOCATION:
Front fenders.
CORRECTION:
Double coat. Respray at two-year inspection.
NO GUARANTEE ON AREAS INVOLVED.

MODEL:
Datsun 240Z
PROBLEM:
Severe corrosion. Foam rubber and poor access.
LOCATION:
Front fenders and rear wheelhouse lip. (see T-B No. 240)
CORRECTION:
Nil. Saturate areas in question. Repeat at two-year inspection.
THESE AREAS NOT GUARANTEED.

MODEL:
Fiat (All)
THOSE LISTED BELOW ARE THE VERY CRITICAL AREAS
MODEL:
Fiat 124 Sport Spider
PROBLEM:
Mud, dirt, and salt build-up.
LOCATION:
Rear section of rocker panels because of large manufacturing opening.
CORRECTION:
Respray at two-year inspection.
NO GUARANTEE.

MODEL:
Fiat 127 and 128
PROBLEM:
Remove sponge rubber glued to sail panels and rear quarters. Poor factory rustproofing.
LOCATION:
Forward wheel arch area.
CORRECTION:
Nil.
NO GUARANTEE ON THIS VEHICLE.

MODEL:
Jaguar XKE
PROBLEM:
No access — along top of fenders.
LOCATION:
Bright work seam, upper fender headlight to cowl. See Tech Manual — Imported Car Section.
CORRECTION:
Nil.
THIS AREA NOT GUARANTEED.

MODEL:
Jensen Interceptor
PROBLEM:
No access due to manufacturer's body design.
LOCATION:
Rear quarters — carpet glued on.
CORRECTION:
Nil.
THIS VEHICLE NOT GUARANTEED.

MODEL:
Mercedes 220 through 280
PROBLEM:
Foam rubber.
LOCATION:
Enter front of hood.
CORRECTION:
Impossible to remove foam rubber.
NO GUARANTEE ON THIS AREA.

MODEL:
Peugeot — All Models
PROBLEM:
Body construction.
LOCATION:
Front fender area open hole above manufacturer's opening in box section.
CORRECTION:
Process with extreme care.
NOTE:
Overlap seam areas. Remove dum dum in headlight area, spray and replace. Remove cowl section cover. Respray at two-year inspection.
NO GUARANTEE ON THESE AREAS.

MODEL:
Porsche 914 and 911
PROBLEM:
No access.
LOCATION:
Front fender, upper rear section.
CORRECTION:
Nil.
NO GUARANTEE ON THESE AREAS.

MODEL:
Porsche 914 and 911
PROBLEM:
Styrofoam.
LOCATION:
Hood and trunk lid.
CORRECTION:
Impossible to remove.
NO GUARANTEE ON THESE AREAS.

MODEL:
Porsche 911
PROBLEM:
No access.
LOCATION:
Front suspension rust area, extreme forward section, underside.
CORRECTION:
Refer to Tech Bulletin no. 179, Page 34:00.
Foreign Car Section.
THESE AREAS NOT GUARANTEED.

MODEL:
Renault 15
PROBLEM:
Critical corrosion areas.
LOCATION:
Eyebrow and fender support areas.
CORRECTION:
Double coat during original process; respray during two-year inspection.
NO GUARANTEE ON THESE AREAS.

MODEL:
Volkswagen 411 and 412
PROBLEM:
Styrofoam.
LOCATION:
Hood, trunk lid, rear dog legs, and rocker panels on 411, rear 10".
CORRECTION:
Unable to remove foam.
NO GUARANTEE ON THESE AREAS.

MODEL:
Volkswagen Beetle and Super Beetle
PROBLEM:
Foam.
LOCATION:
Air intake at sail panel.
CORRECTION:
Remove foam, double coat area. Repeat at two-year inspection.
NO GUARANTEE ON THESE AREAS.

MODEL:
Capri
PROBLEM:
Heat expanding foam.
LOCATION:
Lower quarter panel.
CORRECTION:
Spray entire area, including foam.
NO GUARANTEE ON THIS AREA.

Kendall Refining Company

Lubrication Specialists Since 1881
DIVISION OF WITCO CHEMICAL CORPORATION
Bradford, Pa. 16701

General Letter No. B-K256
August 15, 1975

To: All Kendall Distributors

SUBJECT: Termination — Kendall New Car Rustproofing Policy

Gentlemen:

This is your official announcement of the termination of Kendall's New Car Rustproofing Policy program. Distributors currently using the program are advised to notify their dealers that as of August 25, 1975 Kendall will not accept owner registration coupons. We recommend that you instruct your salesmen to pick up forms now in dealer hands. In some instances you may decide it advisable to notify your dealers by letter.

Kendall will continue to be obligated to registered owners whose cars were rustproofed under the terms and conditions of the policy during the life of the program - July 3, 1972 through August 25, 1975.

The primary reason for the decision is "lack of control" at the dealer level. Owner complaints of dealers failing to service the cavity areas, others of exorbitant and varied prices to their customers, along with dealers who have gone out of business or sold to someone else who will not take care of the required periodic examination, have reached this office. Complaints of this nature were more numerous than anticipated and in our opinion were detrimental to Kendall's reputation.

We regret any inconvenience this decision may cause you. Although Kendall does stand in back of the performance 100%, the success of a rustproofing program like this one is contingent upon complete and proper application of the Kendall products involved.

Sincerely,

W.A. Knapp/vm

FORD RUST VICTORY

On 25 June 1976, the Hon. Judge Harold Lande ruled for the plaintiff in the small claims case of **Danson A.J. - vs - Chateau Motors Ltd.** and **Ford Motor Company.** Mr. Danson had sought compensation for the premature rusting of his 1972 Mercury Cougar. Chateau Motors, the dealer, and Ford, the manufacturer, argued that their responsibility to Mr. Danson had ended with the expiration in late 1973 of the Ford Company "12 months or 12,000 miles" new car warranty. Judge Lande, after noting the general one-sidedness and unfairness of this "take it or leave it" standard warranty, agreed that Chateau Motors and Ford had no contractual responsibility to Danson. Rather, Ford's responsibility was for damage caused to Mr. Danson by its own "acts of negligence."

Addressing himself to the general problem of premature rusting, Judge Lande concluded,

The extreme weather conditions under which automobiles are driven in our Canadian winters as well as the surface conditions of the highways which are covered with salt and other chemicals, require that the quality of automobiles sold for use under these conditions should be sufficient to meet these exigencies of our Canadian climate. This is particularly so, since the automobile manufacturer has had sufficient experience in recent years with these conditions and, therefore, should apply his sophisticated knowledge and the ample research at his disposal to fortify his product to withstand these extremes. **He has knowingly neglected to do so....** In our opinion, all of this constitutes a defect in manufacture....(pp. 7-8)

The reasoning in this judgement gives hope to Ford owners across Canada whose cars suffer from premature rusting. Therefore, the A.P.A. urges all owners of rusted 1972 or newer model year Fords in the provinces not covered by class action suits (Ontario, Nova Scotia, and New Brunswick are covered) to file small claims actions against Ford.

DANSON A.J. MD., - vs - CHATEAU MOTORS LTD and FORD MOTOR CO. OF CANADA LTD., Provincial Court, District of Montreal, No. 530-32-001898-757, Judge Harold Lande.

JUDGEMENT

The Petitioner claims from the Respondents, as manufacturer and vendor respectively, the sum of $300.00 being the cost of replacing the left front fender of his automobile which has rusted very badly;

The Petitioner purchased a New Ford "Cougar" from the Respondent Château Motors Ltd., on August 30, 1972. He also, at his own expense, had the car undercoated by the Ziebart process which guarantees against rust for ten years. Despite this extra precaution, the car started showing evidences of rust about 2½ years after the date of purchase and by August 1975, after 24,000 miles, the left front fender was badly rusted from top to bottom;

The Respondents claim that they are not responsible for this type of deterioration after their new car warranty has expired. This warranty covered a period of one year of 12,000 miles of operation, whichever came first. Since the trouble manifested itself after termination of both of these events, their liability under the contract has ceased;

The following are excerpts of the pertinent parts of the warranty undertaking.

BASIC WARRANTY

"Ford Motor Co. of Canada Ltd. and the selling dealer jointly warrant with respect to each 1972 Model passenger car... sold by Ford, that for a period of 12 months or 12,000 miles, whichever occurs first, the Selling Dealer will repair or replace any part that is found to be defective in factory materials or workmanship... these will be made free of charge for both parts and labour...The repairs, replacements, adjustments and services provided in these warranties constitute the owner's exclusive remedy."

From the foregoing it can be seen that the vendor's warranty (which is very similar to that of most automobile vendors) is much more restrictive than the general rules of warranty in our Civil Code. The former says, in effect, that even if the car falls apart the day after it is delivered, the purchaser cannot cancel the contract or demand a reduction in price, but can only call upon the vendor to repair the defects, and after the warranty period has expired the buyer has no recourse whatsoever;

The automobile has today become an integral and necessary part of the standard of living of most people in North America. However, there are only four manufacturers of automobiles in the U.S. and Canada, all of whom present the consumer with essentially the same warranty contract with the attitude of "take it or leave it". The conditions attached to the sale of foreign cars offer little improvement. The individual consumer is thus faced with a quasi-monopolistic vendor from whom he is obliged to acquire this almost indispensible consumer product and who alone dictates all the conditions of sale, by-passing the general laws of warranty which exist in our common law, and setting up a law unto himself;

However, the present claim can be considered not only on a contractual but also on a delictual basis. In fact the Supreme Court of Canada has already decided that there is nothing repugnant in the

84

"cumul" of both recourses in the same action. **(Ross - vs - Dunstall, 1921 — 62 S.C.R. 393)** at page 415 Mignault J. states:

> "In my opinion whether the civil responsibility incurred proceeds from a contract or rests on a quasi-delict, matters very little in this case."

In this case it was held that the manufacturer who was not a party to the contract of sale could be held responsible for "faute délictuelle" and the vendor for "faute contractuelle". Thus Duff J. says at page 396 of the judgment:

> "I cannot understand why a delictual responsibility towards whom the negligent manufacturer has no contractual relation may not co-exist with contractual responsibility towards those with whom he has.

At page 419 of the same judgment, Mignault J. says:

> "The authors, and chiefly Pothier (Vente, Nos. 212 and following, Obligations, No. 168), explain that the seller is legally presumed to know the defects when the thing sold is one in which the seller usually deals or one manufactured by him. The mere dealer is generally allowed to rebut the legal presumption of knowledge by showing that in fact it was impossible for him to discover the defect, **but the manufacturer is not listened to when he pleads ignorance of the defect, for he is held to have guaranteed the product created by him as free from latent defect,** spondet peritiam artis, **and** as Pothier observed **his ignorance of the defect in the thing manufactured by him is in itself a fault.** Imperitia culpae annumeratur.
>
> (emphasis is ours)

Hence, whilst the dealer may have contracted himself out of his liability for the present claim, the manufacturer may still be held responsible delictually whether he was or was not a party to the contract as vendor;

The foregoing principle has been followed in Quebec jurisprudence. See the case of **Lazanik - vs - Ford Motor Co. of Canada Ltd.** (Challies J.) S.C.M. No 623-564, Judgement June 15, 1965. (unreported)

In **Gougeon - vs - Peugeot Canada Limitée,** 1973, C.A. 824 where the purchaser of an automobile sued the manufacturer to cancel the sale after the expiry of the warranty, Kaufman J., speaking for the Court concluded.

> "Appellant was not obliged - nor indeed limited - to seek redress from Peugeot Canada Ltée in virtue of the conventional guarantee which existed.

In the case of **Insurance Company of North America - vs - General Motors of Canada Limited,** (C.P.M. 02-066523-72), Judgment October 1, 1974, the undersigned stated at Page 10:

> "The fact is that the automobile which General Motors delivered to the Defendant Harold Cummings Motors to be, sold to Pierre Pettas had a major defect which was not apparent and for which they are bound by delictual responsibility; the restrictive warranty would not in any case absolve General Motors from its own acts of negligence. C.C. 1509.

The wording of the warranty in this latter case was very similar to that in the present case;

For the foregoing reasons the Court has concluded that even if in law the Ford Motor Company of Canada Limited has no contractual liability under its conventional warranty it can be held responsible for damages suffered if they result from its own delicts or acts of negligence;

At the hearing the Petitioner submitted overwhelming evidence through photographs, verbal testimony and garage estimates of the damages which he suffered. He has satisfied the Court that he bought a new Ford product at the end of August 1972, that two and one half years later after the car had gone some 24,000 miles, rust spots appeared in various places on the left front fender and by the autumn of 1975 the fender had developed rust to such an extent that the only alternative was to replace it with a new one. All of this evidence was uncontradicted. Furthermore, the Respondents made no proof in their own defence;

The body of a new automobile, if properly maintained and free of accidents, should last more than 2½ years. In the case of the Petitioner this was particularly so since, at his own expense, he had the car undercoated by a reputable process when it was new and before he took delivery. Furthermore, the Petitioner is a physician who has satisfied the Court that he has given his car the best of maintenance;

The extreme weather conditions under which automobiles are driven in our Canadian winters as well as the surface conditions of the highways which are covered with salt and other chemicals, require that the quality of automobiles sold for use under these conditions should be sufficient to meet these exigencies of our Canadian climate. This is particularly so, since the automobile manufacturer has had sufficient experience in recent years with these conditions and, therefore, should apply his sophisticated knowledge and the ample research at his disposal to fortify his product to withstand these extremes. He has knowingly neglected to do so. What is more, it is common knowledge that in recent years the manufacturers of American automobiles have permitted a deterioration in the quality of the metal which goes into the body of their product. In our opinion, all of this constitutes a defect in manufacture, a "faute lourde" for which the manufacturer is delictually responsible;

FOR THESE REASONS, the Court:

GRANTS the demand of the Petitioner, and

CONDEMNS the Respondent, Ford Motor Co. of Canada Ltd. to pay Petitioner the sum of $297.00, the proven damages, and cost of $10.00.

CONFIDENTIAL

FORD

SPECIAL REPORT
CAR BODY SHEET METAL CORROSION
NAAO RELIABILITY — QUALITY MEETING

Introduction
Recent reports from the Cleveland District, followed by a telephone survey of Ford Customers Service Division personnel in twenty districts located in Northern areas and along the Eastern and Gulf Coasts, plus results of customer direct mail surveys indicate that **there is a serious vehicle rust problem on our 1969 through 1973 vehicles in a maximum corrosion environment.** Field surveys conducted in Cleveland and Detroit by representatives of the Automotive Assembly Division, Body Engineering Office, Ford Customer Service Division, and Product Development support this opinion. Further evidence of this problem is contained in the recently published annual "Paint and Corrosion Survey."

The General Product Acceptance Specification relating to rust and corrosion for highly visible panels allows no rust in one year and in two years only that rust that can be wiped off. Rust that can be wiped off in one year is permitted for other visible panels. **No metal perforation on exterior appearance panels is permissible for five years.**

The basic design and processing of corrosion protection has remained essentially unchanged in our cars for the past ten years with the exception of additional electrocoat facilities. **Why then has corrosion suddenly developed as a prominent product problem?** The answer at this time must be subjective but is judged to be a product of higher customer expectation and competitive upgrading in corrosion protection such as dip phosphate and primer, multiple coatings including aluminum filled wax and vinyl sealer, zinc chromate primer, and galvanized panels in tailgates. In a severe corrosion environment, our products do not satisfy the GPAS but seem competitive for the one and two year requirement. However, **perforation, which is the category of corrosion failure highest in customer concern, develops from one to two years earlier in our cars than in the competition's.**

The purpose of this Special Report is to specifically cover the major areas of corrosion now identified on Ford products in the post warranty period and to discuss those corrective actions that are released or under investigation. Since the size of the problem relative to the total vehicle population has not been accurately established, additional investigations are discussed.

Description of Problem and Plan to Determine Scope
In severe corrosion environments in the U.S. and Canada, corrosion perforation of body sheet metal is occurring in the following areas prior to the five year GPAS requirement.
Door inner and outer panel.
Quarter panel and wheelhouse.
Tailgate inner and outer panel.
Quarter and pillar to rocker panel joint.
Station wagon spare tire well and storage compartment.
Deck lid inner and outer panel.
Fender.

Four surveys have been conducted in the past month. These surveys were recognized to have statistical limitations due to sample size and method of sample selection. However, results of these surveys, when combined with previous survey data, Arizona Proving Ground corrosion test results, and Customer Service Division reports have provided a listing of individual body sheet metal corrosion locations. Customer Service Division will complete an analysis of expenditures of extended policy funds by district, model year, carline, and major sheet metal panel by November 30, 1973.

Statistically organized field surveys are planned in order to obtain a more accurate definition and scope of known problems, detect new problems, and provide a basis for field feed back of the effectiveness of corrective design and process changes. Survey participants will be included from all affected offices. Phase 1 completion is expected by December 15, 1973 with subsequent surveys to be regularly scheduled.
(Source: Ford Quality Control Meeting, October 19, 1973.)

Corrective Action to Date

Corrective action has eliminated four corrosion perforation problems identified in annual "Paint and Corrosion Survey."

- Quarter panel at fuel filler (Ford and Mercury — all models) effective January, 1971.
- Spare wheelwell (Ford, Mercury, Torino and Montego — wagons) effective October, 1973.
- Quarter panel rear extension (Ford, Mercury, Torino and Montego — wagons) effective October 1973.
- Lower back panel (Mustang — all models) effective July 1, 1974. In addition the Excel Program was effective in all assembly plants July 1, 1973 to monitor body sealing operations.

Unresolved Problems Pending Corrective Action

A joint effort involving Automotive Assembly Division, Body Engineering Office Ford Customer Service Division, Metal Stamping Division and Product Development is in progress to establish appropriate corrective action for the remaining presently identified corrosion problems.

- Quarter panel (all carlines — all models) perforations occur along the lower periphery — 2 to 3 years.
- Front and rear door inner and outer panel (all except electrocoat cars — all models) perforations occur along lower surfaces — 2 to 3 years.
- Tailgate inner and outer panel (Torino, Montego, Ford, Mercury — wagons) perforations occur along lower surfaces — 2 years. Perforations occur along lower surfaces — 2 years.
- Tailgate window regulator mounting panel (Torino, Montego, Ford, Mercury — wagons) perforation causes detachment of lower end — 2 to 3 years.
- Rocker panel to quarter panel joints (all carlines — all models) perforation is occurring at joints due to galvanic action caused by moisture entry through sealer cracks and skips — 2 years.
- Deck lid inner and outer panel (Ford, Mercury, Torino and Montego — all models less wagons) perforations occur along the bottom edges — 3 years.
- Front fender (Pinto, Mustang, Maverick, Comet — all models) perforations occur along top surface and lower rear corner — 2 to 3 years.
- Quarter storage compartment (Ford and Mercury — wagons) perforations occur on lower surface — 2 to 3 years.
- Quarter wheelhouse (all carlines — all models) perforations occur at front and rear — 2 to 3 years "D" pillar at belt.(Ford, Mercury, Torino and Montego — wagons) perforations occur at the rear outer corners — 2 years.
- Rear floor pan extension to quarter panel (Maverick, Comet — all models and Ford, Mercury, Torino, Montego — wagons) perforation occurring along the lower vertical surface — 3 years.

- Hood inner and outer panel (Pinto — all models) perforations occur along leading edge — 3 years.
- Pillar to rocker panel (all carlines — all models) perforations occur at joint — 3 years.

Future Model Programs

The design of corrosion protection on forward programs conceptually follows current programs, at times modified by field experience. Performance is evaluated after the fact on one through five year old customer-owned vehicles by means of annual field surveys. Control of sheet metal corrosion in future model programs requires a Design Verification Plan for measuring the effectiveness of corrosion protection prior to vehicle signoff.

The existing Arizona Proving Ground accelerated corrosion test (P3-76) is used to gain information each year on new model prototype and early production vehicles. This test provides general information only because at present a correlation between the Arizona Proving Ground test and field service has not been established. The Body Engineering Office and Product Development are studying the test vs. field experience to determine proper correlation for subsequent GPAS utilization.

Other means of evaluating performance of corrosion protection at the prototype and early production stage are being considered; for example laboratory salt spray testing of complete doors, tailgates, hoods, and deck lids.

Improvements in corrosion protection will be accomplished by reexamination of current practice in specifying barrier and sacrificial coatings, expanded use of spray-on vinyl sealer (ESB-M4G191) as a replacement for zinc rich primer, plus improved water drainage in doors, quarters, tailgates, deep wells, etc. through sheet metal design configuration and optimum drain hole size, shape, and placement.

Consideration will be given to the use of special barrier protection for vehicles assembled in plants that normally supply customers in severe corrosion producing areas.

Work Plan Summary

The following actions are scheduled for completion in the near future as indicated:

First Cleveland area survey	(A)	9-12-73
Second Cleveland area survey	(A)	9-19-20-73
Detroit area survey	(A)	9-22-73
Cleveland area Wixom car survey	(A)	10-15-17-73
Ford vs. competition corrosion protection study		11-15-73
Detroit area statistical survey		11-15-73
Interim action proposal		11-20-73

Customer Service Division
    extended policy analysis   11-30-73
Statistical field survey to determine
    problem frequency   12-15-73
Corrective action and cost-effectiveness   1-21-74

A follow-up meeting to review the results of the above actions will be scheduled the week of January 21, 1974.

DESIGN LIABILITY

The two key cases in the field of auto design liability, involving the concept of crashworthiness are *Larsen v. General Motors Corporation*, 391 F. 2nd 495 (8th Cir., 1968) and *Evans v. General Motors Corporation*, 359 F. 2nd 822 (7th Cir., 1966). In *Larsen,* the Eighth Circuit ruled that the manufacturer has a duty to use reasonable means in vehicle design to reduce the incidence and severity of injuries to occupants in the case of a crash. The *Evans* court imposed no such duty since it found that participation in a collision is not one of the intended purposes of the auto.

This issue of crashworthiness has subsequently been litigated in several jurisdictions. The following cases follow the *Larsen* rationale:

Grundmanis v. British Motor Corporation, 308 F. Supp. 303 (E.D. Wis., 1970).

Mickle v. Blackmon, 166 S.E. 2nd 173 (Supreme Court S.C., 1969).

Gray v. General Motors Corporation, 434 F. 2nd 110 (8th Cir., 1970).

Dyson v. General Motors Corporation, 298 F. Supp. 1064 (E.D. Penn. 1969).

Those following *Evans* are:

Schemel v. General Motors Corporation, 384 F. 2nd 802 (7th Cir., 1967)

Shumard v. General Motors Corporation, 270 F. Supp. 311 (S.D. Ohio, 1967).

Willis v. Chrysler Motor Corporation, 264 F. Supp. 1010 (S.D. Tex., 1967).

Automobile Design Liability, by Richard Goodman, The Lawyer's Co-operative Publishing Company, 1970, 884 pages, $35.00. This is a background reference source for anyone dealing with the field of automobile design liability. It contains an abundance of information including: key legal doctrines and major cases in the auto products liability field, Federal Motor Vehicle Safety Standards, state maintenance and equipment regulations, and lists of experts witnesses and consultants. Goodman also discusses the important doctrine of crashworthiness.

16 AM. Jr., *Proof of Facts* s 1, (1965). "Automobile Design Hazards", Ralph Nader. In this article, Mr. Nader discusses the major legal avenues available in auto design litigation. Various hazardous design features (e.g. directional instability, door latches, etc.) are also explored. For those unfamiliar with the field of auto design liability litigation, this is a good background source.

IF YOUR CAR IS ON THIS LIST
YOU MAY BE LIVING DANGEROUSLY
10 MOST DANGEROUS CAR RECALLS*

GM	Chevrolet V-8s	1965-69	Engine mounts may separate causing sudden loss of control.	GM will install free new safety device, but not new mounts.
GM	All full-sized	1971-72	Steering mechanism may jam.	GM will install protective shielding.
GM	Chevrolet Vega	1971-72	Defective rear axle; wheels may fall off.	GM will replace rear axle where necessary.
GM	Chevrolet Vega	1971-72	Defective carburetor may jam throttle.	GM will install new idler bracket where necessary.
GM	Chevrolet Vega	1972	Defective exhaust; car may burst into flames.	GM will install new muffler system where necessary.
Ford	Torino & Montego	1972	Rear axle defect, wheel may fall off.	Ford will replace axle and bearing where necessary.
AMC	Most models	1972-73	Defective brake pedal link fastener can cause total loss of brakes.	AM will replace link where necessary.
Chrysler	Cricket	1971-72	Defective steering gear assembly can cause loss of steering control.	Chrysler will replace with modified rack bar assembly.
Ford	Most models	1972-73	Defective power steering assembly can result in loss of control.	Ford will install lockpin missing in assembly.
GM	Corvair	1961-69	Defective heaters can cause carbon monoxide poisoning.	GM will inspect but owner must pay for repairs.

*NOTE: These are only 10 of the most dangerous car recalls. Many others have been recalled. If you think yours might be among them, or if you suspect unrecalled defects in your car, please send the details to us.
(Source: National Highway Traffic Safety Administration, Washington, U.S.A.)

DEFECT INVESTIGATIONS

Over 47 million cars have been recalled by their manufacturers for built-in defects, many of them deadly. Fires can break out. Engine mounts can break. Heaters can leak deadly carbon monoxide. Brakes can fail. Power steering can freeze.

Please check this list. If you car is on it, you may be living dangerously. If you haven't had it repaired, get to your dealer, fast. In most cases he'll repair or safeguard it free. If he refuses, notify the manufacturer.

Those cases listed thereon are the subjects of current safety-related investigations being conducted by the APA. When an investigation is begun, it should **not** be assumed that a defect exists; only that a safety-related problem has been reported with sufficient indication of its existence to justify investigation.

MANUFACTURER/ MAKE	MODEL	YEAR	COMPONENT	POSSIBLE PROBLEMS
Ford	Fairlane, Mustang	1966-1970	Drop-in Fuel Tank	Certain Vents exposed to rupture by shifting luggage
Ford	F-250	1968-1969	16 x 5.5 Two piece wheel	Lock ring gutter failure
All Manufacturers	Travel Trailers	1965-1970	Axles, wheels and tires	Overloading of suspension
Ford	Ford full-size Lincoln, Mercury and Thunderbird	1965-1969	Front lower control arm	Failure of front lower control arm at ball joint area
General Motors	Chevrolet ½ ton Van and passenger cars	1969	Steering tie rod end	Suspected fatigue failure in thread section
Ford	Full-size	1969	Ignition switch	Poor connection between harness plug and switch
Ford	Ford, Mercury	1965-1971	15 x 5.5 single piece wheel	Bead seat failure
Ford	Galaxie	1968-1970	Front wheel spindle	Fatigue crack in heel area
Ford Chrysler, GM, and International Harvester	School Bus	Pre-1966	Hydraulic brake line	Steel hydraulic brake line failure due to corrosion

MANUFACTURER/ MAKE	MODEL	YEAR	COMPONENT	POSSIBLE PROBLEMS
General Motors	GMC and Chevrolet Pickup	Various	15" single piece wheel	Bead seat failure
Ford	All	1967-1971	Brake master cylinder	Failure of cylinder due to corrosion
Volkswagen	All	Pre-1966	Heater	Engine fume intrusion into passenger compartment
Ford	Ford, Mercury	1970	15 x 6.5 single piece wheel	Disc failure
Chrysler	All "C" Body	1969-1972	Bulkhead electrical connector	Becomes disconnected
General Motors	Chevrolet Impala	1968-1970	Steering wheel	Breakage at hub
General Motors	Chevrolet Vega	1971-1973	Steering relay rod	Lockup due to foreign object
International Harvester	Scout 800A and 800B	1970-1973	Clutch cable	Breakage due to bending fatigue
Mack Trucks	F-700 Series	1970-1972	Tilt cab pivot lock plate	Plate breakage
Ford	Full-Size	1970-1971	Hood latch	Failure of latch mechanism
International Harvester	1600, 1700s and 1800 Loadstar Chassis	Various	Rear axle U-Bolt	Low torque
Chrysler	Plymouth Valiant and Dodge Dart ("A" Body)	1970-1972	Brake proportioning valve	Rear wheel lockup under normal brake operation
Winnebago	D24 Motor Home	1970-1971	Front tires, wheels springs and axles	Suspension ratings are possibly exceeded by unloaded weights of vehicle front ends with standard or optional equipment, plus normal occupant and luggage loads
Action Industries	25-Foot Swinger Motor Home	1971	Front tires, wheels springs and axles	As above

MANUFACTURER/ MAKE	MODEL	YEAR	COMPONENT	POSSIBLE PROBLEMS
Champion Home Builders	24-Foot Motor Home	1971	Front tires, wheels, springs and axles	As above
Boise Cascade	Lifetime Premier 23-Foot Motor Home	1969-1971	Front tires, wheels, springs and axles	As above
PRF Industries	Travco 220 Motor	1970	Front tires, wheels, springs and axles	As above
Ford	Pinto	1971-1974	Rack and pinion steering	Bending of steering assembly on wheel impact causes binding
Ford	All with 4-Barrel Carburetors	1968-1974	Non-metallic fast idle cam	Breakage causes jamming of throttle in open position
Ford	School Bus	1966-1974	Brake drum	Breakage causes loss of brakes
Nissan	Datsun 510 and 1200	1969-1971	Plastic connector and filler hose	Leakage allows fuel or fumes to enter passenger compartment
Nissan	Datsun 510	1968-1971	Front suspension transverse link	Breakage due to improper shipping may allow loss of control
General Motors	All with Rochester Carburetors	1965-1972	Carburetor float	Engine flodding caused by loss of float buoyancy
Western Auto	Wizard A-5030	Various	Auto jack stand	Failure to meet load rating
Globe Fabricated	JS-100	Various	Auto jack stand	Failure to meet load rating
International Harvester	Scout II, 1110-1300-D, 1010-1310, 4x4	1970-1973	Brake lining	Brake pull and fade upon application
General Motors	Chevrolet Chevelle V8 engine	1965-1969	Engine mount	Secondary effects from shearing of engine mounts
Kar-Rite	Jack Stand- Model 1052, Rated at 4,000 pounds	All	Jack stand	Alleged unsatisfactory performance

MANUFACTURER/ MAKE	MODEL	YEAR	COMPONENT	POSSIBLE PROBLEMS
Volvo	Volvo	1973	Front bumper bracket	Failure of front bumper support bracket
Ford	Mercury Capri	1971-1973	Seat failure	Failure in reclining mechanism allowing seat to rotate rearwards and could result in loss of vehicle control
Ford	Mustang II	1974	Exhaust heat transfer to rear passenger compartment	Routing of exhaust system in rear axle area results in scorching and charring of the underside of the rear seat and melting of the floorboard insulation
Ford	Mercury Capri	1971-1973	Seat latch and seat belt	Inboard seat belt abrasion by seat latch
General Motors	All Light Duty	1966-1971	Rear axle control arm	Cracking and splitting at welds
International Harvester	Travelall	1971-1973	Steering arm ball	Movement during braking may cause loss of control
Toyota	Corona	1973	Front disc brake rotors	Corrosion and glazing encountered during shipping
Ford	Mercury Capri	1973	Fuel and evaporation line connectors	Molded tubing connectors may crack
Skyline Corporation	19½-Foot Nomad Travel Trailer	1971	Shackle bolt	Inadequate thread engagement with lock nut
Chrysler	All Six-Cylinder	1971-1972	Exhaust manifold	cracking
Ford	B and F-500 thru 700	1971-1972	Throttle linkage	Seizure of bell-crank at firewall linkage
General Motors	Cadillac, Eldorado and Oldsmobile Toronado	1967-1970	Front wheel lugs	Incorrect torque

MANUFACTURER/ MAKE	MODEL	YEAR	COMPONENT	POSSIBLE PROBLEMS
Ford	B-700 School Bus	1969-1970	Right front spring	Failure of main and second leaf
General Motors	Cadillac	1969-1970	Air-conditioner blower relay	Failure may cause overheating of electrical harness
General Motors	GMC and Chevrolet Pickup Truck	1971-1972	Steering tie rod end	Separation of ball from socket
Ford	Fairlane and Ranchero Mercury Montego Ford Falcon Mercury Comet	1965-1969 1965-1969 1965-1970 1965-1970 1965-1970	Engine mounts	Secondary effects from shearing of engine mounts
Toyota	Corona and Corolla	1971	Hood latch	Failure of secondary latch
Ford	Pinto	1972-1973	Assembly aid tab on rear wheel well	Tab may contact and cut tire
General Motors	Buick Opel	1964-1971	Fuel tank and system	Fuel system integrity
General Motors	All Passenger Cars	1967-1973	Power steering gear	Binding spool valve
Champion Builders	Concord 28-Foot Motor Home	1973	Gas tank	Location and installation of gas tank may cause overloading
Volvo	142, 144, 145, 164 and 1800E	1971-1973	Bosch fuel injectors	Fuel leaks from pressurized system on to engine exterior
Volkswagen	VW Type 3 prior to August 1971 Porsche 914 1.8, 1.7 and 2.0 Liter Engine VW Type 4 1.7 Liter Engine	1970-1972	Bosch fuel injectors	As above
Renault	Model 17 Sports Coupe	1971-1973	Bosch fuel injectors	As above
General Motors	Chevrolet Corvette	1963-1974	Rear wheel bearing	Failure due to insufficient lubrication
International Harvester	Travelall	1974	Battery cable	Rubbing or chafing causes spark or short

MANUFACTURER/ MAKE	MODEL	YEAR	COMPONENT	POSSIBLE PROBLEMS
Ceat S.P.A.	Mercurio 10.00x22	Various	Tire	Failure in bead area
General Motors	Pontiac All V8 Equipped Engines	1966-1972	Timing gear and chain	Failure of timing gear and chain
Toyota Motor Sales	Corolla Equipped with 1600cc Engine	1971-1973	Throttle	Alleged throttle sticking

(Source: National Highway Safety Administration, Washington, D.C.)

CHAPTER IV

THE ART OF
COMPLAINING

CHAPTER IV

THE ART OF
COMPLAINING

Complaining is a discouraging business. Tempers flare, harsh words are spoken, and both of the complaining parties usually take a solemn oath never to do business together again.

Not all complaints have to fall into the above category. Actually, there is an art to complaining that brings quick results and leaves tempers intact.

Most dealers hire specialists to deal with customer complaints. This is the last person you should deal with. Customer relations specialists are never in a policy-making position. They are required to apply warranty service within the strict confines of the manufacturer's or dealer's warranty. They know of a hundred and one reasons to justify the cancellation of your guarantee. Since they hear complaints all day, only the most incredible, hard-luck borderline cases get accepted under warranty.

The service manager is another individual not very helpful in settling warranty disputes. His job is to fix cars, not repair them gratuitously.

Whenever you are dissatisfied with a dealer's service, the best man to see is the owner of the dealership. This is the man everyone is afraid of. This is the man who likes to boast of his complaint-free servicing. This is also the man least likely to turn you away when you complain directly to him. The owner really does not want to hear customer complaints, but since very few complaints find their way to his office, he will probably attempt to settle those complaints that directly involve him.

When dealing with dealers it is always a good idea to emphasize that the only reason you bought your car from this particular dealer was because of the good reputation he has in the community. Tell him how impressed you were with the competence and honesty of the garage — until you began having your present problems. Conclude by asking the dealer to personally verify your story before deciding to meet your demands. Before ending the conversation, repeat firmly and politely your demands.

If your problem has not been settled after a few days, send the dealer a registered letter, politely repeating your demands (see sample complaint letter). If after five days the dealer does not make a reasonable offer, send a final registered letter claiming the amount for corrective repairs if the car is only partially defective, or claim the entire purchase price, if the car is a real lemon. Make photocopies of this final letter and send copies to different government representatives on the local and federal level, consumer groups, and government consumer protection agencies.

By now, no more than two weeks have passed since you first approached the dealer. You now are faced with 3 choices. One: you can admit that it was all a bluff and that you may as well keep your defective car. Two: you may get the car repaired elsewhere and sue the dealer in small claims court for the cost of corrective repairs. Your last alternative is to sue the dealer in the provincial court for your full purchase price plus expenses. This final alternative may not be desirable if provincial court cases have more than a few months waiting period. In Quebec and Ontario provincial court cases may take up to 6 months to be heard, while cases before the small claims court are usually disposed of in a few weeks.

Getting compensation from an automobile company is not difficult if the initial complaint is drafted correctly. First, send out a registered letter that lists in a polite fashion (of course, you may believe the guy to be the biggest crook the Lord ever created, just don't say so in your letter) all the defects and request that corrections be made.

The same type of polite, registered letter can be used for complaints against insurance companies, car repair shops, used car dealers, tire retailers, and credit companies. If satisfaction is not obtained, deposit a copy of the registered letter with the clerk of the local small claims court. Consumers living in the Maritimes and New Brunswick where small claims courts do not exist (as a result, consumers are ripped off more there than elsewhere in Canada.

When will these provinces join the rest of Canada in protecting their citizens with small claims courts?) are urged to contact the regional offices of the Federal Department of Consumer and Corporate Affairs where mediation services by the ministry often are very effective. In fact, regional Consumer and Corporate Affairs information officers do more to help consumers in their particular regions, despite an almost total absence of legislation with which to prosecute (Yes, Virginia, some businessmen are still afraid of the federal government), than the Ottawa bureau of Box 99 which is less in touch with regional particularities and consumer problems.

When the case goes before the small claims court plead your case in a polite, but firm manner. Remember, the judge also drives a car. Chances are that he has been cheated too. If you win, you will have joined the ranks of Canada's consumer radicals. If you lose, well, next time you will be more experienced, perhaps have a better case, or, just become a better pleader. In any case the experience of going to the small claims court and using the judiciary is one inexpensive "thrill" that is difficult to forget. Remember, the only difference between you and a lawyer is 4 years of schooling and the fact that the lawyer gets paid whether he wins or loses.

THE ART OF EFFECTIVE COMPLAINING

1. **Write your complaint.** (Letters intrude into the office routine, calls are forgotten, and meetings can be denied).

2. **Involve others.** (Dishonest dealers dislike publicity and are afraid of anything that could turn into a group action).

3. **Act promptly.** (Most complaints can be settled within 2 weeks. Take legal action if no settlement within 1 month of the initial complaint).

4. **See the top man.** (If pollution flowed upstream, companies would cease polluting. Only the dealer can change policy and make compromises. The salesman sells; the service manager services; and the public relations department explains company policy).

5. **Be polite and firm.** (Tell the dealer you chose his place because he's the best dealer in town — But now you're having second thoughts).

6. **Use guerilla warfare.** (Send copies of your complaint to the APA, the provincial and federal ministers of transport, consumer affairs, newspaper "action-lines", radio "open-line" shows, the police, health department, fire department, and if the dealer has a roaming watchdog, call the dog catcher).

7. **Use the courts.** (Small claims courts are particularly lethal when used against unscrupulous dealers, so save all letters and documents).

8. **Form your own consumer group.** (There is power with numbers, especially if many of the discontented consumers have been taken by the same dealer).

9. **Be persistent.** (Complain to at least 10 different agencies each day. Call the dealer daily. If the phone is not answered, send a night telegram).

10. **Keep your sense of humor.** (If you are too serious or menacing, you may scare people away).

The following four general rules for an efficient and succesful complaint strategy should be helpful in dealing with car dealers, or any other businessman.

Write the Complaint
Telephone calls are forgotten as soon as the receiver is put down. Registered letters, though, intrude into the daily office routine,

while telephone calls and personal visits can later be denied. A letter also helps you to formulate your complaint in clear, precise terms, for maximum impact. Try to keep your complaint within the confines of a two-page, double-spaced letter. Keep copies of all correspondence since this will help you later if you go before the provincial small claims court.

Involve Others
Dishonest businessmen do not like publicity. Who knows, other unhappy customers may pick up the case. Write letters to your newspaper's "action-line", or, directly to the editor. Some consumer complaints are so universal that many newspapers do feature stories on business abuses as a warning to their readers. The summer months are best for this approach.

Call "open-line" radio shows but be careful not to libel anybody. Call your deputy and ask him to call the dealer for you. Call the police, fire department and city health inspectors. If your dealer has a watchdog, call the dog catcher.

Sometimes, it can be fun to form your own Consumer Action Group. Call a press conference and invite others with similar problems to write you (use a post office box, and give your home telephone number only to journalists). You will be surprised to see how quickly the dealer responds to your demands when you represent a dozen of his own discontented customers.

Use Humor
Although it may be difficult, try to interject a bit of humor into your negotiations. Businessmen often polarize their positions if the consumer comes on too strong.

Use the Courts
Consumers are using more frequently the small claims court to settle disputes with merchants. In fact, some businessmen will settle out of court rather than risk the publicity of a court proceeding. In some jurisdictions, lawyers are not allowed to plead and the judge handles the case himself. Since cases brought before the small claims court are quickly settled, and court costs are low, these courts are handling an increasing amount of consumer litigation.

SAMPLE COMPLAINT LETTER

Registered
Without Prejudice

Mr. Honest Abe,
Honest Abe's Used Cars,
500 Melrose Blvd.,
Montreal, P.Q.

Dear Mr. Abe,
   I bought my.....................on ....
Since I purchased this car from you I have discovered the
following defects:

1. ....
2. ....
3. ....
4. ....
5. ....

   I have repeatedly asked that you fix these defects under
warranty. This has not been done.

   This car was purchased from your dealership with the understanding that it was a reliable means of transportation that
would suit my needs.

   I therefore, request that you correct the defects mentioned
above, failure which, I shall correct the defects elsewhere and
hold you responsible.

   Awaiting your earliest convenient reply, I remain,

Sincerely yours,

Charlotte Consumer.

HOW TO START A CONSUMER GROUP

1. RENT A POST OFFICE BOX.

2. WRITE A PRESS RELEASE.

3. CALL A PRESS CONFERENCE.

4. INVITE CONSUMER COMPLAINTS, VOLUNTEERS, AND PROFESSIONAL GUIDANCE.

5. ELECT A BOARD OF DIRECTORS.

6. INCORPORATE THE ASSOCIATION AS NON-PROFIT WITH LOW MEMBERSHIP FEES.

7. START SOLVING CONSUMER COMPLAINTS.

8. CALL SECOND PRESS CONFERENCE WITH DETAILS AS TO NUMBER AND TYPE OF COMPLAINTS RECEIVED.

9. ESTABLISH CONTACT WITH GOVERNMENT AND PRIVATE AGENCIES.

10. CONTACT INDUSTRY AND GOVERNMENTAL "WHISTLE-BLOWERS".

11. FIND HONEST LEGAL FIRM. (YOU MAY HAVE SEVERAL LAWSUITS BY NOW).

12. KEEP THE ASSOCIATION SMALL.

13. CALL A MONTHLY PRESS CONFERENCE EXPOSING A DOCUMENTED ABUSE.

CONSUMER PRESSURE TACTICS

The following consumer pressure tactics have been used successfully by individual motorists as well as organized consumer groups throughout North America and Europe. Some of the more original tactics have been perfected by the late radical labor organizer, Saul Alinsky, who spent his life organizing labor in America.

Parallel Auto Show
Whenever the local dealers present their annual auto exhibition present a free parallel exhibition using public facilities. Exhibit cars that are prematurely rusted, or, that have other obvious defects.

109

Demand that the media give equal time whenever other auto exhibit is publicized. Choose ten worst cars, ten worst dealers, elect miss "Lemon," and even raffle off a scrapped car to some deserving dealer.

Malpractice Award

Give a malpractice award to that segment of the auto industry that distinguishes itself as most deserving.

SAMPLE: PRESS RELEASE
CENTER FOR AUTO SAFETY

For Immediate Release

CENTER FOR AUTO SAFETY GIVES AUTOMOTIVE ENGINEERING MALPRACTICE AWARD TO GM'S COLE

The Center for Auto Safety today announced the selection of Edward N. Cole, President of General Motors Corporation, as the first recipient of the annual Automotive Engineering Malpractice Award.

The Ralph Nader-affiliated auto safety group announced Cole's selection for the award at a press conference in Union Square (opposite the Hotel St. Francis) at 12:30 today. The annual award will be given by the Center for Auto Safety to the individual whose actions or inactions have had the most detrimental effect on auto safety. The press conference was preceeded by a picket, comprised of local consumer groups, protesting Cole's presentation with an award of opposite intent — inside the hotel Cole was being given the National Motor Vehicle Safety Advisory Council's first annual award to an individual for contributions to auto safety.

The Washington-based Center said it would attempt to present Cole with a statute constructed of remnants of defective GM parts. The award consisted of a Pontiac "spinner" hubcap with protruding, unshielded, ornamental, knife-like blades; a piece of baling wire to signify GM's disregard for consumers in failing to replace defective engine mounts but rather installing wire-like restraint cables; a broken power brake vacuum check valve; a defective GM cruise control lever; a vial of carbon monoxide symbolizing two large GM safety defect notification campaigns: the first for carbon monoxide leakage into the passenger compartment of $2\frac{1}{2}$ million 1965-69 Chevrolets, the second for the defective heaters on 600,000 Corvairs. The last item in the statute is a piece of gravel, representing an object which could cause steering lockup on any 1971 or 1972 full-sized GM car.

"This should serve as a fitting reminder to Mr. Cole of the large numbers of persons who are killed and injured each year by defective GM vehicles," commented a representative of the Center.

Details of Cole's and GM's automotive engineering errors will be covered in full at the press conference.

In addition, information on two newly discovered GM violations will be released.

Midnight Telegrams

For dealers who refuse to answer their phone or otherwise respond to consumer complaints send a telegram. Send it "night-letter" rate (it's cheaper), and keep a copy.

Picketing

One of the most dangerous consumer tactics that can be employed, it should be used only as a last resort. Picketing always presents the danger of mob rule that can lead to criminal charges, or a court injunction. Injunctions are counter-productive because they can create outrageous legal expenses that will fast dry up a consumer group's finances. If picketing is used as a pressure tactic, be sure to get a permit, ask for police protection, call the media, use no more than 10 picketers, and picket peacefully.

Misleading Advertising Complaints

An excellent pressure tactic to use in conjunction with other tactics. Don't expect to have the complaint taken seriously by an industry agency, though. The depositing of this type of complaint is useful in attracting media attention, getting additional consumer support, and tying up a company's lawyers and public relations people for weeks.

Press Conference

Write a press release (2 pages, double-spaced, with telephone number) announcing a future press conference dealing with the formation of a consumer protection group formed to combat the abuses you have personally experienced. Send out the release 3 days before holding the press conference. The day of the press conference, rent a meeting hall, dress conservatively, and meet the press around 2 PM so as to get on the 6 o'clock news. Be brief and precise. Present visual "treats" for the cameraman like signs, a car painted like a lemon, or fellow members of the group. If no one comes to the press conference, send out the text of your speech to all media people and list a post office box where people may write.

"Lemon" signs

As a last resort, put several lemon signs on your car and park it near the manufacturer or dealer. This tactic often gets quick results. Before getting out the paint and paper, though, check with the local university law society (free legal advice) whether such a sign could provoke an injunction or contravene a municipal by-law. If trouble starts later, the law society may feel obliged to help out.

Classified Ads

Dealers and manufacturers use the classified ads to sell their cars. Any consumer placing satirical ads to critize his own car is profaning sacred ground and attracts the attention of the car manufacturers, local dealers, and journalists looking for a human interest story.

This consumer tactic was especially useful to one irate Nova Scotia rusty Ford owner who placed the following ad in one of the local newspapers:

> RUSTED
> 1973 FORD CUSTOM
> 44,000 miles, requires about $2200 worth of rust repairs and uses about 2 quarts of oil every 200 miles and gets about 8 miles per gallon. Does not at present pass safety inspection. Owner wants rid of. 865-7148.
> x1x17

As a result of this ad campaign which cost approximately $13.50, Joe MacDonald, who placed the ad, received more than 200 telephone calls from other angry Ford owners and eventually found enough support to establish a Rusty Ford Owners Association that now is pressing for a global settlement from Ford for all Ford owners victimized by Ford's rusting defect. The only negative result of MacDonald's ad was one telephone call from a local Ford salesman requesting that the ad be withdrawn because it was hurting his sales. The ad ran two days.

Complain to the Local Paper
Visit the news desk and try to interest a reporter in the story. Remember, chances are he has been cheated by garages and dealers fairly often himself.

"Action" Column
These consumer help columns are of limited value. Most of them receive far too many requests for help to be really effective. Staffers may have become so jaded by hard luck stories that motorists' complaints may have a very low priority. Another disadvantage with "action" columns is that the business community and other journalists tend to disregard the impact the columns may have with the general public.

Creative Hysteria (Mau-Mauing the Dealer)
As a last resort, it is often useful to appear completely irrational and dangerous to the dealer in private while maintaining a serene and peaceful comportment in public. This tactic is especially effective if you practice it by hanging around the showroom while the salesmen are showing new cars to customers.

While waiting for repairs that should be done under warranty, take a lunch along to the dealership and eat it inside one of the showroom cars (peanut butter and jelly sandwiches are the most cost-effective). Repairs will probably be completed in record time.

Write a Book About the Car
This will consolidate correspondence, alert the public and media, and possibly help pay for the legal expenses involved in a lawsuit. Eileen Greslik of Toronto, Ontario, has written an automotive morality play in her book detailing the troubles she has experienced with her defect-prone, updated Toyota. Proceeds from the book have financed her lawsuit.

Burning the Car
This is another last resort tactic that attracts the media and dramatizes the problem. A few years ago in California, Eddy Campos burned his new Lincoln Continental in front of Ford's regional headquarters. Public sympathy and media interest was so great that donations began pouring in from across North America. With these donations, Campos founded Motorists United, a non-profit consumer protection association for motorists. Be sure to check fire and pollution regulations before attempting a similar protest.

Government Hearings
Testify at government hearings investigating the automotive industry. This tactic will add pressure on the company as well as alert legislators to the problem.

Harass the Dealer's Bank
This is a last resort quasi-legal tactic that is a group exercise. Find out which bank the dealer or garage uses and then send in a dozen individuals to open savings accounts with the minimum $5 deposit. Then have the same people go back and close their accounts. Keep opening and closing accounts until most of the bank's staff is tied up in the savings department alone, then ask for a heart to heart talk with the bank manager. Remember, don't threaten and never say that it is a planned harassment campaign.

Contact the Sales Tax People
Businessmen do not like visits from the sales tax investigator. The investigator probably has difficulties with his own dealer. Many dealers are confused over all the different sales tax procedures so an investigation by one agent will usually turn up something. Even if there is no violation of the law, the dealer will need a week to recover.

Contact the Income Tax Inspection Division
Calling in the Taxation Department on a car dealer is like waving a cross in front of a vampire, the effect is immediate. Most business-

men are following tax plans established by their accountants without fully understanding what they mean. Therefore, visits by the Tax Inspector brings on a surge of pain because the dealer is poorly equipped to respond to precise inquiries as to his tax situation. The inspector may also be another aggrieved automobile owner.

Call the Health Department
Bathrooms are a good place to start. Even if there are no serious violations, the visit will have been unnerving enough.

Ask for Police Assistance
Usually the police have no powers to resolve civil disputes involving repair charges or the quality of used cars. In some areas, though, the police are well aware of the dishonest practices of certain car dealers or garages in their territory. Often the police will use their power of persuasion to convince the garage to release the car without being paid. Even if the police cannot do anything, their subsequent report can be used in court to show the dealer's attitude and to describe the events leading up to the lawsuit.

Cancel the Check
If possible, give the dealer a check and cancel the check later. Be sure to inform the dealer by registered mail that the reason the cheque was cancelled was to liberate your car. Offer to re-negociate the bill at the dealer's earliest convenience.

Foreign Press Releases
Japanese and European automakers are extremely sensitive to consumer criticism of their products directed against the parent company within their country of origin. By translating criticism into Japanese, German, French, Italian, or Swedish, and diffusing the material through that country's foreign correspondents, generally found at the National Press Building, Washington, D.C., major local scandals can be easily created.

CLASS ACTIONS

Class action lawsuits are initiated by one person on behalf of a group of individuals seeking compensation from the same party for the same reasons. Although recent United States Supreme Court decisions have made class action lawsuits there more difficult to set up, they still remain an effective means whereby Canadian consumers can sue an automobile manufacturer together in one joint lawsuit and thereby minimize legal costs.

Just the simple act of filing a class action lawsuit often pressures the automobile manufacture to give compensation in an out-of-court settlement.

A good example of a manufacturer bowing to class action pressure is the Ford Motor Company's recent decision to settle out of court a class action lawsuit, brought by 39 Michigan Ford owners claiming compensation for the premature rusting of their vehicles. Ford gave the plaintiffs $27,500 to drop the lawsuit.

Class action lawsuits require professional legal representation. Most U.S. lawyers, though, will take on a class action prosecution on a contingency basis where they take no fees, but share in the final award. In Canada, contingency fees are illegal.

The best places to find other car owners with similar problems is newspaper "action" columns, or the Automobile Protection Association.

Remember, there is no Canadian legislation authorizing class actions. So, any legal decision is likely to set a precedent. The only automobile class action ruled upon was in the GM Firenza class action where Judge Osler allowed the procedure. GM has appealed the decision. Presently the Ford Motor Company of Canada is the defendant in 4 class actions brought in Ontario, Nova Scotia and New Brunswick for damages of more than $400 million caused by the premature rusting of its 1969-1976 models.

SMALL CLAIMS COURTS

Businessmen dislike being sued before the small claims courts. There are few delays, lawyers are not always present and judges are experienced in hearing small claims. In some local court jurisdictions, the judge may have already heard similar cases against the same garage, car dealer, or automobile manufacturer. If you lose, the costs are minimal.

Because fraud is the foundation of the automobile industry in North America, consumers are victimized indiscriminately. Judges too, are fair game, and frequently find themselves the target of incompetent mechanics, or, manufacturing defects. Usually, judges suffer this exploitation in silence, rather than create a disturbance. However, since these same judges preside over trials involving car dealers, they bring with them a keen sense of curiosity, cynicism, and prejudice based upon their own experiences (does anybody believe that judges are objective?). Therefore, as long as judges continue to get cheated by the automobile industry in their personal dealings, consumers will still find the courts understanding and equitable.

Of course, some judges may find their personal feeling against the automobile industry too over-powering and subsequently decide to recuse themselves from hearing the case. Recently, two small claims court judges refused to preside over cases where consumers were asking $300 compensation each from Ford and

Fiat because of damage due to premature rusting. Both judges had similar problems and publicly withdrew from the cases amid much courtroom laughter. In fact, the only persons not laughing in the courtroom were the representatives sent to testify on behalf of Ford and Fiat.

Many cases don't make it to trial, but are settled out of court as soon as the dealer gets a subpeona and thereby finds out his customer is serious in pursuing his claims. Records show that almost one-third of these cases are settled out of court.

Finally, small claims courts are especially effective to consumer groups as a type of deferred class action. For example, Vega owners victimized by self-destructing motors and a biodegradable body have taken out hundreds of small claims court lawsuits against GM and its dealers throughout the United States and Canada, using GM "secret" warranty extentions on these items as the primary evidence for their claims. Initially, the judges were snowed under by GM's service representatives denying that such a warranty extension existed, and some consumers lost their cases. However, other more alert judges found out the warranty extensions actually did exist and awarded compensation to the Vega owners bringing suit.

Each case that was won was then given extensive publicity in the media due to the efforts of consumer groups in exploiting the victories. This publicity attracted other Vega owners to the courts to such an extent that now GM has found itself in the middle of a Vega owners revolt. As a result of these small claims court victories, General Motors has decided to settle most of its Vega cases out of court rather than spend its time constantly before the courts.

This same tactic has been used successfully against Ford for premature rusting, General Motors for defective transmissions and imported car manufacturers for updating model years.

It is an effective tactic that radicalizes the judicial system and the general motoring public as well. And since many small claims court judges also preside over courts of higher jurisdiction, a continuing series of small claims court victories helps pave the way for consumers bringing similar cases before superior courts.

It should also be noted that small claims courts allow consumers to subpeona important internal company documents that the manufacturer would prefer to keep secret. Many of the secret warranty extension documents found in this book were obtained by subpeona through the small claims court.

LAWSUIT MATERIALS

Sooner or later, you will file a lawsuit as the last resort to obtain compensation. Whether the action is initiated before the small claims court or higher judicial body, solid documentation is essential to winning the case. Usually, the dealer will be badly prepared and will not expect to see confidential internal company documents or industry research materials brought into the case.

The following documents have been used successfully by North American consumer groups before the courts. If some of these documents are unobtainable before the trail, they may still be subpeonaed from the manufacturer.

Extended warranties or customer "goodwill" guidelines
These secret warranty extensions are admissions by the manufacturers of the existence of substandard mechanical components. Under a strict interpretation of product liability, the manufacturer cannot limit his liability to mileage, elapsed time, or number of prior owners. Be sure to subpeona the exact document as listed in this book.

The United States Motor Vehicle Safety Act, Department of Transportation, Washington, D.C., or Canadian Motor Vehicle Safety Act (1971), Ministry of Transport, Ottawa, Ontario.
This federal law states the government's powers and defines the responsibilities of auto manufacturers in correcting factory defects and complying with safety standards.

NHTSA Recall Register, Department of Transportation, Washington, D.C. or Canadian Recall Register, Ministry of Transport, Ottawa, Ontario.
The Department of Transportation's National Highway Traffic Safety Administration publishes these quarterly guides which summarize *all* motor vehicle safety-related defects that have culminated in recall campaigns. The Canadian Recall Summary appears irregularly.

NHTSA Defect Investigations
Based upon consumer complaints, industry leaks, and independent investigation, the NHTSA publishes this monthly list of suspected defects to encourage motorist input into the inquiry. Note that an investigation is not an admission by the government or the automobile manufacturer that a defect actually exists.

FADA Guide to Used Car Prices
This booklet is ideal for convincing judges that you overpaid the dealer or that the vehicle was sold for the wrong year. Insurance companies offering unfair prices as compensation for vehicles

"totaled" after major accidents should be confronted with this booklet in negotiating fairer compensation.

PDI Inspection Sheet
Every new car has to be carefully checked out by the dealer before delivery to the purchaser. This verification procedure is called the Pre-delivery Inspection and is paid for by the automobile manufacturer. The dealer is required to fill out a PDI sheet and keep it with the owner's file at the dealership. Many dealers do not carry out the PDI and pocket the profit instead. This practice may account for the poor condition of a new car throughout its first 6 months of use.

Dealer Franchise Agreement
Car dealers are *not* independent businessmen. In fact, the automobile manufacturers, through tough franchise agreements, keep a strict control over almost everything the dealer does. The dealer franchise agreement will indicate whether the dealer follows company policy in his sales or services operations.

Warranty Claims Sheet
Each dealer has to claim his warranty costs from the manufacturer by submitting computer-coded warranty claims sheets. These forms will show if the dealer was paid for warranty work that was not done or if what was alleged to have been a "minor" engine adjustment was actually a complete motor overhaul.

Warranty Interpretation Manual
This dealer guide will show how dealers should process warranty claims. This guide is useful in showing if the dealer actually followed the correct procedures.

Dealer and Manufacturer Advertising
For both new and used car sales, checking the advertising can uncover contradictions, exaggerations, misleading statements, or just plain lies. Very useful in cases where a new or used car sales is to be cancelled. It also can be used to dispute claims for reliability, economy, or gas mileage. Recently, the Ford Motor Company was forced by a small claims court judge to pay the owner of a 1974 Bobcat $300 to cover the difference in gas mileage between what Ford advertised and what the driver actually got.

Dealer Invoice
This document shows how much the dealer paid for the vehicle and if there was a claim for transport damage. About one-third of all new cars are damaged in transport.

118

Prior Sales Contracts
These verify the price at which a used car was initially sold,
when it was sold, the mileage, and what reconditioning was done
to the vehicle. This information is essential in the cancellation of
used car sales. Also try to bring in the previous owner of the
vehicle to testify to the poor condition of the car.

Service Work Orders
Can be used to discover what reconditioning was done to the
vehicle, at what mileage, and at what cost to the dealer.

The Mitchell Manual, 4926 Savannah St., San Diego, California
In disputes over car repairs, this guide shows parts cost and time
alloted to perform repairs. This information can be devastating to
garages who habitually "boost" repair bills or charge for fictitious
"shop supplies". Costs are computed for Canadian garages.

Owner's Manual
This booklet is useful to show how carefully a car was maintained.

WHERE TO GO FOR HELP

I - Federal Government Agencies

**National Highway Traffic Safety Administration, Department of
Transportation, Washington, D.C. or the Director, Road and Motor
Vehicle Traffic Safety, Ministry of Transport, Ottawa, Ontario,
K1A 0N5.**
These people will tell you all you ever wanted to know about
your automobile, but were afraid to ask. Actually, the NHTSA is
responsible for the recall of more than 47 million vehicles for safety
related defects. Staff engineers may be useful as expert witnesses
in lawsuits alleging the presence of automotive defects.

**Federal Trade Commission, Washington, D.C. or The Minister of
Consumer and Corporate Affairs, Place du Portage, Hull, Quebec.**
This federal agency is interested in monitering the advertising
claims of companies and investigating their sales practices. Although
the FTC and CCA do not have any real teeth and work chiefly
through "cease and desist" orders and persuasion, some automakers
may prefer to change their advertising or warranty practices rather
than get "gummed" by the FTC or CCA.

II - MLAs and MPs
Each elected representative tries to maintain close contact with the
electors of his/her district hoping to exploit popular causes that
will facilitate re-election. Consumer complaints are often investigated, settled, or publicized by these politicians because they wish
to show "the folks back home" that local issues are important.

Federal and provincial members of parliament can also be instrumental in establishing public hearings and drawing up legislation covering automobile industry abuses. One drawback in complaining to politicians, though, is the possibility that the garage or dealer may be a financial contributor to the politician's election campaign. This problem can be overcome by using the media to publicize the cause so much that political action is rewarded by public support.

III - Small Claims Courts
See page 115 for a full description.

IV - Independent Consumer Agencies

Center for Auto Safety, 1223 Dupont Circle Building, Washington, D.C. 20036, (202) 659-1126.
The Center for Auto Safety was founded in 1970 with a grant from Consumers Union. Its purpose is to probe the relationship between unsafe car design and highway deaths and injuries, to press for safer car design, and to monitor the effectiveness of government efforts to enact vehicle safety standards. Operating out of offices in Washington, D.C., the Center keeps extensive files on consumer complaints about automobiles and is in continual contact with the auto industry and other private and federal sources.

Product Liability Action Resource (PLAR)
In the course of its research, the Center has acquired considerable expertise and a wide range of valuable information which is made available to subscribers through PLAR. The service offers technical reports and research studies, lists of attorneys handling similar cases, lists of potential expert witnesses, and complete records of Federal recalls and defect investigations.

Specific Services

Motor Vehicles
1. Names, addresses and telephone numbers of attorneys involved in related litigation;

2. List of engineers who have served as expert witnesses in litigation;

3. Review of recall campaigns for related defects;

4. Information on investigations of the subject model auto;

5. A compilation of the relevant Federal Motor Vehicle Safety Standards;

6. Any relevant petitions, docket submissions, tests, or compliance investigations from the Department of Transportation (DOT);

7. Highway safety literature relating to the subject defect;

8. Information on any detailed investigations of accidents involving the subject vehicle;

9. Internal service bulletins that relate to the defect sent by the manufacturers to their dealers;

10. Copies of corroborative letters from the files at DOT and the Center for Auto Safety;

11. Names and addresses of persons who have complained of similar or related defects to the Center for Auto Safety, DOT, and Ralph Nader.

Mobile Homes

The Center recently published a book-length exposé of the mobile home industry, including extensive documentation of severe fire and wind hazards. Copies of **Mobile Homes: The Low-Cost Housing Hoax** are available from the Center for $10.95.

In the area of mobile home fires, the Center offers:

1. Information regarding specific mobile home construction and safety standards existing at time the unit was built;

2. Lists of attorneys who are handling or have handled similar lawsuits;

3. Detailed technical information regarding the flammability of mobile home interior finishes;

4. Detailed technical information regarding the aluminum wiring fire hazard, and names of potential expert witnesses on the subject;

5. Information about possible sources of ignition, including faulty wiring, gas explosions, and furnace and water heater malfunctions;

6. Information regarding escape and rescue provisions (e.g. egress windows) in mobile homes.

In addition, there is on file substantive technical information about mobile home susceptibility to windstorm damage.

Highways

The Center monitors Federal and State highway activities regarding the road design for safety. In December, 1974, it published a 300-page report on highway safety, **The Failure of America's Roadside Safety Program** (available from the Center for $12.50).

The Center offers to attorneys handling highway safety design cases:

1. Specific information on roadside design;

2. Names of potential expert witnesses on proper roadside design;

3. Copies of design and construction standards relevant to a particular site;

4. Analysis of the respective Federal and State roles in designing and constructing Federal-aid roads.

Bi-Monthly News Bulletin

The Center's PLAR bi-monthly news bulletin, IMPACT, keeps subscribers informed about current defects and recalls, Federal regulatory actions, and the Center's monitoring activities.

Subscription charges

The Product Liability Action Resource fees are designed to make the service self-sufficient. The subscription fee is $50.00 per year for an individual attorney and for firms with 5 or fewer lawyers. For firms with more than 5 lawyers, the charge is $250.00. In addition to this membership charge, subscribers are billed a modest $25.00/hour fee for initial research performed by the Center on each request. Follow-up services will be supplied without additional charge, except when the Center's technical staff generates substantial original analytical material. The subscription fee includes the charge for IMPACT.

Automobile Protection Association, 292 ouest Boul. St. Joseph, Montréal, Canada (514) 273-2477, 5318.
See the Preface for a description of the APA.

V - Other Agencies

Consumer protection agencies are seldom well-financed and often are very financially unstable. For this reason alone, many of the following consumer protection groups may have changed location or simply disappeared by the time this list is published. If such is the case, please write the publisher so that a correction can be made.

The Better Business Bureau is to be used only if no other independent consumer agency can provide help.

HELPFUL AGENCIES RECEIVING
CONSUMER COMPLAINTS

The Automobile Protection Association, 292 St. Joseph Boulevard West, Montreal, Québec. (514) 273-2477.
The Consumers Association of Canada, 251 Laurier Street West, Suite 801, Ottawa, Ontario, K1P 5Z7.
The Department of Consumer and Corporate Affairs, Box 99, Ottawa, Ontario.
The Ministry of Transport, Road and Motor Vehicle Traffic Safety, Ottawa, Ontario, K1A 0N5.

Provincial Consumer Protection Bureaus
Department of Provincial Affairs, Confederation Building, St. John's, Newfoundland.
Consumer Services Division, Department of Provincial Secretary, Provincial Administrative Building, P.O. Box 2000, Charlottetown, P.E.I.
Consumer Services Bureau, Brookfield Building, 53 Inglis Street, Sydney, N.S.
Department of Provincial Secretary, Centennial Building, Box 32, Room 348, Fredericton, N.B.
Consumer Protection Bureau, 7th floor, 800 Place d'Youville, Quebec, Quebec.
Consumer Protection Bureau, 201 Cremazie Blvd. West, Montreal 354, Quebec.
Consumer Protection Bureau, 555 Yonge Street, Toronto 284, Ontario.
Consumer Bureau, Legislative Building, 210 Osborne Street North, Winnipeg, Manitoba.
Consumer Affairs Department, 1739 Cornwall, Regina, Saskatchewan.
Consumer Affairs Branch, 502 I.B.M. Building, 10808-99th Avenue, Edmonton, Alberta.
Consumer Affairs Officer, Room 12, LXAW Courts Building, Attorney-General's Office, Victoria, B.C.

Federal Government Consumer Consultants
Royal Trust Building, 139 Water Street, St. John's, Newfoundland.
639 Ralston Building, 1557 Hollis Street, Halifax, N.S.
Hardware Building, Queen & Regent Street, Fredericton, N.B.
800 De Maisonneuve East, Dupuis Building, Montreal, Quebec.
706 Global Building, 480 University Avenue, Toronto 101, Ontario.
412 Federal Building, 269 Main Street, Winnipeg 1, Manitoba.
Derrick Building, 4th floor, 1825 McIntyre Street, Regina, Saskatchewan.
Federal Building, 9820-107th Street, Edmonton 14, Alberta.
626 Customs Building, 1001 West Pender Street, Vancouver 1, B.C.

Better Business Bureaus

Better Business Bureau of Newfoundland and Labrador, P.O. Box 516, St-John's, Newfoundland. (709) 722-2447.

Better Business Bureau of the Maritimes, Duke St. Tower, Scotia Square, Halifax, N.S. (902) 422-6581.

Better Business Bureau of Quebec, 475 Richelieu Street, Quebec, Quebec, (418) 523-2555.

Better Business Bureau of Montreal, 1155 Dorchester Blvd. West, Montreal 2, Quebec. (514) 861-1731.

Better Business Bureau of Ottawa and Hull, 237 Queen Street, Ottawa 4, Ontario. (613) 233-1191.

Better Business Bureau of Hamilton and District, 155 James Street South, Hamilton, Ontario. (416) 526-1225.

Better Business Bureau of Metropolitan Toronto, 85 Richmond Street West, Toronto 1, Ontario. (416) 363-7111.

Better Business Bureau of Metropolitan Winnipeg, Room 204, 365 Hargrave Street, Winnipeg 2, Manitoba. (204) 943-1486.

Better Business Bureau of Calgary, Suite 404, 630 8th Avenue, S.W. Calgary 2, Alberta. (403) 269-3905.

Better Business Bureau of Edmonton, Mutual Life Building, 11765 Jasper Avenue, Edmonton, Alberta. (403) 482-2341.

Better Business Bureau of the mainland of British Columbia, 12th floor, 100 West Pender Street, Vancouver 119, B.C. (604) 682-2711.

Better Business Bureau of Vancouver Island, Suite 110, 645 Fort Street, Victoria, B.C. (604) 386-6348.

RUSTY FORD OWNERS ASSOCIATION
Key contact people

New Brunswick Rusty Ford Owners Association

c/o   Isidore Barr
Inflation Fighters
306 Pacific Ave
Moncton, N.B.   Tel: (506) 389-3547

James Letcher,   Legal counsel
Barrister
19 Church St,
Moncton, N.B.   Tel: (506) 855-2070

Nova Scotia Rusty Ford Owners Association

c/o   Joe MacDonald
88 Zinck Ave
Lower Sackville, N.S.

Robert Stroud   Legal counsel
MacKay, White, Stroud & Langley
Box 577
559 E. River Road
New Glasgow, N.S.   Tel: (902) 752-8336

124

Ontario Rusty Ford Owners Association

c/o   Tom Beeney
      R.R. 2
      Georgetown, Ont.

      Jeff Lyons   Legal counsel
      Lyons, Arbus,
      Box 291
      Commercial Union Tower
      Toronto-Dominion Ctr.
      Toronto, Ont.   Tel: (416) 869-0123

LEGAL CONTACTS

APPEL, GOLFMAN, COHEN, COOPER and CASTONGUAY
1440 Ste-Catherine west, Ch. 426, Montréal   Tel: (514) 871-8801

APPEL, David, Consumer lawsuits
COHEN, Ron, Misleading advertising, Class action
CASTONGUAY, Jacques, Consumer lawsuits
GOLFMAN, Robert, Corporate law
COOPER, Robert, Consumer law

Consumer lawsuits

CONNALLY, Thomas,
90 Sparks St., Suite 224,
Ottawa, Ont.   Tel: (613) 236-7981

KRAM, Ron, Toronto   Tel: (416) 961-6881

STROHL, Arnold
1117 Ste Catherine West, Montréal   Tel: (514) 849-1288

Class Action

LETCHER, James,
19, Church St., Moncton, New Brunswick   Tel: (506) 855-2070

LYONS, Jeff
LYONS, ARBUS,
Box 291, Commercial Union Tower,
Toronto-Dominion Ctr, Toronto, Ont.   Tel: (416) 869-0123

STROUD, Robert
MACKAY, WHITE, STROUD & LANGLEY
559 E. River Rd., Box 577, New Glasgow, N.S.   Tel: (902) 752-8336

CHAPTER V

"SECRET" WARRANTY EXTENSIONS

CHAPTER V

"SECRET"
AUTO WARRANTY EXTENSIONS

Most consumers are aware of the 12,000 mile warranty applied to new cars. However, automobile manufacturers also have a system of secret warranty extensions for vehicles which have defective components. These warranty extensions often offer free parts and labor up to 5 years or 50,000 miles regardless of the number of prior owners.

The following "secret" warranty extensions are presently in force. Nevertheless, most manufacturers will deny that extended warranties exist. If this happens write Box 99, Department of Consumer and Corporate Affairs in Ottawa for copies of internal company documents sent to the Government by the APA.

Also, if the extended warranty's arbitrarily established time limit has elapsed, consumers may still demand that the dealer or manufacturer pay part of the repairs. Usually a small claims court lawsuit will bring quick results if all else fails.

DEFECTIVE GM TRANSMISSIONS

General Motors, encountering some problems with leaking transmissions on its 1973, 1974, and some 1975 models as a result of switching to a new type of transmission fluid, warrants cars with the problem for up to five years or 50,000 miles.

GM was forced to stop using whale oil in its automatic transmission fluid because of a ban on the killing of sperm whales. Beginning in 1973, it adopted an alternate transmission oil.

Reports have come in from all GM divisions that the new fluid resulted in corrosion of a part of the automatic transmission oil cooler inside the radiator. This caused transmission fluid to leak into the cooling system while antifreeze got into the transmission.

John C. Bates, GM service director, said the 400 series hydramatic transmission, used in about 2.1 million '73-'74 standard models, resulted in about 5,000 leakages. On the company's 350 series automatic transmissions for its intermediates and compacts, about 500 failures ave been reported.

According to **Automotive News** the reports of failures have been trending downward since November and December.

GM changed production of its transmission coolers last November, strengthening them with more silver in the solder.

GM is also planning to get less corrosive fluids into the marketplace. Bates said if they were introduced in July, they would fully replace current transmission fluids sold by retailers and dealers by the end of the year.

Although no formal extension of its one-year, 12,000 mile warranty has been announced to cover cars with the leakage problem, Bates said he expects dealers to be formally notified of one shortly.

Problems with the leaky transmission can require an overhaul costing as much as $400. GM has been footing the bill for cars with this problem, despite having made no formal policy statement to dealers.

FORD RUSTING GUARANTEE EXTENDED

Ford claims to have fixed for free over 39,000 1969-1972 cars and light trucks for premature rusting under its "Limited Service Program J-67", Ford General Field Bulletin 550. Under this program Ford states:

"In our continuing effort to assure customer satisfaction we are announcing a service program covering body rust on 1969-1972 model cars and light trucks.

This is a limited service program **without dealership notification** and should be administered on an individual complaint basis. In effect, it enables you to handle body rust complaints without utilizing your extended policy funds.

Under this program there will be 100 percent coverage of repair cost through the first 24 months and 75 percent from the 25th to the 36th month without regard to mileage. Approved claims should be noted J-67".

CHRYSLER PAINT WARRANTY EXTENDED

The Chrysler company had quality control problems with the paint used on its 1972 and 1973 models. Paint problems were especially severe on cars with the "Purple People Eater" paint style. Chrysler extended warranty through its Technical Bulletin.

WHAT TO DO?

Warranty extensions are made by manufacturers to compensate consumers for defective parts that either fail prematurely or never function properly from the start.

The APA lawyers advise consumers never to accept an automobile manufacturer's warranty limitations, whether it be for 5 years as with some Toyota and Vega-Astre warranty extensions, or the normal 12,000 miles—12 month warranty. The lawyers feel that since the warranty extensions are for repairs caused by defective parts, dealers and car manufacturers cannot arbitrarily limit the extent of their liability. The law holds manufacturers responsible for their negligence regardless of what a dealer or factory representative may say to the contrary. Therefore, be wary of "goodwill" settlements where the dealer or manufacturer agrees to assume only 50 percent of the bill, or agrees to pay only for parts but not for the labor to install the parts. This type of "Goodwill" is hard to accept since the labor would not be necessary if the part was not defective.

Consumers wishing to contest a repair bill that may be excessive or covered by a secret warranty extension should take the following steps:

1. Write a registered letter to dealer and car manufacturer asking that repairs be covered by the warranty or by an extended warranty.
2. If the request is refused, pay for repairs and then make a a claim for reimbursement through the provincial small claims court.

3. Be sure to send a subpeona to the manufacturer ordering the deposit of all internal documents relating to the warranty extension for that model car.

The APA keeps on file a list of small claims court cases where consumers have forced manufacturers to extend their warranties for cars well after the normal warranty has expired. Some court judgements have extended the warranty beyond the normal warranty period.

DEFECTIVE AUTOMOBILE COMPONENTS

In addition to maintaining a system of secret auto warranty extensions, automobile manufacturers also compile confidential summaries of the major defective components used in each model year for each model car assembled.

The Ford Motor Company, for example, holds regular monthly meetings to discuss the reliability and quality of each car model as reflected by the number of warranty claims reported. The APA has obtained copies of those reports submitted to the "North American Automotive Operations Reliability — Quality Meeting" held by Ford on October 19, 1973, November 16, 1973, and again on January 17, 1974. These highly confidential internal Ford documents show, for example, that Ford approved 33 "extended policy programs" between 1971 and 1973 that cost the company $24.8 million.

In addition to outlining the various "secret" warranty extensions paid for by Ford, the internal reports also give details on more than 2000 separate defects affecting Ford models from 1969 to the 1974 model year. Ford owners who have paid for the repair of any defective mechanical components are urged to read the following selected documents carefully to determine if Ford has classified that component as defective. If so, a registered letter should be sent to the Ford Motor Company demanding a reimbursement for the repairs. If Ford refuses to give reimbursement, a small claims court lawsuit should be initiated using Ford's own confidential documents as proof.

KEY COMPANY ADDRESSES

American Motors Canada Ltd.
Brampton, Ontario
(416) 451-6780

British Leyland
Burlington, Ontario

Chrysler Canada Ltd.,
Windsor, Ontario
(519) 252-3651

Citroen Canada Ltd.
5465 Royalmount
Montréal, P.Q.

Datsun Automobiles Co.,
New Westminster, B.C.

Fiat Motors of Canada Ltd.,
1750 Brimley Road,
Scarborough, Ontario
(416) 291-6491

Ford Motor of Canada Ltd.
Oakville, Ontario.
(416) 845-2511

General Motors of Canada Ltd.,
Oshawa, Ontario
(416) 644-5000

Honda Canadian Motors Ltd.,
50 Emblem Court
Agincourt, Ontario.
(416) 291-6401

Mazda Motors of Canada Ltd.
75 Nugget Ave.,
Agincourt, Ontario.
(416) 291-2138

Peugeot Canada Ltd.,
2550 Trans Canadienne,
Pointe-Claire, P.Q.
697-7310

Renault Canada Ltée.,
1305 Marie-Victorin,
St-Bruno, P.Q.
653-3661

Toyota Canadian Motor Sales Ltd.,
1291 Bellamy Road,
Scarborough, Ontario.
(416) 438-6320

Volkswagen Canada Ltd.,
Golden Mile Road,
Toronto, Ontario.

Volvo Canada Ltd.,
175 Gordonbaker Road,
Willowdale, Ontario.
(416) 493-3700

SECRET WARRANTY EXTENSIONS (TAKEN FROM ORIGINAL CONFIDENTIAL DOCUMENTS)

Published By
GENERAL MOTORS LTD.
TOYOTA USA LTD.
FORD OF CANADA LTD.
FORD OF USA LTD.

GENERAL MOTORS VEGA AND ASTRE
1971-1974

GMP-325-3M 6-74-MBF

VEGA-ASTRE "SPECIAL POLICY"
REQUEST FOR REIMBURSEMENT —
SPECIAL ENGINE OVERHEAT POLICY

This Special Policy applies to all 1971 through 1974 Vegas/Astres regardless of previous or present ownership and is retroactive for Overheat Services previously performed for which the owner may have been charged for all or part of these services. Charges for parts and/or labour which may have been performed by a General Motors Dealer or an Independent Service Station prior to June 1, 1974 will be considered for adjustment.

Engine components eligible for Special Policy considerations include Head Gasket, Cylinder Head, Engine Block Replacement, Engine Block Reconditioning, Fitted Block Replacement, Partial Engine Assembly Replacement, necessary related gaskets and labour allowances for installing the components.

The cost of parts and labour in connection with Maintenance Services normally considered owner responsibility as outlined in the applicable Owner's Manual, General Motors New Vehicle Warranty are excluded from the provisions of this Policy.

Purchasers must provide authentic documentation of repairs and proof of ownership of the vehicle in question.

Dealers are to assist owners in completing this application and insure all documentation required is attached.

Vegas/Astre engine must' have the coolant recovery system installed prior to submitting this application. Forward all applications to Zone Office for Zone Approval.

TOYOTA: EXTENDED POLICY 1

(1971-1972 TOYOTA COROLLAS WITH 2T-C MOTORS)

Nature of repair applicable for extended policy:
Head Crack

Applicable Vehicle Models:

Warranty coverage of 5 years/50,000 miles for Vehicles with Frame Numbers Prior no:	For Vehicles within the Frame Number Range indicated below, 36 months, 50,000 mile warranty is applicable.
TE 21 059163	TE 21 059164 to 080836
TE 21 607044	TE 21 607045 to 631898
TE 27 049464	TE 27 049465 to 075030
TE 28 508364	TE 28 508365 to 530459
TA 12 062087	TA 12 062088 to 119325
	TA 12 700001 to 702941

Policy period and coverage:
Refer to the above Applicable Vehicle Models column.

Expiration date: June 30, 1975

OPERATION CODE F.R.H. DESCRIPTION OF REPAIR

Operation Code and flat rate hr.   **Please refer to the Toyota Flat Rate Manual.**

Failed Part No.

Authorization Number: HWG-3339

TOYOTA U.S.A.

SECRET MOTOR WARRANTY

Remarks:	This Bulletin replaces Extended Policy Bulletin
Feuille 153	
Nature of repair application for extended policy:	Replace engine block in accordance with the Toyota Service Bulletin referenced above.
Applicable Vehicle Models:	All vehicles 2T-C engines prior to engine number 2T-0571850 or prior to frame numbers indicated below: TE 21 036625 TE 28 541264 TE 21 649076 TA 12 143028 TE 27 081612 TA 12 717221 TE 27 410638
Policy period and coverage:	100% parts and labor for 24 months or 24,000 miles
Expiration date: June 30, 1975	
OPERATION CODE F.R.H. DESCRIPTION OF REPAIR	
Operation Code and flat rate hr.	**Please refer to the Toyota Flat Rate Manual.**
Failed Part No.	
Authorization Number:	EP 3-A
Remarks:	This Bulletin replaces Extended Policy Bulletin.

FORD U.S.A.
SECRET RUST WARRANTY, AUGUST 25, 1972

All Regional and District Managers, Ford Customer Service Division.

Limited Service Program J-67 for body rust on 1969 — 1972 model cars and light trucks — District Information Only.

Announcement of limited service program covering body rust on 1969-1972 model cars and light trucks.

In our continuing effort to assure customer satisfaction we are announcing a service program covering body rust on 1969-1972 model cars and light trucks.

This is a limited service program **without dealership notification** and should be administered on an individual complaint basis. In effect, it enables you to handle body rust complaints without utilizing your extended policy funds.

Under this program there will be 100 percent coverage of repair cost through the first 24 months and 75 percent from the 25th to the 36th month without regard to mileage. Approved claims should be noted J-67.

Your cooperation in administering this as a limited service program will assure maximum benefits for all Districts.

FORD SECRET WARRANTY DOCUMENTS

Some of Ford's secret documents relate to manufacturing defects experienced by Canadian Ford owners.

FORD EXTENDED POLICY PROGRAM NO. 88

*Revised

CAPRI HEATING-VENTILATING SYSTEM

ELIGIBLE VEHICLES:
*All 1971, 1972 and **1973 Capris,** built prior to **April 1,** 1973.

DESCRIPTION:
*This EPP has been established to correct problem of inadequate heater and/or ventilation modulation and operator control.

REPAIR PROCEDURE:
*Under the provisions of this EPP, dealers will make repairs with the procedures published in **72 B 45 Item No. 4.**

PART NUMBERS:
Please refer to the above-noted Technical article and the Parts Catalogue.

LABOUR TIME OPERATION:
Labour operation No. SP-18476-B-72.
Time: 2.2 hours

REIMBURSEMENT POLICY:
The coverage for 1971, 1972 and 1973 model Capris is extended to December 31, **1973** with no restriction on time or mileage.

CLAIMS SUBMISSION INSTRUCTIONS:
Show "Program 788" in the instruction area of the claim, 18476 in the CAUSAL PART NO. box and 788 in the PROBLEM CODE box.

PARTS DISPOSITION:
Replaced parts should be treated as normal warranty parts and handled in accordance with the provisions of Subject 3.1 of the current Warranty and Policy Manual.

EFFECTIVE DATES OF EPP:
*Provisions of this EPP are effective from **April 30, 1973** until December 31, **1973** regardless of vehicle mileage.

*Attachment to 73 M 24.

SIGNIFICANT EXTENDED POLICY PROGRAMS, FORD

Component	Maximum Coverage (Months)	Vehicle Lines	Model Years	Estimated Program Costs (Mils.)
Valve Guide Wear	24/24	Cars & Light Trucks	1970-1972	$ 3.4
A/C Compressor	24/-	Torino & Montego	1972	3.2
330 HD FT Engine Bore Wear	-/50	Medium Trucks	1969-1973	2.9
361 & 391 PT Eng. Bore Wear & Oil Cons.	30/50	Med. & Heavy Trucks	1970-1973	2.1
C-4 A/T Band Slippage	24/40	Cars & Light Trucks	1971-1972	1.8
Body Rust	36/-	Cars & Light Trucks	1969-1972	1.3
Bonded Ventless Window Glass	24/-	Cars Except Maverick	1969-1970	1.2
A/C Evaporator Core	36/-	Ford & Mercury	1970-1972	1.1
Rear Axle "Chuckle"	24/24	Cars & Light Trucks	1972	1.1
Quarter Panel Rust around Fuel Filler	24/-	Ford & Mercury	1969-1971	0.4
Power Window Motor and Drive Assy.	30/-	T'Bird & Mark III	1969-1970	0.3
Subtotal				$18.8
All Other			1967-1974	3.6
Total				$22.4

SPECIAL ADJUSTMENT BULLETIN NO. 71 EXCESSIVE OIL CONSUMPTION

ELIGIBLE UNITS:
All 1971 and 1972 Capri and Pinto and 1972 Cortina with 2.0 litre engines.

DESCRIPTION:
This SAB has been established to correct problems of excessive oil consumption.

REPAIR PROCEDURE:
Oil consumption problems should be confirmed using the evaluation procedure published with Service Management Letter 70 M 3.

Repairs made under the terms of this program should involve the installation of new exhaust valve stem seals (all models) and replacement of the oil dipstick with a revised part as required (Cortina and Capri only).

DEFECTIVE FORD COMPONENTS (TAKEN FROM ORIGINAL CONFIDENTIAL DOCUMENTS)

Published by
FORD CANADA LTD.
FORD ENGLAND LTD.
FORD USA LTD.

MAJOR CUSTOMER PRODUCT PROBLEMS

Problem Area	Car Lines	Description	No. of Review
Current Model Problems			
Paint	All except Ford & Mercury	Mis-match and poor application	Nov.
Electrical Malfunctions	All except Mav., Comet & Pinto	Inoperative accessory and Interior/exterior lights	Dec.
Air Conditioning	All	W/S fogging, leaks and compressor failures	Dec.
High Speed Vibration	T'Bird, Mark IV, Lincoln, Must. and Mercury	Improper tire balance	Dec.
Driveability	All with 2.3L, 2.8L and 250 CID	Dieseling, stalling and rough idle	Nov.
Wind Noise & Water Leaks	Lincoln, T'Bird, Mark IV, Torino, Montego	Improper glass adjustment and poor sealing	-
Driveline Clunk	All	Noise on shift engagement	-
Front Suspension	All except Mav. Comet & Pinto	Noise and mis-alignment	-
Power Steering Gear	All w/XR-50 gear	Sticks and binds	Jan.
Locks, Handles and Mechanism	Linc., Mustang, Comet, Torino, Montego & Cougar	Inoperative and improper adjustment	Jan.
Starter Interlock/ Seat Belts	All	No-start and twisted belts	Dec.
Sheet Metal	Ford, Mercury, Mark IV, Lincoln, Mustang, Comet and Montego	Poor fits, dents, dings, rough metal finish	Nov.
Radio	Mercury, T'Bird, Mark IV, Lincoln Montego	Inoperative, static, poor reception	-
Shift Cable	Torino, Montego, T'Bird, Mark IV, Cougar	Cable freeze-up	-
Automatic Transmission	All	Erratic shifting	Dec.
Brakes	All	Master cylinder internal leakage	-
Solid State Ignition	All with 460, 400 CID engine	Module failure	Oct.

Past Model Problems

Rust and Corrosion	All 1969-1973 car lines	Body rust & perforations	Oct.
Exhaust Manifold	1971-73 351W	Manifold cracking	Jan.
Valve Guides	1972-73 400 CID	Excessive guide wear	Jan.

CHAPTER VI

USED CAR RATINGS

CHAPTER VI

USED CAR RATINGS

The following used car ratings are based upon consumer complaints, garage interviews, and reports from 17 different European and American testing agencies. Although some used cars are harshly criticized, this criticism does not mean that every single car in that model category will have the same defect. Even though a certain model may be listed as "Not Recommended", it may still be a good buy if an independent mechanic approves the vehicle before it is sold.

USED CAR PRICE

This price is the actual retail selling price these cars command in Montreal and Toronto. To find the retail value of a used car in other provinces, add on the following percentages:

Newfoundland 10%, Nova Scotia 5%, Prince Edward Island 5%, New Brunswick 5%, Quebec 0%, Ontario 0%, Manitoba 5%, Saskatchewan 5%, Alberta 10%, British Columbia 10%, Northwest Territory 10%, Yukon 10%.

Remember that a car dealer will always sell these cars for the amount listed. However, no car dealer will buy these cars for their full retail prices. To determine the wholesale price (dealer to dealer), subtract 30 percent from the retail figure. A $2,000 used car will be sold between dealers for $1,400 for a gross profit of $600. A smart shopper could cut the retail price down to $1,700 and still give the dealer a comfortable $300 profit.

The "Black Book" and "Red Book" used car listings have not been consulted because of their close affinity to the automobile industry and the contradictions found in their prices.

For this book, prices have been determined by consumer interviews, newspaper advertising, automobile auction reports, and negotiating for consumers throughout Canada.

FREQUENCY OF REPAIRS

The modern automobile has more than 15,000 separate moving parts. Some parts are weaker than others. Whenever consumers complain that one particular part constantly breaks down, the APA lists that component as having a higher than average frequency of repair rate.

Certain components, such as disc brakes, have a higher than average breakdown rate primarily because of the salt and extreme climate found in Canada. Many manufacturers are working on this problem.

GAS MILEAGE

Gas mileage rates are only an indication of what a particular model may do under optimum conditions. Mileage ratings are expressed in Canadian gallons.

TECHNICAL DATA

The technical data category may not be precise for every variation of a particular model. Thus, the data is to be used only as an approximation of available options.

SAFETY DEFECTS

Over 47 million vehicles have been recalled for safety-related defects. It has been estimated that 30 percent of the recalled cars are never brought into the dealer for correction. If your car has been recalled for safety defects, the automobile manufacturer must correct that defect regardless of your car's mileage, year, or number of different owners.

Check your used car for defects. Better that it be the manufacturer who pays for corrective repairs, rather than taking the money from your pocket.

150

BODY RUSTING

Many used cars may appear to be excellent buys, but, after a few weeks of ownership, huge rust perforations may appear through the new paint job applied by the used car dealer.

RECOMMENDATIONS

Certain used cars have so many things going against them that they are risky buys for consumers wanting the most quality for the least amount of money.

Before deciding on a used car, check out its mechanical condition with a competent independent mechanic. **Do not depend upon this book's recommendation alone.** Some good cars may not be listed since these car ratings cannot cover every car manufactured. For additional information on any car not listed, please call the Automobile Protection Association in Montreal at: (514) 273-2477.

MILEAGE/PRICE TABLE

The price of a used car can vary considerably depending upon its mileage. So as to take the mystery out of mileage/price computations, the following mileage/price table has been calculated. Remember, an average car does about 12—15,000 miles a year. Be suspicious of any used cars showing less than the normal amount of mileage.

MILEAGE DEDUCTION TABLE

Model year

Mileage	1970	1971	1972	1973	1974	1975	1976
0 to 15,000	+$200	+$150	+$100	+$50	+$25	—	—
15,001 to 20,000	+$175	+$125	+$75	+$25	—	—	-$50
20,001 to 25,000	+$150	+$100	+$50	—	—	-$50	-$100
25,001 to 30,000	+$125	+$75	+$25	—	—	-$100	-$150
30,001 to 35,000	+$100	+$50	—	—	-$50	-$150	-$200

Mileage	1970	1971	1972	1973	1974	1975	1976
35,001 to 40,000	+$75	+$25	—	—	-$100	-$200	-$250
40,001 to 45,000	+$50	—	—	-$50	-$150	-$250	-$300
45,001 to 50,000	+$25	—	—	-$100	-$200	-$300	-$350
50,001 to 55,000	—	—	-$50	-$150	-$250	-$350	-$400
55,001 to 60,000	—	—	-$100	-$200	-$300	-$400	-$450
60,001 to 65,000	—	-$50	-$150	-$250	-$350	-$450	-$500
65,001 to 70,000	—	-$100	-$200	-$300	-$400	-$500	-$550
70,001 to 75,000	-$50	-$150	-$250	-$350	-$450	-$550	-$600
75,001 to 80,000	-$100	-$200	-$300	-$400	-$500	-$600	-$650
80,001 to 85,000	-$150	-$250	-$350	-$450	-$550	-$650	-$700
85,001 to 90,000	-$200	-$300	-$400	-$500	-$600	-$700	-$750
90,001 to 95,000	-$250	-$350	-$450	-$550	-$650	-$750	-$800
95,001 to 100,000	-$300	-$400	-$500	-$600	-$700	-$800	-$850

1970 DOMESTIC MODEL RATINGS

This was the year that the sub-compacts were really first introduced, the intermediates began to lose sales to the compacts of the Valiant variety, and the luxury cars had one of their most popular years.

General Motors
General Motors' best models for that year were the Camaro ($1,000),

Nova ($700), Firebird ($1,000), Laurentian ($900), Tempest ($900), Buick Le Sabre (1,000), and the Oldsmobile Delta (1,000).

Some of GM's lemons of that period were the Vauxhall ($50) and the Cadillac Calais ($1,600).

Ford
Best of the Ford lot was its Maverick and Comet (600), although Ford's intermediates had excellent mechanical components. Its luxury cars were a disaster for that year. All of Ford's vehicles and light trucks were severely eaten up by premature rusting, so very few may still be around that are worth buying.

Chrysler
In 1970, Chrysler was certainly king of the compacts with its Valiant and Dart ($900) classed as the best compact cars around. Chrysler's Simca ($50) was an imported nightmare, and its luxury Imperial model ($800) was problem-prone.

American Motors
This is the year when American Motors almost might have gone on welfare. Sales were so bad that the company had to give away free television sets in order to get rid of its cars. Best cars were the Javelin ($900), Gremlin ($600), and the Hornet ($700). The ambassador ($500) was probably put together by a mad scientist, its reputation for reliability was so erratic.

MAJOR RECALL CAMPAIGNS

National Highway Safety Administration, Washington, D.C.

American Motors Corporation

Make	Model	Model Year	Brief Description of Defect (Manufacturer's Corrective action)	No. of Pages on File	Number of Vehicles Recalled
			American Motors Corporation		
American Motors	Rebel Ambassador Gremlin AMX Javelin	1970	Possibility that locking pawl used on bucket seat back may have been produced with steel of improper specifications. It was determined that locking pawl would not pass Federal Motor Vehicle Safety Standard 207. (Correct by replacing with proper type pawl.)	14	2,498

Make	Model	Model Year	Brief Description of Defect (Manufacturer's Corrective Action)	No. of Pages on File	Number of Vehicles Recalled
American Motors	Model 7010 Rebel	1970	Possibility that rear suspension lower control arm may fail because bushing hole may not be of proper dimension. Can cause metal fatigue after extensive or hard usage which will affect rear axle stability. (Correct by replacing lower control arm and bushing.)	14	3,581
American Motors	7108 Hornet Sportabout	1971	Possibility that rear auxiliary floor pan supports were improperly located. Fastening screws could slightly penetrate gas tank and gasoline would leak from tank when full or when vehicle is parked on an incline.	14	5,704
American Motors	Hornet—7101 Gremlin—7140	1971 1971	Door latch assemblies may not latch, lock, or unlock. (Correct by replacing parts.)	14	19,111
American Motors	Matador & Ambassador	1972 1973	Possibility that headrest on models with individual seats do not consistently comply with rear-impact, energy-absorbing requirements of Federal Motor Vehicle Safety Standard No. 201. (Correct by inspecting and installing rubber grommets to allow softer flexing of headrest.)	3	17,693
American Motors	Hornet Matador Gremlin Javelin Ambassador	1972 1973	Possibility that brake pedal link was secured with incorrect fastener. If nut is not specified type, it may possibly work loose permitting link to separate from brake pedal.	4	270,815
Jeep	CJ5 & CJ6	1972	Possibility that dimmer switch may accumulate dirt and salt from splash of roadway, causing terminals to corrode. (Correct by inspecting and replacing dimmer switch terminals in down position and installing rubber insulators on terminals.)	16	10,357
Jeep	CJ5 & CJ6	1972	Possibility that after several quick returns of brake pedal to its resting place, master cylinder stop plate may become fatigued from repeated impact and breaks. This will permit push rod to disengage from master cylinder and cause brakes to no longer perform. (Correct by inspecting and replacing with push rod and plate of new design.)	4	15,819
Jeep	Wagoneer	1971	Possibility that right rear brake line could wear through, due to rubbing.	12	5,029

154

Make	Model	Model Year	Brief Description of Defect (Manufacturer's Corrective Action)	No. of Pages on File	Number of Vehicles Recalled
American Motors	Jeep CJ-5 CJ-6	1974	Possibility that vehicles were assembled with suspension spring lock nuts with insufficient locking action to properly engage threads of mating bolt. If condition exists, nut, and subsequently bolt, can be lost, resulting in separation of one end of spring from frame with possible vehicle control problems.	3	19,088
American Motors	Pacer	1975	Possibility that fuel line retainer clip was improperly installed which would allow fuel hose to bear against front engine/suspension crossmember, causing abrasion and hose failure with subsequent fuel leakage.	3	13,676

MAJOR RECALL CAMPAIGNS
National Highway Traffic Safety Administration, Washington, D.C.
Chrysler Motors Corporation

Make	Model	Model Year	Brief Description of Defect (Manufacturer's Corrective Action)	No. of Pages on File	Number of Vehicles Recalled
Dodge Plymouth	Dart Valiants equipped with standard drum brakes	1970	Possibility that front portion of brake master cylinder was damaged or improperly assembled in production. Also possible that primary cup in front brake portion may have been cut, or a thin washer between cup and piston may have been omitted.	12	19,160
Dodge	Polara Monaco	1970	Possibility that bumper jack hook under some conditions may not properly engage front bumper flange and allow vehicle to fall during jacking operations. (Correct by replacing hook where necessary.)	5	81,932
Plymouth	Cricket	1971 1972	Possibility that under certain unusual types of road conditions sufficient loading can be generated in steering linkage to overstress and bend steering gear rack bar. If condition exists, could result in binding in gear and eventual loss of steering control. (Correct by inspecting and replacing with modified rack bar assembly.)	9	42,000
Plymouth	Fury	1972	Possibility that front bumber guard may not be adequately attached to bumper to withstand loads imposed during jacking. If condition exists, guard could pull off during jacking. (Correct by inspecting and replacing with new bumper jack hook.)	2	56,371

155

Make	Model	Model Year	Brief Description of Defect (Manufacturer's Corrective Action)	No. of Pages on File	Number of Vehicles Recalled
Plymouth Dodge	Satellite Coronet Charger	1973 1973	Possibility that front brake hose may rest against frame due to misalignment of brake hose frame mounting bracket.	2	14,000
Plymouth	Valiant Satellite Fury	1972 1973	Possibility of fuel leakage due to metal fatigue and cracking at extruded fuel pump outlet and/or seal of fuel pump integral filter.	2	149,056
Dodge	Dart Coronet Charger Polara w/6-cylinder	Manfd July thru Dec. 1972	Metal fatigue is caused by deficiencies in pump and fuel line vibration. Leak at fuel filter is result of inadequate seating. Either of these defects could result in engine compartment fire.		
Imperial Chrysler Plymouth Dodge	All All Fury Monaco	1974	Possibility that vehicles may not have full heater and defrosting capability and may not comply with Federal Motor Vehicle Safety Standard No. 103. Failure is due to heater hose water valve not opening from closed position, or remaining in open position.	2	60,000
Plymouth Dodge Chrysler Imperial	Fury Polara Monaco All All	1974 1974 1974 1974	Possibility that lower control arm may be fractured in area adjacent to lower ball joint, which may permit separation of ball joint from control arm. (Correct by inspecting and reinforcing lower control arm.)	12	159,149
Plymouth Dodge	Valiant Dart	1975 1975	Possibility that floor covering (carpet or rubber mat) may interfere with accelerator pedal. If condition exists, carpet or rubber mat to right of accelerator pedal may impede normal return of accelerator.	5	55,862
Plymouth Dodge Chrysler	Gran Fury Monaco Chrysler Imperial	1975 1975 1975	Possibility that jack furnished with vehicle may have holding pawl failure during jacking. Over-travel of jacking handle and level during lifting motion can result in heavy interference loading between holding and lifting pawls. Loading may cause holding pawl to fail.	2	65,000
Plymouth Dodge	Fury & Gran Fury Coronet & Monaco Police & taxi fleet	1975 1975	Possibility that front suspension lower control arm strut (passenger side only) attachment to frame may loosen and disengage as result of heavy breaking loads and high degree of suspension movement experienced in severe fleet service.	2	32,000

MAJOR RECALL CAMPAIGNS

National Highway Traffic Safety Administration, Washington, D.C.
General Motors Corporation

Make	Model	Model Year	Brief Description of Defect (Manufacturer's Corrective Action)	No. of Pages on File	Number of Vehicles Recalled
Buick	Skylark Sportwagon and GS	1970	Possibility that carburetor throttle operating cable may have been kinked or bent during assembly. This could result in cable binding and prevent throttle from closing.	10	19,917
Chevrolet	Chevelle Monte Carlo	1970	Incorrect tire-information decal may have been installed.	10	16,712
Pontiac	Firebird Trans-AM	1970	Possibility that idle stop solenoid bracket nut on carburetor could interfere with movement of air-valve-switch-activating lever, possibly preventing throttle from closing.	5	1,406
Buick Pontiac Oldsmobile	Regular passenger size cars with chassis wheels 15" x 6"	1971	Possibility of welds breaking where wheel spider (disc) attaches to rim. Fatigue cracking may occur around spot welds of disc-to-rim attachment and could possibly result in eventual separation of disc from rim.	14	30,885
Chevrolet	Vega	1971 1972	Possibility that vehicles equipped with standard engine and monojet (single-barrel) carburetor may experience breakage of idle stop solenoid bracket.	13	350,000
Chevrolet	Vega	1971 1972	Possibility that rear axle shaft may have insufficient thrust button length.	19	526,000
Buick Oldsmobile	Electra Riviera 88 & 98	1972 1972	Possibility that improperly manufactured steering pitman arm was installed in production.	19	41,711
Pontiac	Grand Prix	1972	Possibility that electrical fire may occur in mounted console area due to loose retainer. Battery may tip.	8	42,689
Chevrolet Pontiac Oldsmobile Buick	Biscayne Bel Air Impala Caprice Catalina Bonneville Grandville 88 & 98 Le Sabre Centurion Electra Riviera	1971 1972 1971 1972 1971 1972 1971 1972	Possibility that while driving on unpaved road surfaces (particularly roads which are heavily graveled, extremely wavy or filled with chuck holes) at speeds which cause car to pitch excessively, front crossmember may scoop up loose stones or gravel and throw them into engine compartment. One of these stones could lodge between steering coupling and frame and cause increased steering effort or interference with steering control of car when steering wheel is turned to left.	30	3,707,064

157

Make	Model	Model Year	Brief Description of Defect (Manufacturer's Corrective Action)	No. of Pages on File	Number of Vehicles Recalled
Cadillac	"C" cars except Eldorados	1971 1972	Possibility that due to lack of lubricant in steering linkage idler assembly combined with exposure to road splash containing deicing salts and close shaft to bushing clearance, corroding and binding condition may occur.	15	381,421
Cadillac	Calais DeVille Brougham	1972	Possibility that left rear axle shaft may be a fraction too long.	10	37,500
Pontiac	A, B, C, G & X	1973	Possibility that fuel line accumulator welch plug may become dislodged, allowing fuel to siphon from fuel tank onto surface under car when engine is not running.	15	685,434
Cadillac	All except Eldorado	1973 1974	Possibility, that due to lack of lubricant in the steering idler arm assembly together with exposure to road salt, corroding and binding condition may result which could allow idler attachment to break away from frame.	13	270,400
Chevrolet	Chevelle El Camino	1973	Possibility that steering linkage may over-travel and cause severe front wheel toe-in. Condition can occur when steering wheel is turned to extreme left position while vehicle is in reverse and right front tire strikes object such as curb or parking block. Operation of vehicle in this condition can damage right hand inner tie rod end assembly which eventually could result in loss of steering control of right front wheel.	30	155,418
Pontiac	Le Mans Grand Prix	1973			
Buick	Century	1973			
Oldsmobile	Cutlass	1973			
GMC	Sprint	1973			
Pontiac	Grand Prix Grand Am	1973	Possibility that electrical short caused by unused wiring harness lamp socket could result in current flow through air conditioner temperature control cable, causing wiring to heat up which can ignite the cable housing and cause fire in passenger compartment.	15	75,010
Chevrolet	A, B, F, X Series C, P, K-10, G-20 Series trucks	1973 1974	Possibility that single diaphragm brake vacuum power booster was assembled with dimensional discrepancies in vacuum power booster housing which may reduce torque required to unlock front half of housing from rear half. If condition exists, low unlocking torque coupled with	18	1218,387
Pontiac	A, F, X Series	1973 1974			
Oldsmobile	A Series X Series	1973 1974			

158

Make	Model	Model Year	Brief Description of Defect (Manufacturer's Corrective Action)	No. of Pages on File	Number of Vehicles Recalled
Buick	A Series	1973	other variations in assembly may cause housing to rotate and disengage from locking tabs resulting in separation of two halves of booster and complete loss of brakes.		
	X Series	1973			
Cadillac	All series & commercial chassis	1974	Possibility that secondary hood latch may not engage if vehicle is driven with primary hood latch not engaged or inadvertently released.	13	234,278
Chevrolet	A, B, F, & G Series	1974	Possibility that front upper control arm inner bushing retainer nuts may loosen and come off.	11	782,111
Pontiac	A, B, F, & G Series				
Chevrolet	Corvette	1974	Possibility that fuel tank return line fitting may have thin wall section that could break.	15	2,937
Chevrolet	Monte Carlo Chevelle El Camino	1975	Possibility that rear axle was assembled with rear axle shaft outer bearing (rear wheel bearing) with thrust plates that were not heat treated. If inner or outer thrust plates of bearings are not hardened, rollers can wear through and allow rear axle shaft to move with respect to axle housing.	38	220,982
Pontiac	Le Mans Grand AM	1975			
Buick	Century Regal	1975			
Oldsmobile	Cutlass	1975			
GMC	Sprint	1975			
Chevrolet	Monza 2+2	1975	Possibility that strength of J bolt (hook) furnished may be inadequate in event of severe frontal collision when spare tire is mounted on rear compartment floor.	10	98,631
Buick	Skylark hatchback	1975			
Oldsmobile	Starfire	1975			
Chevrolet	Camaro equipped w/ 350 CID V8 engine & air conditioning	1975	Possibility of failure of flexible fan blade exists.	9	31,073
Chevrolet	Chevette	1976	Possibility that right rear brake pipe at connector to junction block located on rear axle differential cover may be subject to fatigue failure.	5	4,107

159

MAJOR RECALL CAMPAIGNS

National Highway Traffic Safety Administration, Washington, D.C.

Ford Motor Company

Make	Model	Model Year	Brief Description of Defect (Manufacturer's Corrective Action)	No. of Pages on File	Number of Vehicles Recalled
Ford	Thunderbird Ford Fairlane Mustang/ equipped with front seat belt assembly	1970	Possibility that seat belt retractor locking mechanism may be erratic in locking action. (Correct by replacing where necessary with proper seat belt retractor mechanism.)	5	86,300
All	Passenger cars (except 1970 Maverick & 1970-1971 convertibles & imports) Ranchero	1970 1971	Possibility that shoulder belt pin connector plastic sleeves which were injection molded contains surface imperfections.	2	4,072,000
Ford Mercury	Cortina Capri	1970 1971	Possibility that steering wheel assembly may lack adequate strength at point of attachment of steering wheel to energy absorbing cylinder that underlies it.	20	15,607
Ford Mercury	Mustang Cougar	1971 1971	Possibility that in welding #2 cross-member to side rails some spot welds were inadvertently missed during production. This could cause separation of #2 cross-member from its support and cause loss of front end alignment, increased tire wear and steering effort. (Correct by welding where necessary.)	9	15,548
Lincoln Ford	Mark III Thunderbird Fordor	1971 1971	Possibility that front and rear inboard seat belt anchors were inadequately welded to floor pan. (Correct by inspecting and properly welding where necessary.)	11	4,600
Ford	Pinto	1971	Possibility that accelerator linkage has interference condition where accelerator pedal is depressed beyond half-throttle position. Could cause accelerator to hold and not return to normal position when pedal is released. (Correct by modifying where necessary.)	7	26,000
Ford	Pinto	1971	Possibility that engine backfire may ignite accumulated fuel vapors in air cleaner assembly, creating possibility of fire damage in engine compartment. (Correct by modifying.)	86	215,823

Make	Model	Model Year	Brief Description of Defect (Manufacturer's Corrective Action)	No. of Pages on File	Number of Vehicles Recalled
Ford	Torino Ranchero	1972	Possibility that rear axle bearing may deteriorate due to high axle shaft deflection. Deterioration of bearing usually will produce sufficient noise and vibration to indicate need for repair; relative movement of axle shaft will result in complete loss of tractive effect as it disengages from differential. (Correct by inspecting and replacing with larger diameter shaft axle and new bearing.)	41	407,244
Mercury	Montego	1972			
Ford Lincoln Ford Truck	Torino, Ranchero Thunderbird Mercury Mark IV F-100, F-250, F-350, w/power steering	1972 1973	Possibility that power steering gear assemblies were built with worm and valve assembly torsion rod lock pin inadvertently omitted. If condition exists, could result in loss of steering control. (Correct by inspecting and installing pin where necessary.)	18	1,033,800
Ford	Torino	1973	Possibility that in process of connecting center link to idler arm cotter pin was omitted, which holds attaching nut in position should nut be installed loose.	3	58,832
Ford Mercury	Torino Maverick Montego Comet Cougar	1973 1974	Possibility that 2V carburetor used on 302,351 and 400CID engines with automatic transmission may have misalignment between transmission linkage lever and adjusting screw assembly and throttle lever tab. If condition exists, it may cause contact between screw threads and edge of throttle lever tab and cause throttle to stick.	8	74,884
Ford Lincoln	Thunderbird Mark IV	1973	Possibility that starter cable was improperly routed during assembly.	11	41,462
Ford Mercury Lincoln Ford	Torino Ford Thunderbird Montego Cougar Continental Mach IV Ranchero Trucks	1974 1974 1974 1974	Possibility that vehicles equipped with speed control option may have vent solenoid armature bind within servo assembly because of undersize brass eyelet that guides armature. Should condition occur, speed control system will maintain or, if binding occurs in acceleration mode, increase speed of vehicle without prior warning even though driver attempts to disengage system.	5	127,208

Make	Model	Model Year	Brief Description of Defect (Manufacturer's Corrective Action)	No. of Pages on File	Number of Vehicles Recalled
Ford	Ford Torino Elite F-100	1974	Possibility that Firestone HR 7 78-15 tires installed may have been undercured during vulcanizing process. Condition results in localized overheating at tire shoulder or lower sidewall that could cause chunking and/or separation, resulting in rapid loss of air during operation.	3	35,711 (177,555 tires)
Ford Mercury	Granada Monarch	1975	Possibility that front suspension upper control arm could fatigue fracture with extended usage due to being manufactured from steel of less than acceptable material thickness.	10	32,003
Ford Mercury	Maverick Granada Comet Monarch	1975	Possibility that dash panel to engine wiring harness located between carburetor and valve rocker arm cover was routed incorrectly.	2	8,460

1971 MODELS

VEGA

All data based on two-door coupe

Used Car PRICE* $300

Based on standard equipped car with automatic transmission, and radio. Price assumes excellent condition.

*Subtract 25 dollars for each month after October, for current price.

Statistical Comparison:
Very rapid depreciation.
Expensive parts cost.
Parts often unavailable.
Below average fuel economy.

TECHNICAL DATA

Wheelbase .... 97 in.
Length 169.7
Weight .... 2,200 lbs
Width .... 65.4 in.
Standard Engine.. 4 cyl.
Standard Brakes...Disc-Drum
Gasoline Mileage 27.1
(With regular fuel)

Frequency or Repairs:
Brake problems, motor overheating, excessive oil consumption, and transmission failure.

Body:
Excessive rusting appearing after only a few months use. Ziebart refuses to guarantee Vegas and Astres.

Safety Defects:
Possibility of defective throttle lever, wheels, steering, Rochester carburetor and power brake vacuum check valve.

Recommendation:
Not recommended. If the rust and sticking accelerator don't get you, the depreciation will. Make GM pay for motor and fender defects through small claims court.

···

CHEVY II NOVA

All data based on four-door sedan

Use Car PRICE* $900

Based on standard equipped car with automatic transmission, and radio. Price assumes excellent condition.

*Subtract 25 dollars for each month after October, for current price.

Statistical Comparison:
Excellent parts availability.
Below average depreciation.
Average parts cost.
Excellent fuel economy.

TECHNICAL DATA

Wheelbase .... 111 in.
Length .... 189.4 in.
Weight .... 3,200 lbs.
Width .... 72.4 in.
Standard Engine.. 6 cyl.
Standard Brakes.. Drum
Gasoline Mileage 23.3
(With regular fuel)

Frequency of Repairs:
Good motor, transmission, brakes and suspension. Troubles reported with carburetor and ignition system.

Body:
Very solid construction. Very few complaints.

Safety Defects:
Possibility of defective throttle lever, wheels, steering, Rochester carburator and power brake vacuum check valve.

Recommended:
An ideal used car for a small family.

CHEVROLET (Full-sized)
Biscayne, Bel Air, Impala, Caprice

All data based on four-door sedan

Used Car PRICE* $1,100

Based on standard equipped car with automatic transmission, and radio. Price assumes excellent condition.

*Subtract 25 dollars for each month after October, for current price.

Statistical Comparison:
Excellent parts availbility.
Below average depreciation.
Average parts cost.
Excellent fuel economy.

TECHNICAL DATA

Wheelbase .... 121.5 in.
Length .... 216.8 in.
Weight .... 4,000 lbs.
Width .... 79.5 in.
Standard Engine... 6 cyl.
Standard Brakes... Disc-Drum
Gasoline Mileage 15.2
(With regular fuel)

Frequency or Repairs:
Minor problems with carburetor and manual transmission. Excellent motor, automatic transmission and brakes.

Body:
Rusting problems. Also frequent complaints of rattles.

Safety Defects:
Possibility of defective throttle lever, wheels, and steering. Check for defective engine mounts. Possibility of defective power brake vacuum check valve, Rochester carburetor, steering wheel and engine mount restraint.

Recommended:
An excellent, inexpensive family car.

***

PONTIAC VENTURA II

All data based on four-door sedan

Use Car PRICE* $1,000

Based on standard equipped car with automatic transmission, and radio. Price assumes excellent condition.

*Subtract 25 dollars for each month after October, for current price.

Statistical Comparison:
Average depreciation.
Low parts cost.
Good parts availability.
Average fuel economy.

TECHNICAL DATA

Wheelbase .... 111 in.
Length .... 194.5 in.
Weight .... 3,000 lbs.
Width .... 72.4 in.
Standard Engine... 6 cyl.
Standard Brakes... Drum
Gasoline Mileage 19.3
(With regular fuel)

Frequency of Repairs:
Some minor engine problems, but overall mechanical components are good.

Body:
Good construction, but some rust and water leakage.

Safety Defects:
Possibility of defective tires, steering, throttle lever, and wheels. Also possibility of defective Rochester carburetor and power brake vacuum check valve.

Recommendation:
Not recommended. Try the Nova instead.

PONTIAC LE MANS

All data based on four-door sedan

Used Car PRICE* $1,200

Based on standard equipped car with automatic transmission, and radio. Price assumes excellent condition.

*Subtract 25 dollars for each month after October, for current price.

Statistical Comparison:
Average parts cost.
Average parts availability.
Below average fuel economy.
Rapid depreciation.

TECHNICAL DATA

Wheelbase .... 116 in.
Length .... 206.8 in.
Weight .... 3,400 lbs.
Width .... 76.7 in.
Standard Engine .... 6 cyl.
Standard Brakes .... Drum
Gasoline Mileage 15.9
(With regular fuel)

Frequency of Repairs:
Some small problems with motor and transmission. Brakes, electrical system and carburetor are excellent.

Body:
Some rusting around doors. A few rattles reported.

Safety Defects:
Possibility of defective tires, steering, throttle lever and wheels. Also possibility of defective Rochester carburetor and power brake vacuum check valve.

Recommendation:
Recommended.

...

PONTIAC (Full-sized)
Catalina, Executive, Bonneville, Laurentian and Parisienne

All data based on four-door sedan

Used Car PRICE* $1,300

Based on standard equipped car with automatic transmission, and radio. Price assumes excellent condition.

*Subtract 25 dollars for each month after October, for current price.

Statistical Comparison:
Average depreciation.
Low parts cost.
Good parts availability.
Average fuel economy.

TECHNICAL DATA

Wheelbase .... 123.5 in.
Length .... 220.2 in.
Weight .... 4,200 lbs.
Width .... 79.5 in.
Standard Engine V8
Standard Brakes .... Disc-Drum
Gasoline Mileage 12.9
(With regular fuel)

Frequency of Repairs:
Suspension and carburetor problems.

Body:
Rusting and rattles.

Safety Defects:
Possibility of defective tires, steering, throttle lever, and wheels. Also possibility of defective Rochester carburetor and power brake vacuum check valve.

Recommendation:
Recommended. A good family car.

169

Buick Division
General Motors

BUICK (Full-sized)
Le Sabre, Centurion, Electra

All data based on four-door sedan

Used Car PRICE* $1,300

Based on standard equipped car with automatic transmission, and radio. Price assumes excellent condition.

*Subtract 25 dollars for each month after October, for current price.

Statistical Comparison:
Average fuel economy.
Excellent parts availability.
Low parts cost.
Average depreciation.

TECHNICAL DATA

Wheelbase	124 in.
Length	220.74 in.
Weight	4,200 lbs.
Width	79.72 in.
Standard Engine	V8
Standard Brakes	Disc-Drum
Gasoline Mileage	14.2

(With regular fuel)

Frequency of Repairs:
Excellent mechanical components. Brakes, suspension and motor are very durable.

Body:
The only weak point. Premature rusting around doors. Rattles are common.

Safety Defects:
Possibility of defective wheels and steering. Le Sabre model may have defective headlamp switch. Also possibility of defective Rochester carburetor and power brake vacuum check valve.

Recommendation:
Recommended, but check the safety defects.

***

Oldsmobile Division
General Motors

OLDSMOBILE (Full-sized)

All data based on four-door sedan

Used Car PRICE* $1,200

Based on standard equipped car with automatic transmission, and radio. Price assumes excellent condition.

*Subtract 25 dollars for each month after October for current price.

Statistical Comparison:
Average depreciation.
Good parts availability.
Average parts cost.
Good fuel economy.

TECHNICAL DATA

Wheelbase	124 in.
Length	220.2 in.
Weight	4,200 lbs.
Width	79.5 in.
Standard Engine	V8
Standard Brakes	Disc-Drum
Gasoline Mileage	14.1

(With regular fuel)

Frequency of Repairs:
Excellent motor, transmission and brakes. Minor problems with suspension.

Body:
Excellent body construction.

Safety Defects:
Possibility of defectives wheels and steering. Also possibility of defective carburetor and power brake vacuum check valve.

Recommendation:
Recommended. A good buy as a family car.

FORD PINTO

All data based on two-door sedan

Used Car PRICE* $600

Based on standard equipped car with automatic transmission, and radio. Price assumes excellent condition.

*Subtract 25 dollars for each month after October, for current price.

Statistical Comparison:
Rapid depreciation.
Average parts cost.
Average parts availability.
Average fuel economy.

TECHNICAL DATA

Wheelbase ....94 in.
Length ....163 in.
Weight ....2,100 lbs.
Width ....69.4 in.
Standard Engine..4 cyl.
Standard Brakes..Drum
Gasoline Mileage 27.7
(With regular fuel)

Frequency of Repairs:
Good brakes and electrical system. Problems with transmission, carburetor, and motor.

Body:
Need for frequent door adjustments. Body is rust-prone.

Safety Defects:
Possibility accelerator may stick, clutch cable may cause loss of oil and engine damage or car may burst into flames.

Recommendation:
Not recommended. Car will easily fall to pieces.

***

FORD MAVERICK

All data based on four-door sedan

Used Car PRICE* $800

Based on standard equipped car with automatic transmission, and radio. Price assumes excellent condition.

*Subtract 25 dollars for each month after October, for current price.

Statistical Comparison:
Low depreciation.
Inexpensive parts.
Average parts availability.
Good fuel economy.

TECHNICAL DATA

Wheelbase ....109.9 in.
Length ....186.3 in.
Weight ....2,700 lbs.
Width ....70.6 in.
Standard Engine..6 cyl.
Standard Brakes..Drum
Gasoline Mileage 23.8
(With regular fuel)

Frequency of Repairs:
Excellent motor and electrical system. Problems with brakes, carburetor, and automatic transmission.

Body:
Excessive rusting in front fenders around door, on hood, and in trunk.

Safety Defects:
Possibility of defective 15 x 5.5 and 15 x 6.5 single-piece wheel, brake master cylinder, 4 barrel carburetor, power brake vacuum check valve, and gas tank.

Recommendation:
Not recommended. A waste of money.

FORD MUSTANG

All data based on two-door hardtop

Used Car PRICE* $1,000

Based on standard equipped car with automatic transmission, and radio. Price assumes excellent condition.

*Subtract 25 dollars for each month after October, for current price.

Statistical Comparison:
Rapid depreciation.
Average parts cost.
Average parts availability.
Terrible fuel economy.

TECHNICAL DATA

Wheelbase .... 109 in.
Length .... 189.5 in.
Weight .... 3,200 lbs.
Width .... 74.1 in.
Standard Engine .... 6 cyl.
Standard Brakes .... Drum
Gasoline Mileage 16.9
(With regular fuel)

Frequency of Repairs:
Problems with suspension, transmission, and heating system. Excellent motor, and electrical system.

Body:
Excessive rusting. "J-67" warranty extension applies.

Safety Defects:
Possibility of steering defects, wheel defects and defective master cylinder, and power brake vacuum check valve.

Recommendation:
Not recommended. Ford should not have changed the first 1965 Mustang.

***

FORD TORINO, MONTEGO

All data based on four-door sedan

Used Car PRICE* $600

Based on standard equipped car with automatic transmission, and radio. Price assumes excellent condition.

*Subtract 25 dollars for each month after October, for current price.

Statistical Comparison:
Very rapid depreciation.
Average parts cost.
Average parts availability.
Below average fuel economy.

TECHNICAL DATA

Wheelbase .... 117 in.
Length .... 206.2 in.
Weight .... 3,400 lbs.
Width .... 76.4 in.
Standard Engine .... 6 cyl.
Standard Brakes .... Drum
Gasoline Mileage 17.4
(With regular fuel)

Frequency of Repairs:
Problems with brakes, transmission, suspension and steering.

Body:
Excessive rusting. Complaints of rattles and paint peeling.

Safety Defects:
Possibility of defective seat belts, hood latch, 15 x 5.5 single-piece wheel, brake master cylinder, 4 barrel carburetor, and power brake vacuum check valve.

Recommendation:
Not recommended. Corrosion problems too extensive.

Ford Division
Ford Motor Company

FORD (Full-sized)
Custom, Galaxie, LTD

All data based on four-door sedan

Used Car PRICE*...$700

Based on standard equipped car with automatic transmission, and radio. Price assumes excellent condition.

*Subtract 25 dollars for each month after October, for current price.

Statistical Comparison:
Rapid depreciation.
Low parts cost.
Excellent parts availability.
Good fuel economy.

TECHNICAL DATA

Wheelbase ....121 in.
Length ....216.2 in.
Weight ....4,100 lbs.
Width ....79.3 in.
Standard Engine...6 cyl.
Standard Brakes...Drum
Gasoline Mileage 16.3
(With regular fuel)

Frequency of Repairs:
Problems with idler arms. Some complaints concerning carburetor and suspension.

Body:
Excessive rusting in front fenders and around doors. Not one of Ford's better ideas. Also paint quality inferior to other models.

Safety Defects:
Possibility of defective seat belts, power brake vacuum check valve, 15 x 5.5 and 15 x 6.5 single-piece wheel, 4 barrel carburetor, master cylinder and hood latch mechanism.

Recommendation:
Not recommended. An average car with serious rust problems. Warranty extension "J-67" applies.

· · ·

Plymouth Division
Chrysler Corporation

PLYMOUTH VALIANT
Duster and Scamp

All data based on four-door sedan

Used Car PRICE*...$1,200

Based on standard equipped car with automatic transmission, and radio. Price assumes excellent condition.

*Subtract 25 dollars for each month after October, for current price.

Statistical Comparison:
Low depreciation.
Low parts cost.
Excellent parts availability.
Excellent fuel economy.

TECHNICAL DATA

Wheelbase ....108 in.
Length ....188.4 in.
Weight ....3,000 lbs.
Width ....71.1 in.
Standard Engine...6 cyl.
Standard Brakes...Drum
Gasoline Mileage 21.8
(With regular fuel)

Frequency of Repairs:
Excellent mechanical components. Some transmission, brake and clutch problems.

Body:
Excellent body construction, except for front fender rusting.

Safety Defects:
Possibility of defective brake linings and front wheel bearings. Also possibility of defective exhaust manifold, power brake vacuum check valve, and brake proportioning valve.

Recommendation:
Recommended. One of the best cars made. Six cylinder motor is best.

Dodge Division
Chrysler Corporation

DODGE DART
Demon and Swinger

All data based on four-door sedan

Used Car PRICE*...$1,200

Based on standard equipped car with automatic transmission, and radio. Price assumes excellent condition.

*Subtract 25 dollars for each month after October, for current price.

Statistical Comparison:
Low depreciation
Below average parts cost
Excellent parts availability.
Excellent fuel economy.

TECHNICAL DATA

Wheelbase ....111 in.
Length ....196.2 in.
Weight ....3,000 lbs.
Width ....69:7 in.
Standard Engine...6 cyl.
Standard Brakes...Drum
Gasoline Mileage 21.2
(With regular fuel)

Frequency of Repairs:
Serious brake problems. Transmission and clutch complaints. Excellent motor, carburetor, and electrical system.

Body:
Excellent body construction. Very rust-resistant, except for front fender rust perforations.

Safety Defects:
Possibility of defective brake linings and defective front wheel bearings. Also possible defective power brake vacuum check valve cracking exhaust manifold, and brake porportioning valve.

Recommendation:
Recommended. One of the best cars on the market. Six cylinder superior to eight.

...

Plymouth Division
Chrysler Corporation

PLYMOUTH SATELLITE
Belvedere, Sebring

All data based on four-door sedan

Used Car PRICE*...$1,000

Based on standard equipped car with automatic transmission, and radio. Price assumes excellent condition.

*Subtract 25 dollars for each month after October, for current price.

Statistical Comparison:
Average depreciation.
Average parts cost.
Average parts availability.
Below average fuel economy.

TECHNICAL DATA

Wheelbase ....117 in.
Length ....204.6 in.
Weight ....3,400 lbs.
Width ....78.6 in.
Standard Engine...6 cyl.
Standard Brakes...Drum
Gasoline Mileage 17.8
(With regular fuel)

Frequency of Repairs:
Problems with brakes, suspension, and electrical system.

Body:
Excessive rusting. Also complaints of rattles.

Safety Defects:
Possibility of defective brakes, front seats, disc brakes, and power steering. Possibility of defective power brake vacuum check valve and exhaust manifold cracking.

Recommendation:
Not recommended. Dodge Dart a better buy.

DODGE (Full-sized)
Polara, Monaco, Brougham

All data based on four-door sedan

Used Car PRICE* $900

Based on standard equipped car with automatic transmission, and radio. Price assumes excellent condition.

*Subtract 25 dollars for each month after October, for current price.

Statistical Comparison:
Rapid depreciation.
Average parts availability and cost.
Below average fuel economy.

TECHNICAL DATA

Wheelbase	122 in.
Length	220.2 in.
Weight	3,900 lbs.
Width	79.2 in.
Standard Engine	V8
Standard Brakes	Disc-Drum
Gasoline Mileage	15.2
(With regular fuel)	

Frequency of Repairs:
Serious complaints concerning brakes. Also problems with suspension and transmission.

Body:
Very rust prone, but good paint quality. Front fenders rust prone.

Safety:
Possibility of defective front brakes and windshield defroster. Also possibility of defective power brake vacuum check valve and exhaust manifold cracking (V6).

Recommendation:
Not recommended. Too big, too wasteful, and too fragile.

...

PLYMOUTH FURY

All data based on four-door sedan

Used Car PRICE* $900

Based on standard equipped car with automatic transmission, and radio. Price assumes excellent condition.

*Subtract 25 dollars for each month after October, for current price.

Statistical Comparison:
Average depreciation.
Average parts cost.
Average parts availability.
Below average fuel economy.

TECHNICAL DATA

Wheelbase	120 in.
Length	215.1 in.
Weight	3,900 lbs.
Width	79.6 in.
Standard Engine	6 cyl.
Standard Brakes	Drum
Gasoline Mileage	16.9
(With regular fuel)	

Frequency of Repairs:
Brake, suspension, and electrical system problems.

Body:
Rusting and paint peeling. Front fenders rust-prone.

Safety Defects:
Possibility of defective brakes, exhaust manifold and power brake vacuum check valve.

Recommendation:
Not recommended. A lot of old police cars around.

AMC HORNET

All data based on four-door sedan

Used Car PRICE* $1,000

Based on standard equipped car with automatic transmission, and radio. Price assumes excellent condition.

*Subtract 25 dollars for each month after October, for current price.

Statistical Comparison:
Average depreciation.
Average parts availability.
Average parts cost.
Good fuel economy.

TECHNICAL DATA

Wheelbase .... 108 in.
Length .... 179.26 in.
Weight .... 2,800 lbs.
Width .... 70.58 in.
Standard Engine.. 6 cyl.
Standard Brakes... Disc-Drum
Gasoline Mileage 21.4
(With regular fuel)

Frequency of Repairs:
Serious clutch and fuel system problems. Problems reported with both automatic and standard transmissions.

Body:
Frequent complaints concerning rattles, rusting, and exterior body construction.

Safety Defects:
Possibility of defective door locks and leaking gas tank. Also possible defective power brake vacuum check valve.

Recommendation:
Not recommended. Frequent mechanical failures.

...

AMC GREMLIN

All data based on two-door sedan

Used Car PRICE* $700

Based on standard equipped car with automatic transmission, and radio. Price assumes excellent condition.

*Subtract 25 dollars for each month after October, for current price.

Statistical Comparison:
Average depreciation.
Average parts availability.
Average parts cost.
Good fuel economy.

TECHNICAL DATA

Wheelbase .... 96 in.
Length .... 161.25 in.
Weight .... 2,700 lbs.
Width .... 70.6 in.
Standard Engine.. 6 cyl.
Standard Brakes... Drum
Gasoline Mileage 24.9
(With regular fuel)

Frequency of Repairs:
Same problems as 1970 model, with the manual transmission still causing problems.

Body:
As with Ambassador, this model has an improved construction.

Safety Defects:
Possibility of defective door lacks and leaking gas tank. Also, possibility of defective power brake vacuum check valve.

Recommendation:
Recommended, though don't pay very much for it.

176

AMBASSADOR

All data based on four-door sedan

Used Car PRICE* $800

Based on standard equipped car with automatic transmission, and radio. Price assumes excellent condition.

*Subtract 25 dollars for each month after October, for current price.

Statistical Comparison:
Rapid depreciation.
Average parts availability.
Average parts cost.
Below average fuel economy.

TECHNICAL DATA

Wheelbase .... 122 in.
Length .... 210.78 in.
Weight .... 3,400 lbs.
Width .... 77.24 in.
Standard Engine V8
Standard Brakes .... Drum
Gasoline Mileage 16.9
(With regular fuel)

Frequency of Repairs:
Improved fuel system and better assembled body. Suspension problems still prevalent. Some problems with brakes.

Body:
Much improved assembly. Little exterior rusting, though exhaust system vulnerable to rust.

Safety Defects:
Possibility of leaking gas tank, and a defective jack. Also possibility of defective power brake vacuum check valve.

Recommendation:
Not recommended. Dart or Valiant a better buy.

177

VEGA

All data based on two-door sedan

Used Car PRICE* $500

Based on standard equipped car with automatic transmission, and radio. Price assumes excellent
condition.

*Subtract 25 dollars for each month after October, for current price.

Statistical Comparison
Very rapid depreciation.
Expensive parts cost.
Parts often unavailable.
Below average fuel economy.

TECHNICAL DATA

Wheelbase	97 in.
Length	169.7 in.
Weight	2,200 lbs.
Width	65.4 in.
Standard Engine	4 cyl.
Standard Brakes	Disc-Drum
Gasoline Mileage	26.3

(With regular fuel)

Frequency of Repairs:
Brake problems, major motor problems, excessive oil consumption. Reports of transmission failures.

Body:
Body was made for Florida, not Quebec. Very excessive rusting all over vehicle. Ziebart refuse to
guarantee Vega and Astre.

Safety Defects:
Possibility of defective muffler, throttle cable, and rear axle. Also possibility of defective steering
relay rod.

Recommendation:
Not recommended. GM should be ashamed of itself for making this car. Many court claims won against
GM for defective motor and fenders for 1971-1974 models. Warranty extended.

...

CHEVY II NOVA

All data based on four-door sedan

Used Car PRICE* $1,200

Based on standard equipped car with automatic transmission, and radio. Price assumes excellent
condition.

*Subtract 25 dollars for each month after October, for current price.

Statistical Comparison:
Excellent parts availability.
Below average depreciation.
Average parts cost.
Excellent fuel economy.

TECHNICAL DATA

Wheelbase	111 in.
Length	189.4 in.
Weight	3,200 lbs.
Width	72.5 in.
Standard Engine	6 cyl.
Standard Brakes	Drum
Gasoline Mileage	21.2

(With regular fuel)

Frequency of Repairs:
8 cylinder is the better model. 6 cylinder has brakes, motor and carburetor problems.

Body:
Solid construction with little rusting.

Safety Defects:
Possibility of defective steering and engine mounts. May not have Canadian Motor Vehicle Safety Act
stickers. Also possibility of defective Rochester carburetor and engine mounts restraint.

Recommendation:
Not recommended. Too many mechanical problems.

181

CHEVELLE

All data based on four-door sedan

Used Car PRICE* $1,600

Based on standard equipped car with automatic transmission, and radio. Price assumes excellent condition.

*Subtract 25 dollars for each month after October, for current price.

Statistical Comparison:
Low depreciation.
Average parts cost.
Average fuel economy.
Excellent parts availability.

TECHNICAL DATA

Wheelbase	116 in.
Length	201.5 in.
Weight	3,300 lbs.
Width	75.4 in.
Standard Engine	6 cyl.
Standard Brakes	Disc-Drum
Gasoline Mileage	15.2
(With regular fuel)	

Frequency of Repairs:
8 cylinder motor better than 6. Minor brake problems. Excellent mechanical components

Body:
Excessive rusting all over vehicle.

Safety Defects:
Possibility of defective steering and engine mounts. Also possibility of defective Rochester Carburetor, and engine mounts restraint.

Recommendation:
Recommended. Not as good as full-sized Chevrolet. Watch out for premature rusting.

...

CHEVROLET (Full-sized)
Biscayne, Bel Air, Impala

All data based on four-door sedan

Used Car PRICE* $1,300

Based on standard equipped car with automatic transmission, and radio. Price assumes excellent condition.

*Subtract 25 dollars for each month after October, for current price.

Statistical Comparison:
Excellent parts availability.
Low depreciation.
Average parts cost.
Average fuel economy.

TECHNICAL DATA

Wheelbase	121.5 in.
Length	219.9 in.
Weight	
Width	79.5 in.
Standard Engine	6 cyl.
Standard Brakes	Disc-Drum
Gasoline Mileage	15.1
(With regular fuel)	

Frequency of Repairs
Minor problems with transmission, and brakes.

Body:
Some rusting around fenders. Solid body construction.

Safety Defects:
Possibility of defective steering and engine mounts. Also possibility of defective Rochester carburetor, and engine mounts restraint.

Recommendation:
Recommended. First verify engine mounts.

**Pontiac Division
General Motors**

1972

PONTIAC VENTURA II

All data based on four-door sedan

Used Car PRICE* $1,300

Based on standard equipped car with automatic transmission, and radio. Price assumes excellent condition.

*Subtract 25 dollars for each month after October, for current price.

Statistical Comparison:
Average depreciation.
Low parts cost.
Good parts availability.
Below average fuel economy.

TECHNICAL DATA

Wheelbase .... 111 in.
Length .... 194.5 in.
Weight .... 3,300 lbs.
Width .... 72.4 in.
Standard Engine .... 6 cyl.
Standard Brakes .... Drum
Gasoline Mileage 15.2
(With regular fuel)

Frequency of Repairs:
Serious problems with motor, carburetor and transmission.

Body:
Excessive rusting, rattles and water leakage in rear trunk.

Safety Defects:
Possibility of electrical fire, defective steering, tire, engine mounts, and non-compliance with Canadian Motor Vehicle Safety Act. Also possibility of defective Rochester carburetor.

Recommendation:
Not recommended. May present serious safety hazards.

...

**Pontiac Division
General Motors**

1972

PONTIAC LE MANS

All data based on four-door sedan

Used Car PRICE* $1,500

Based on standard equipped car with automatic transmission, and radio. Price assumes excellent condition.

*Subtract 25 dollars for each month after October, for current price.

Statistical Comparison:
Average parts cost.
Average parts availability.
Rapid depreciation.
Below average fuel economy.

TECHNICAL DATA

Wheelbase .... 116 in.
Length .... 207.2 in.
Weight .... 3,400 lbs.
Width .... 76.7 in.
Standard Engine .... 6 cyl.
Standard Brakes .... Drum
Gasoline Mileage 15.7
(With regular fuel)

Frequency of Repairs:
Much improved motor and transmission. Minor problems with carburetor and pollution control device.

Body:
Some rusting and paint peeling.

Safety Defects:
Possibility of defective steering and motor mounts. May also catch on fire. Rochester carburetor could be defective.

Recommendation:
Not recommended. Car may be hazardous to your health.

183

Buick Division
General Motors

1972

BUICK (Full-sized)
Le Sabre, Centurion, Electra

All data based on four-door sedan hardtop

Used Car PRICE* $1,600

Based on standard equipped car with automatic transmission, and radio. Price assumes excellent condition.

*Subtract 25 dollars for each month after October, for current price.

Statistical Comparison
Excellent parts availability.
Average parts cost.
Average depreciation.
Below average fuel economy.

TECHNICAL DATA

Wheelbase .... 124 in.
Length .... 220.9 in.
Weight .... 4,400 lbs.
Width .... 79.7 in.
Standard Engine V8
Standard Brakes .... Disc-Drum
Gasoline Mileage 13.6
(With regular fuel)

Frequency of Repairs:
All mechanical components of good quality. Some minor transmission problems.

Body:
Body construction improved greatly. Still some rusting around doors.

Safety Defects:
Possibility of defective steering components, and Rochester carburetor.

Recommendation:
Recommended. One of GM's best.

***

Pontiac Division
General Motors

1972

PONTIAC (Full-sized)
Catalina and Executive

All data based on four-door sedan

Used Car PRICE* $1,500

Based on standard equipped car with automatic transmission, and radio. Price assumes excellent condition.

*Subtract 25 dollars for each month after October, for current price.

Statistical Comparison:
Average depreciation
Low parts cost
Good parts availability
Below average fuel economy

TECHNICAL DATA

Wheelbase .... 123.5 in.
Length .... 220.2 in.
Weight .... 4,300 lbs.
Width .... 79.3 in.
Standard Engine V8
Standard Brakes .... Disc-Drum
Gasoline Mileage 11.8
(With regular fuel)

Frequency of Repairs:
Excellent motor and carburetor. Minor problems with transmission.

Body:
Good body construction. Some rattles still present. Minor paint problems.

Safety Defects:
Possibility of defective Rochester carburetor.

Recommendation:
Recommended. A much improved vehicle.

184

Ford Division
Ford Motor Company

1972

FORD PINTO

All data based on two-door sedan

Used Car PRICE* $800

Based on standard equipped car with automatic transmission, and radio. Price assumes excellent condition.

*Subtract 25 dollars for each month after October, for current price.

Statistical Comparison:
Rapid depreciation.
Average parts cost.
Average parts availability.
Average fuel economy.

TECHNICAL DATA

Wheelbase .... 94.2 in.
Length .... 163 in.
Weight .... 2,100 lbs.
Width .... 69.4 in.
Standard Engine .... 4 cyl.
Standard Brakes .... Disc-Drum
Gasoline Mileage 27.1
(With regular fuel)

Frequency of Repairs:
Good suspension and brakes. Problems with motor and transmission.

Body:
Problems with rattles, leakage, and severe rusting around doors, fenders, and trunk.

Safety Defects:
Possibility of defective bolts, rear wheel well, and rack and pinion steering.

Recommendation:
Not recommended. Too small, too rusty, and too expensive.

...

Ford Division
Ford Motor Company

1972

FORD MAVERICK

All data based on four-door sedan

Used Car PRICE* $1,000

Based on standard equipped car with automatic transmission, and radio. Price assumes excellent condition.

*Subtract 25 dollars for each month after October, for current price.

Statistical Comparison:
Rapid depreciation.
Low parts cost.
Good parts availability.
Good fuel economy.

TECHNICAL DATA

Wheelbase .... 109.9 in.
Length .... 186.3 in.
Weight .... 2,700 lbs.
Width .... 70.6 in.
Standard Engine .... 6 cyl.
Standard Brakes .... Drum
Gasoline Mileage 22.5
(With regular fuel)

Frequency of Repairs:
Excellent motor and transmission. Problems with brakes and carburetor.

Body:
Excessive rusting in front fenders, around door, and in rear trunk.

Safety Defects:
Unsafe placement of rear gas tank according to U.S. Army Engineers, and also defective 4 barrel carburetor.

Recommendation:
Not recommended. Premature rusting too extensive.

Ford Division
Ford Motor Company

FORD MUSTANG

All data based on two-door hardtop

Used Car PRICE* $1,200

Based on standard equipped car with automatic transmission, and radio. Price assumes excellent condition.

*Subtract 25 dollars for each month after October, for current price.

Statistical Comparison:
Rapid depreciation.
Average parts cost.
Average parts availability.
Terrible fuel economy.

TECHNICAL DATA

Wheelbase	109 in.
Length	189.5 in.
Weight	3,200 lbs.
Width	74.1 in.
Standard Engine	6 cyl.
Standard Brake	Drum
Gasoline Mileage	14.1

(With regular fuel)

Frequency of Repairs:
Problems with transmission and suspension. Excellent brakes and electrical system. Motor may have valve guide defects.

Body:
Excessive rusting around doors front fenders, and trunk.

Safety Defects:
Unsafe placement of rear gas tank, also possibility of defective 4 barrel carburetor.

Recommendation:
Not recommended. Ford "J-67" warranty extension applies.

...

Ford Division
Ford Motor Company

FORD TORINO, MONTEGO

All data based on four-door sedan hardtop

Used Car PRICE* $900

Based on standard equipped car with automatic transmission, and radio. Price assumes excellent condition.

*Subtract 25 dollars for each month after October, for current price.

Statistical Comparison:
Very rapid depreciation.
Average parts cost.
Average parts availability.
Below average fuel economy.

TECHNICAL DATA

Wheelbase	118 in.
Length	207.7 in.
Weight	3,700 lbs.
Width	79.3 in.
Standard Engine	6 cyl.
Standard Brakes	Drum
Gasoline Mileage	13.4

(With regular fuel)

Frequency of Repairs:
Problems with brakes, transmission, and suspension. Good electrical system and motor.

Body:
Excessive door and fender rusting. Complaints of rattles and paint peeling.

Safety Defects:
Possibility of defective rear axle, seat belts, and wheel bearings. Also possibility of defective 4 barrel carburetor, and rear axle assembly.

Recommendation:
Not recommended. This model can be very expensive to repair rusting damage. Ford extended rust warranty ("J-67").

186

Ford Division
Ford Motor Company

1972

FORD (Full-sized)
Custom, Galaxie, LTD

All data based on four-door sedan

Used Car PRICE* $1,000

Based on standard equipped car with automatic transmission, and radio. Price assumes excellent condition.

*Subtract 25 dollars for each month after October, for current price.

Statistical Comparison:
Rapid depreciation.
Low parts cost.
Excellent parts availability.
Good fuel economy.

TECHNICAL DATA

Wheelbase	121 in.
Length	218.4 in.
Weight	4,100 lbs.
Width	79.2 in.
Standard Engine	6 cyl.
Standard Brakes	Drum
Gasoline Mileage	14.2
(With regular fuel)	

Frequency of Repairs:
Excellent brakes, and electrical system. Problems with idler arms and carburetor. Motor has valve guide defects.

Body:
Numerous rusting and paint problems, especially along fenders doors, and rear trunk.

Safety Defects:
Possibility of defective bumper jacks, and 4 barrel carburetor.

Recommendation:
Not recommended. An average car with serious rust problems. Ford "J-67" warranty extension applies.

...

Plymouth Division
Chrysler Corporation

1972

PLYMOUTH VALIANT
Duster and Scamp

All data based on four-door sedan

Used Car PRICE* $1,600

Based on standard equipped car with automatic transmission, and radio. Price assumes excellent condition.

*Subtract 25 dollars for each month after October, for current price.

Statistical Comparison:
Very low depreciation.
Low parts cost.
Excellent parts availability.
Excellent fuel economy.

TECHNICAL DATA

Wheelbase	108 in.
Length	188.4 in.
Weight	2,900 lbs.
Width	71 in.
Standard Engine	6 cyl.
Standard Brakes	Drum
Gasoline Mileage	23.3
(With regular fuel)	

Frequency of Repairs:
Minor problems with brakes, transmission and anti-pollution device. Excellemt mechanical components.

Body:
Excellent body construction. Rusting perforations of front fenders.

Safety Defects:
Possibility of defective alternator and front seats. Also possibility of defective exhaust manifold and brake proportioning valve.

Recommendation:
Recommended. An excellent new or used car buy. Six cylinder engine is preferred. Verify fender rusting.

187

DODGE DART
Demon and Swinger

All data based on four-door sedan

Used Car PRICE* $1,500

Based on standard equipped car with automatic transmission, and radio. Price assumes excellent condition.

*Subtract 25 dollars for each month after October, for current price.

Statistical Comparison:
Very low depreciation.
Below average parts cost.
Excellent parts availability.
Excellent fuel economy.

TECHNICAL DATA

Wheelbase .... 111 in.
Length .... 196.2 in.
Weight .... 2,900 lbs.
Width .... 69.6 in.
Standard Engine... 6 cyl.
Standard Brakes... Drum
Gasoline Mileage 16.8
(With regular fuel)

Frequency of Repairs:
6 cylinder better than 8. All other mechanical components excellent except automatic transmission. Some problems with brakes locking in emergency stops.

Body:
Excellent body construction. No rusting except for front fenders.

Safety Defects:
Possibility of defective alternator and front seats. Also possibility of defective exhaust manifold, and brake proportioning valve.

Recommendation:
Recommended. There is no better car available.

...

PLYMOUTH SATELLITE
Sebring

All data based on four-door sedan

Used Car PRICE* $1,200

Based on standard equipped car with automatic transmission, and radio. Price assumes excellent condition.

*Subtract 25 dollars for each month after October, for current price.

Statistical Comparison:
Average depreciation.
Average parts cost.
Average parts availability.
Below average fuel economy.

TECHNICAL DATA

Wheelbase .... 117 in.
Length .... 204.6 in.
Weight .... 3,400 lbs.
Width .... 78.6 in.
Standard Engine... 6 cyl.
Standard Brakes... Drum
Gasoline Mileage 16.4
(With regular fuel)

Frequency of Repairs:
Problems with suspension (loose), brakes, and cooling system.

Body:
Some minor rusting. Body construction not up to average, especially front fenders.

Safety Defects:
Possibility of defective speedometer, suspension, and power steering. Also possibility of defective six cylinder exhaust manifold.

Recommendation:
Not recommended. Dart or Fury a better buy.

Dodge Division
Chrysler Corporation

DODGE (Full-sized)
Polara and Monaco

All data based on four-door sedan

Used Car PRICE* $1,300

Based on standard equipped car with automatic transmission, and radio. Price assumes excellent condition.

*Subtract 25 dollars for each month, after October, for current price.

Statistical Comparison:
Rapid depreciation.
Average parts availability and cost.
Below average fuel economy.

TECHNICAL DATA

Wheelbase . . . . 122 in.
Length . . . . 219.4 in.
Weight . . . . 4,000 lbs.
Width . . . . 79.6 in.
Standard Engine . . . . 8 cyl.
Standard Brakes . . . . Disc-Drum
Gasoline Mileage 13.7
(With regular fuel)

Frequency of Repairs:
A much improved car. Brakes are still a minor problem.

Body:
Still very rust-resistant. Complaints concerning exterior finish. Front fenders rust-prone.

Safety Defects:
Possibility of defective front suspension and power steering.

Recommendation:
Not recommended.

...

Plymouth Division
Chrysler Corporation

PLYMOUTH FURY (Full-sized)

All data based on four-door sedan

Used Car PRICE* $1,400

Based on standard equipped car with automatic transmission, and radio. Price assumes excellent condition.

*Subtract 25 dollars for each month after October, for current price.

Statistical Comparison:
Below average depreciation.
Average parts cost.
Average parts availability.
Below average fuel economy.

TECHNICAL DATA

Wheelbase . . . . 120 in.
Length . . . . 217.2 in.
Weight . . . . 4,000 lbs.
Width . . . . 79.9 in.
Standard Engine . . . . 6 cyl.
Standard Brakes . . . . Drum
Gasoline Mileage 14.1
(With regular fuel)

Frequency of Repairs:
A much improved car, but still problems with steering, brakes and electrical system. Excellent motor and transmission. Some high-speed vibration.

Body:
Some rusting, but body construction much improved. Front fenders rust-prone.

Safety Defects:
Possibility of defective bumper jack, and six cylinder exhaust manifold.

Recommendation:
Recommended. Make sure vehicle is not an ex-taxi or police car.

AMC HORNET

All data based on four-door sedan

Used Car PRICE* $1,200

Based on standard equipped car with automatic transmission, and radio. Price assumes excellent condition.

*Subtract 25 dollars for each month after October, for current price.

Statistical Comparison:
Below average depreciation.
Average parts cost.
Average parts availability.
Good fuel economy.

TECHNICAL DATA

Wheelbase .... 108 in.
Length .... 179.3 in.
Weight .... 2,700 lbs.
Width .... 70.6 in.
Standard Engine .... 6 cyl.
Standard Brakes .... Drum
Gasoline Mileage 21.1
(With regular fuel)

Frequency of Repairs:
Same problems as '71 model. Motor is excellent.

Body:
Improved construction, but still causes problems.

Safety Defects:
Possibility of defective disc brakes and brake pedals.

Recommendation:
Not recommended.

...

AMC GREMLIN

All data based on two-door sedan

Used Car PRICE* $1,100

Based on standard equipped car with automatic transmission, and radio. Price assumes excellent condition.

*Subtract 25 dollars for each month after October, for current price.

Statistical Comparison:
Below average depreciation.
Average parts cost.
Average parts availability.
Good fuel economy.

TECHNICAL DATA

Wheelbase .... 96 in.
Length .... 161.3 in.
Weight .... 2,600 lbs.
Width .... 70.6 in.
Standard Engine .... 6 cyl.
Standard Brakes .... Drum
Gasoline Mileage 24.1
(With regular fuel)

Frequency of Repairs:
Problems with carburetion, brakes, and transmission. Good motor electrical system, and automatic transmission.

Body:
Solidly constructed, few rust problems.

Safety Defects:
Possibility of defective disc brakes, brake pedals, and lamp reflection.

Recommendation:
Recommended. Much improved over '71 model.

AMBASSADOR

All data based on four-door sedan

Used Car PRICE* $1,200

Based on standard equipped car with automatic transmission, and radio. Price assumes excellent condition.

*Subtract 25 dollars for each month after October, for current price.

Statistical Comparison:
Rapid depreciation.
Average parts availability.
Average parts cost.
Average fuel economy.

TECHNICAL DATA

Wheelbase .... 122 in.
Length .... 210.8 in.
Weight .... 2,780 lbs.
Width .... 77.2 in.
Standard Engine .... 8 cyl.
Standard Brakes .... Drum
Gasoline Mileage 13.4
(With regular fuel)

Frequency of Repairs:
Suspension problems still reported. Exhaust system problems. Transmission complaints. Brakes and motor are good.

Body:
Excellent body construction. Highly rust-resistant.

Safety Defects:
Insufficient Data.

Recommendation:
Not recommended. Not a good year for American Motors.

***

OLDSMOBILE DELTA 88

All data based on four-door sedan

Used Car PRICE* $1,600

Based on standard equipped car with automatic transmission, and radio. Price assumes excellent condition.

*Subtract 25 dollars for each month after October, for current price.

Statistical Comparison:
Average depreciation.
Good parts availability.
Good parts cost.
Average fuel economy.

TECHNICAL DATA

Wheelbase .... 124 in.
Length .... 22.1 in.
Weight .... 4,300 lbs.
Width .... 79.5 in.
Standard Engine V8
Standard Brakes .... Disc-Drum
Gasoline Mileage 13.1

Frequency of Repairs:
Excellent motor, electrical system, and carburetor. Problems with transmission.

Body:
Solid construction. Some paint problems.

Safety Defects:
Possibility of defective steering components, and Rochester carburetor.

Recommendation:
Recommended. Excellent transportation as a family car.

1973
MODELS

VEGA

All data based on two-door coupe

Used Car PRICE* $700

Based on standard equipped car with automatic transmission, and radio. Price assumes excellent condition.

*Subtract 25 dollars for each month after October, for current price.

Statistical Comparison:
Incredibly rapid depreciation.
Unreasonable parts cost.
Parts often unavailable.
Terrible fuel economy.

TECHNICAL DATA

Wheelbase	97 in.
Length	172.2 in.
Weight	2,268 lbs.
Width	65.4 in.
Standard Engine	V4 (140)
Standard Engine	Disc-Drum
Gasoline Mileage	16.9

(With regular fuel)

Frequency of Repairs:
Premature brake wear, high oil consumption, and frequent motor overheating. GM made a secret warranty extension for motor repairs.

Body:
Excessive rusting all over vehicle. Ziebart refuses to guarantee Vegas and Astres. GM warranty extension provides for free fender replacement.

Safety Defects:
Possibility of steering lock-up due to foreign objects, and defective steering relay rod.

Recommendation:
Not recommended. A masochist's dream car. Many motor and rust claims won in small claims court.

...

CHEVY II NOVA

All data based on four-door sedan

Used Car PRICE* $1,300

Based on standard equipped car with automatic transmission, and radio. Price assumes excellent condition.

*Subtract 25 dollars for each month after October, for current price.

Statistical Comparison:
Average depreciation.
Excellent parts availability.
Low parts cost.
Good fuel economy.

TECHNICAL DATA

Wheelbase	111 in.
Length	194.3 in.
Weight	3,169 lbs.
Width	72.4 in.
Standard Engine	V6 (250)
Standard Brakes	Drum
Gasoline Mileage	15.3

(With regular fuel)

Frequency of Repairs:
Excellent motor. Some carburetion problems. Brakes are average. A much improved car. Transmission is failure-prone, so GM extended warranty to 50,000 miles.

Body:
Some rusting problems, but otherwise well constructed. Paint peeling off. Warranty also extended to cover this defect.

Safety Defects:
Possibility of deteriorated motor mounts.

Recommendation:
Recommended. GM's answer to the Ford Maverick for inexpensive and dependable transportation. Claim in court for transmission or paint compensation.

CHEVELLE
Deluxe, Malibu, El Camino, Laguna

All data based on four-door hardtop sedan

Used Car PRICE* $1,900

Based on standard equipped car with automatic transmission, and radio. Price assumes excellent condition.

*Subtract 25 dollars for each month after October, for current price.

Statistical Comparison:
Average depreciation.
Excellent parts availability.
Average parts cost.
Average fuel economy.

TECHNICAL DATA

Wheelbase .... 116 in.
Length .... 206.9 in.
Weight .... 3,545 lbs.
Width .... 76.6 in.
Standard Engine V6 (250)
Standard Brakes .... Disc-Drum
Gasoline Mileage 15.3
(With regular fuel)

Frequency of Repairs:
Minor suspension transmission and steering problems. Excellent V6 motor, and electrical system.

Body:
Good body construction. Premature rusting caused by poor paint quality.

Safety Defects:
Possibility of defective steering.

Recommendation:
Recommended. An excellent buy equal to the Buick. Remember paint and transmission defects covered by extended warranty.

...

CHEVROLET (Full-sized)
Bel Air, Impala, Caprice

All data based on four-door sedan

Used Car PRICE* $1,700

Based on standard equipped car with automatic transmission, and radio. Price assumes excellent condition.

*Subtract 25 dollars for each month after October, for current price.

Statistical Comparison:
Average depreciation.
Excellent parts availability.
Average parts cost.
Average fuel economy.

TECHNICAL DATA

Wheelbase .... 121.5 in.
Length .... 221.9 in.
Weight .... 4,284 lbs.
Width .... 79.5 in.
Standard Engine V8 (350)
Standard Brakes .... Disc-Drum
Gasoline Mileage 12.6
(With regular fuel)

Frequency of Repairs:
Some steering suspension, transmission and pollution control problems. Excellent motor, and electrical system.

Body:
Good construction. Some rusting problems due to bad paint.

Safety Defects:
Possibility of defective steering.

Recommendation:
Recommended. Almost as good as the Chevelle. Use courts for paint and transmission damages.

PONTIAC VENTURA II

All data based on four-door sedan

Used Car PRICE* $1,700

Based on standard equipped car with automatic transmission, and radio. Price assumes excellent condition.

*Subtract 25 dollars for each month after October, for current price.

Statistical Comparison:
Average depreciation.
Low parts cost.
Good parts availability.
Below average fuel economy.

TECHNICAL DATA

Wheelbase .... 111 in.
Length .... 197.5 in.
Weight .... 3,234 lbs.
Width .... 72.4 in.
Standard Engine V6 (250)
Standard Brakes .... Drum
Gasoline Mileage 13.3
(With regular fuel)

Frequency of Repairs:
Carburetion and motor problems. Premature transmission wear, so warranty was secretly extended by GM.

Body:
Frequent problems with rusting and water leaks. Paint defects are chronic, but warranty extended.

Safety Defects:
Rochester carburetor.

Recommendation:
Not recommended. GM has better cars for the same price. Many successful court claims over paint and transmission.

...

PONTIAC (Full-sized)
Catalina, Bonneville, Grandville

All data based on four-door hardtop sedan

Used Car PRICE* $2,000

Based on standard equipped car with automatic transmission, and radio. Price assumes excellent condition.

*Subtract 25 dollars for each month after October, for current price.

Statistical Comparison:
Below average depreciation.
Average parts cost.
Average parts availability.
Below average fuel economy.

TECHNICAL DATA

Wheelbase .... 124 in.
Length .... 224.8 in.
Weight .... 4,505 lbs.
Width .... 79.6 in.
Standard Engine V8 (350)
Standard Brakes .... Disc-Drum
Gasoline Mileage 10.2
(With regular fuel)

Frequency of Repairs:
Excellent motor. Some carburetor, transmission and pollution control problems.

Body:
Solid construction. Some rusting around doors and fenders. Paint defects.

Safety Defects:
Possibly of defective fuel line and rear window defroster.

Recommendation:
Not recommended. Not the car for a gasoline shortage. Use the courts for paint and transmission compensation under extended warranties.

Buick Division
General Motors

BUICK (Full-sized)
Le Sabre, Custom, Centurion

All data based on four-door sedan

Used Car PRICE*..$1,900

Based on standard equipped car with automatic transmission, and radio. Price assumes excellent condition.

*Subtract 25 dollars for each month after October, for current price.

Statistical Comparison:
Low depreciation.
Excellent parts cost.
Excellent parts availability.
Average fuel economy.

TECHNICAL DATA

Wheelbase ....124 in.
Length ....224.2 in.
Weight ....4,899 lbs.
Width ....79.6 in.
Standard Engine...V8 (350)
Standard Brakes..Disc-Drum
Gasoline Mileage 10
(With regular fuel)

Frequency of Repairs:
Excellent motor and electrical system. Some problems with brakes and transmission. Transmission warranty extended.

Body:
Solid construction. Excellent body durability. Some rusting due to serious paint defects. Paint warranty extended.

Safety Defects:
Possibility of defective brakes.

Recommendation:
Recommended. An excellent family-sized car. Verify motor mounts. Many paint and transmission claims won in small claims court.

***

Oldsmobile Division
General Motors

OLDSMOBILE DELTA 88

All data based on four-door sedan

Used Car PRICE*..$1,900

Based on standard equipped car with automatic transmission, and radio. Prices assumes excellent condition.

*Subtract 25 dollars for each month after October, for current price.

Statistical Comparison:
Low depreciation.
Average parts availability.
Average parts cost.
Below average fuel economy.

TECHNICAL DATA

Wheelbase ....124 in.
Length ....226.2 in.
Weight ....4,420 lbs.
Width ....79 in.
Standard Engine...V8 (350)
Standard Brakes..Disc-Drum
Gasoline Mileage 10
(With regular fuel)

Frequency of Repairs:
Excellent mechanical components. Some problems with automatic transmission, but transmission warranty extended.

Body:
Excellent body construction, but rusting and paint wear around doors. Warranty extended for these defects.

Safety Defects:
Insufficient data.

Recommendation:
Recommended. Don't forget to use small claims court for paint or transmission defects.

198

Ford Division
Ford Motor Company   1973

FORD PINTO

All data based on two-door sedan

Used Car PRICE* $1,000

Based on standard equipped car with automatic transmission, and radio. Price assumes excellent condition.

*Subtract 25 dollars for each month after October, for current price.

Statistical Comparison:
Rapid depreciation.
Average parts cost.
Average parts availability.
Below average fuel economy.

TECHNICAL DATA

Wheelbase . . . . 94.2 in.
Length . . . . 164.1 in.
Weight . . . . 2,216 lbs.
Width . . . . 69.4 in.
Standard Engine V4 (98)
Standard Brakes . . . . Disc-Drum
Gasoline Mileage 17.5
(With regular fuel)

Frequency of Repairs:
Good brakes and steering. Problems with suspension, motor and transmission.

Body:
Poor body construction. Much rusting. Some paint problems. Ford extended warranty "J-67" applies.

Safety Defects:
Possibility of defective rack and pinion steering, and rear wheel well.

Recommendation:
Not recommended. Not a "better idea" from Ford. Maverick or Comet is much better car buy. Pinto rusting is worse than other models. Use small claims court for rust and high fuel consumption damages.

...

Ford Division
Ford Motor Company   1973

FORD MAVERICK

All data based on four-door sedan

Used Car PRICE* $1,200

Based on standard equipped car with automatic transmission, and radio. Price assumes excellent condition.

*Subtract 25 dollars for each month after October, for current price.

Statistical Comparison:
Average depreciation.
Low parts cost.
Good parts availability.
Good fuel economy.

TECHNICAL DATA

Wheelbase . . . . 103 in.
Length . . . . 183.3 in.
Weight . . . . 2,852 lbs.
Width . . . . 70.5 in.
Standard Engine V6 (200)
Standard Brakes . . . . Drum
Gasoline Mileage 19.6
(With regular fuel)

Frequency of Repairs:
Motor and transmission are excellent. Some minor problems with brakes. Starting problems caused by gearshift lever, poor contact in ignition. Correct by raising lever in "Park" position.

Body:
Excessive rusting along wheel fender skirts and around doors.

Safety Defects:
Possibility of defective tires, brakes, carburetor, and 4 barrel carburetor.

Recommendation:
Not recommended. Mechanically sound, but rust problems too serious. Ask for warranty extension compensation.

Ford Division
Ford Motor Company

1973

FORD MUSTANG

All data based on two-door hardtop

Used Car Price* $1,500

Based on standard equipped car with automatic transmission, and radio. Price assumes excellent condition.

*Subtract 25 dollars for each month after October, for current price.

Statistical Comparison:
Rapid depreciation.
Average parts availability.
Average parts cost.
Below average fuel economy.

TECHNICAL DATA

Wheelbase .... 109 in.
Length .... 193.8 in.
Weight .... 3,229 lbs.
Width .... 74.1 in.
Standard Engine.. V6 (250)
Standard Brakes... Disc-Drum
Gasoline Mileage 12.1
(With regular fuel)

Frequency of Repairs:
Some carburetor and suspension problems. Average motor and electrical system.

Body:
Excessive rusting around front fender skirts and doors.

Safety Defects:
Possibility that 4 barrel carburetor may cause throttle to jam.

Recommendation:
Not recommended. This behemoth barely resembles first Mustang so popular in 1965.

***

Ford Division
Ford Motor Company

1973

FORD TORINO, MONTEGO

All data based on four-door hardtop sedan

Used Car PRICE* $1,200

Based on standard equipped car with automatic transmission, and radio. Price assumes excellent condition.

*Subtract 25 dollars for each month after October, for current price.

Statistical Comparison:
Rapid depreciation.
Average parts cost.
Average parts availability.
Below average fuel economy.

TECHNICAL DATA

Wheelbase .... 114 in.
Length .... 208 in.
Weight .... 3,838 lbs.
Width .... 79.3 in.
Standard Engine.. V6 (250)
Standard Brakes... Drum
Gasoline Mileage 11.5
(With regular fuel)

Frequency of Repairs:
Transmission, carburetor and brake problems. Good motor.

Body:
Rusting around doors and front fenders. Paint defects caused by faulty design.

Safety Defects:
Possibility of defective power steering, carburetor, brakes and fuel lines.

Recommendation:
Not recommended. Rust, rust, and more rust. Ford's biodegradable car. Ask for secret warranty extension "J-67" compensation.

200

FORD (Full-sized)
Custom, Galaxie, LTD

All date based on four-door hardtop.

Used Car PRICE*...$1,600

Based on standard equipped car with automatic transmission, and radio. Price assumes excellent condition.

*Subtract 25 dollars for each month after October, for current price.

Statistical Comparison:
Rapid depreciation.
Average parts cost.
Excellent parts availability.
Average fuel economy.

TECHNICAL DATA

Wheelbase ....121 in.
Length ....219.5 in.
Weight ....4,292 lbs.
Width ....79.5 in.
Standard Engine..V8 (351)
Standard Brakes...Drum
Gasoline Mileage 11
(With regular fuel)

Frequency of Repairs:
Problems with steering, carburetion and brakes. Good motor and transmission. May have premature valve guide wear. Ford has secret warranty extension for this motor defect.

Body:
Serious rusting problems around doors, fenders, and along wheel fender skirts.

Safety Defects:
Possibility of defective power steering, distributors, and brakes on Meteor models. Defective 4 barrel carburetor may jam throttle in open position.

Recommendation:
Not recommended. Still an average car with serious rust problems. Seek rusting compensation in small claims court under Ford's "J-67" secret warranty extension.

...

PLYMOUTH VALIANT
Scamp and Duster

All data based on four-door sedan

Used Car PRICE*...$1,900

Based on standard equipped car with automatic transmission, and radio. Price assumes excellent condition.

*Subtract 25 dollars for each month after October, for current price.

Statistical Comparison:
Very low depreciation.
Excellent parts availability.
Low parts cost.
Excellent fuel economy.

TECHNICAL DATA

Wheelbase ....108 in.
Length ....195.8 in.
Weight ....2,440 lbs.
Width ....71 in.
Standard Engine...6 cyl.
Standard Brakes...Drum
Gasoline Mileage 21.5
(With regular fuel)

Frequency of Repairs:
Excellent mechanical components. Minor problems with carburetor and brakes.

Body:
Solid construction. No rusting, except for rust-prone front fenders.

Safety Defects:
Possibility of defective transmission fluid, steering, and fuel leakage.

Recommendation:
Recommended. The six cylinder version is the best new or used car on the market. Many motorists have won compensation from small claims court for rusting damages.

201

DODGE DART
Swinger

All data based on four-door sedan

Used Car PRICE* .... $1,900.

Based on standard equipped car with automatic transmission, and radio. Price assumes excellent condition.

*Subtract 25 dollars for each month after October, for current price.

Statistical Comparison:
Very low depreciation.
Average parts cost.
Excellent parts availability.
Average fuel economy.

TECHNICAL DATA

Wheelbase	111 in.
Length	203.8 in.
Weight	2,985 lbs.
Width	69.6 in.
Standard Engine	6 cyl.
Standard Brakes	Drum
Gasoline Mileage	17.8

(With regular fuel)

Frequency of Repairs:
Some carburetion and motor problems caused by pollution control device. Other mechanical components excellent, except for rear brake defects.

Body:
Excellent body construction, no rusting other than front fenders.

Safety Defects:
Possibility of defective transmission fluid, and defective steering.

Recommendation:
Recommended. The best family car on the market. When front fenders rust demand compensation through small claims court.

...

PLYMOUTH SATELLITE
Road Runner, Satellite Custom,
Satellite Sebring

All data based on four-door hardtop

Used Car PRICE* .... $1,700.

Based on standard equipped car with automatic transmission, and radio. Price assumes excellent condition.

*Subtract 25 dollars for each month after October, for current price.

Statistical Comparison:
Average depreciation.
Average parts cost.
Average parts availability.
Below average fuel economy.

TECHNICAL DATA

Wheelbase	117 in.
Length	213.3 in.
Weight	3,625 lbs.
Width	78.6 in.
Standard Engine	V-6 (225)
Standard Brakes	Disc-Drum
Gasoline Mileage	12

(With regular fuel)

Frequency of Repairs:
Problems with brakes, steering and electrical system.

Body:
Good body construction. Very little rusting, except for front fenders.

Safety Defects:
Possibility of defective transmission fluid, defective starter, and fuel leakage.

Recommendation:
Not recommended. Fury is better buy.

DODGE (Full-sized)
Polara and Monaco

All data based on four-door sedan

Used Car PRICE* $1,800

Based on standard equipped car with automatic transmission, and radio. Price assumes excellent condition.

*Subtract 25 dollars for each month after October, for current price.

Statistical Comparison:
Rapid depreciation.
Average parts cost.
Average parts availability.
Below average fuel economy.

TECHNICAL DATA

Wheelbase .... 122 in.
Length .... 226.6 in.
Weight .... 3,980 lbs.
Width .... 79.6 in.
Standard Engine V8 (318)
Standard Brakes .... Disc-Drum
Gasoline Mileage 10
(With regular fuel)

Frequency of Repairs:
Problems with brake, motor, carburetor, and suspension.

Body:
Fair overall body construction, but front fenders are rust-prone by design. Many small claims courts judgments against dealers for $300 - $400 as compensation for defect.

Safety Defects:
Possibility of defective carburetor or air conditioner.

Recommendation:
Not recommended. Fenders and mechanical problems are too frequent.

...

PLYMOUTH FURY
I, II, III

All data based on four-door sedan

Used Car PRICE* $1,700

Based on standard equipped car with automatic transmission, and radio. Price assumes excellent condition.

*Subtract 25 dollars for each month after October, for current price.

Statistical Comparison:
Average depreciation.
Average parts cost.
Average parts availability.
Below average fuel economy.

TECHNICAL DATA

Wheelbase .... 120 in.
Length .... 223.4 in.
Weight .... 3,980 lbs.
Width .... 79.8 in.
Standard Engine V8 (318)
Standard Brakes .... Drum
Gasoline Mileage 11.6
(With regular fuel)

Frequency of Repairs:
Problems with brakes, carburetor and fuel leakage.

Body:
Good body construction. Isolated rusting of front fenders.

Safety Defects:
Possibility of defective carburetor and fuel leakage.

Recommendation:
Recommended. Watch out vehicle is not an ex-taxi or police car by checking for roof holes or dashboard radio mounting screw holes.

American Motors   **1973**
AMC HORNET

All data based on four-door sedan

Used Car PRICE* $1,500

Based on standard equipped car with automatic transmission, and radio. Price assumes excellent condition.

*Subtract 25 dollars for each month after October, for current price.

Statistical Comparison:
Below average depreciation.
Average parts cost.
Average parts availability.
Average fuel economy.

TECHNICAL DATA
Wheelbase .... 108 in.
Length .... 184.9 in.
Weight .... 2,884 lbs.
Width .... 71 in.
Standard Engine V6 (232)
Standard Brakes .... Drum
Gasoline Mileage 19
(With regular fuel)

Frequency of Repairs:
Problems with carburetion, brakes and suspension. Motor and transmission are excellent.

Body:
Excellent body construction. Some rattles reported.

Safety Defects:
Possibility of defective brake master cylinder, and brake pedal.

Recommendation:
Recommended. Station wagon is top choice. Order heavy duty battery for reported cold-weather starting difficulties.

...

American Motors   **1973**
AMC GREMLIN

All data based on two-door sedan

Used Car PRICE* $1,400

Based on standard equipped car with automatic transmission, and radio. Price assumes excellent condition.

*Subtract 25 dollars for each month after October, for current price.

Statistical Comparison:
Below average depreciation.
Average parts cost.
Average parts availability.
Good fuel economy.

TECHNICAL DATA
Wheelbase .... 96 in.
Length .... 165.45 in.
Weight .... 2,702 lbs.
Width .... 70.6 in.
Standard Engine V6 (232)
Standard Brakes .... Drum
Gasoline Mileage 21.6
(With regular fuel)

Frequency of Repairs:
Excellent motor, transmission, and electrical system. Problems with brakes and suspension.

Body:
Excellent body construction. Some paint-peeling reported.

Safety Defects:
Possibility of defective brake master cylinder, brake pedal.

Recommendation:
Recommended. A good compact car with inadequate interior space for tall adults. Verify braking performance.

AMBASSADOR

All data based on four-door sedan

Used Car PRICE* $1,700

Based on standard equipped car with automatic transmission, and radio. Price assumes excellent condition.

*Subtract 25 dollars for each month after October, for current price.

Statistical Comparison:
Above average depreciation.
Average parts availability.
Average parts cost.
Average fuel economy.

TECHNICAL DATA

Wheelbase .... 122 in.
Length .... 212.86 in.
Weight .... 3,814 lbs.
Width .... 77.28 in.
Standard Engine V8 (304)
Standard Brakes .... Drum
Gasoline Mileage 11
(With regular fuel)

Frequency of Repairs:
Excellent motor and transmission. Problems with suspension, and brakes. Exhaust system improved.

Body:
Excellent body construction. Very little rusting.

Safety Defects:
Possibility of defective suspension and brake pedal.

Recommendation:
Recommended, but model discontinued. So plan on visiting scrap yards frequently for parts.

1974
MODELS

1974 RECOMMENDED MODELS

Chevrolet Nova (Acadian) $2,000 (18.8 M.P.G.)
This model has an excellent 6 cylinder engine, offers adequate interior space, and gets good gas mileage. There is the possibility that the rear axle is unsafe. Many lawsuits won against paint and automatic transmission defects.

Chevrolet Chevelle $2,100 (14.3 M.P.G.)
An intermediate car for the whole family. Very few complaints received concerning mechanical components or body construction. Six cylinder is preferred. Possibility of defective seat belts. Also afflicted by inferior paint and defective automatic transmission.

Pontiac Parisienne $2,300 (14.2 M.P.G.)
Since 1971 this car has proven to be economical, durable, and reliable. The 1974 model continues this tradition. Some transmission and paint problems reported.

Oldsmobile Delta $2,300 (12.3 M.P.G.)
Although fuel economy is low and depreciation is above average, the Delta looks so far to be a reliable family-sized car. Premature rust around doors and defective 350 and 400 series automatic transmission.

Ford Maverick (Comet) $1,600 (18.6 M.P.G.)
Since 1970 the Maverick and Comet have performed well. Depreciation is above average. Serious rusting. Fuel economy is good.

Ford Meteor $1,700 (13.5 M.P.G.)
Both the Rideau 500 and Montcalm were excellent used car buys, but major rusting and paint problems are reported. Average fuel economy and an above average depreciation also found with this model.

Plymouth Valiant $2,100 (20 M.P.G.)
One of the best cars Chrysler makes. Six cylinder preferred. Possibility of defective wheel bearings suspension, ignition, brakes and stalling problems. Fenders still rust-prone.

Dodge Dart $2,000 (20 M.P.G.)
The other good car Chrysler makes. Possibility of defective suspension, fenders, brakes, ignition and suspension.

American Motors
American Motors has one of the best new car warranties found in North America. For this reason, the Gremlin, Hornet, and Matador are recommended as excellent used car buys. The Ambassador is not recommended because it has been dropped from production.

Gremlin $1,600 (19 M.P.G.)
Hornet $1,900 (17.6 M.P.G.)
Javelin $2,000 (16.7 M.P.G.)
Ambassador $1,800 (13.6 M.P.G.)

1974 NON-RECOMMENDED MODELS

Chevrolet Vega $900 (27.5 M.P.G.)
This car has an incredible tradition of safety-related and performance-related defects. A bicycle is more reliable. General Motors has extended motor and fender warranty to cover premature rusting and engine overheating. If the dealer refuses to give this compensation, go directly to the small claims court. The Vega and Astre are identical models.

Pontiac Astre $900 (27.5 M.P.G.)
This car is the Vega's twin and has an equally bad tradition.

Cadillac
Possibility of defective heater-defroster, suspension, and brakes. The Cadillac is GM's prestige car that is over-priced and problem-prone. Just the right car to subsidize your local gasoline station and insurance broker.
Calais $4,300 (10.6 M.P.G.)
DeVille $4,800 (10.6 M.P.G.)
Fleetwood $5,300 (10.6 M.P.G.)

Ford Torino (Montego) $1,600 (13.2 M.P.G.)
Severe rusting, transmission, and motor problems. Ford's biodegradable medium-sized car. Next to the Pinto, one of the worst models Ford sells.

Pinto $1,400 (18.3 M.P.G.)
This model may have serious problems with its rack and pinion steering which might cause a binding of the steering assembly. This is the worst car Ford has ever unleashed on an unsuspecting motoring public. Makes the Edsel look like a dream car. Corrosion is so bad, that the Pinto's name is practically synomynous with premature rusting. Gasoline consumption is another problem and some owners have won lawsuits against Ford before the small claims court. One Quebec court case, **Marchand** vs. **Ford Motor Company,** forced Ford to pay $300 to a 1974 Bobcat (Pinto) owner because the car only gave 11 miles to a gallon of gas and Ford advertised 30 miles to a gallon of gas. (Thetford Mines, Judge Bastien No. 235-32-000387-758).

Mustang II $1,900 (16.3 M.P.G.)
Another Ford "better idea" that flopped. Consumers complain of serious vibrations at speeds of 30-60 m.p.h., defective tires, poor gas mileage and premature rusting.

1975 RECOMMENDED MODELS

Ford Maverick (Comet) $2,000 (19.2 M.P.G.)
Two good, dependable cars, but paint and rusting still major problems. Some minor motor problems due to pollution control devices, but gas mileage is good. Both models have rusting defects.

Dodge Dart (Valiant) $2,500 (21.6 M.P.G.)
A great car for a small family. Plenty of passenger room. Very slow depreciation and good parts availability. Very rust-resistant, except for fenders. Problems with stalling, brakes, tires, and vibrations. Unusual number of quality control defects with water leaking into interior topping the list. Problems can be corrected, so both models still recommended.

American Motors
All three models continue to be excellent buys. Buyer Protection Plan gives fair warranty service, but complaints are on the increase.
Gremlin $2,200 (25.2 M.P.G.)
Hornet $2,500 (21.6 M.P.G.)
Matador $2,800 (17.2 M.P.G.)

1975 NON-RECOMMENDED MODELS

General Motors Vega (Astre) $1,400 (25.2 M.P.G.)
GM's first disposable subcompact car. Use either car once, then throw it away.

Ford Pinto (Bobcat) $2,800
Too many quality control defects combined with sloppy exterior finishes. Premature rusting, vibrations, poor gas mileage and inferior paint continue to plague the Pinto.

American Motors Pacer $2,700 (18.5 M.P.G.)
One of the most radically different new cars, the Pacer is very popular due to its distinctive styling, interior space, and slow depreciation. Ziebart technicians predict that rusting could become a major problem. Model not recommended due to seat anchorage defects, inadequate parts supply, high initial cost, poor service, and erratic rate of depreciation.

Chrysler Cordoba
A real problem car. Severe front end vibrations, defective Goodyear tires, paint mis-match, inadequate braking performance, and poor servicing are most frequent complaints.

FOREIGN
USED CARS
1970-1975

DOMESTIC VS IMPORT

There is still a lot of controversy surrounding the relative merits of foreign and domestic cars. Before deciding which car is best, it would be wise to forget all the popular mythology and try to get solid facts.

Almost without exception, foreign car parts will be much more expensive than those for a domestic equivalent, despite the similar initial retail price. A good way to check these prices is to comparison shop prices on certain items one would expect to replace frequently. Exhaust systems, brake pads, tires, and electrical components are the best indicators. Time permitting, verify replacement costs for major items, such as the transmission and motor as well.

Servicing also needs to be investigated since this has traditionally been the "bête noire" of the importer in North America. For example, a vehicle can have the best engineering features in the world, but if the servicing is lousy, that vehicle will quickly deteriorate and fall into a lemon category. Volkswagen, Fiat, and Volvo are well aware of this problem and are trying to improve servicing procedures at the dealership level. British Leyland, though, may be already too far gone for any help to be useful.

Verify how often the vehicle needs to be serviced, and if there is a franchised dealer nearby with mechanics that are both reliable and inexpensive. Of course, no dealer is going to admit that it has recurring problems on a particular model, and thereby lose a potential sale. So check servicing costs with other car owners driving similar models and be on the look out for cars showing the dealer's nameplate on the trunk. Ask owners to evaluate the quality of service found at their dealership. It also might be worthwhile to check with fleet owners about the servicing problems they are encountering with their foreign or domestic vehicle. Finally, question closely regional and national automobile consumer protection groups as to which vehicles receive the most complaints and what mechanical components are the most failure-prone. Remember, that most consumer groups need at least six months worth of complaints in order to properly evaluate new cars.

AVIS FLEET EXPERIENCE (ENGLAND)

Avis compiled the following table based on a year's experience in England with their cars. The high figure for Rover reflects frequent engine trouble costs. This table was first published in **Autocar**, September, 1974.

Model	Percentage of models in fleet	Percentage of total maintenance budget
Hillman Avenger	25.0	12.0
Hillman Hunter	10.0	11.8
Hillman Hunter Estate	10.2	11.8
Ford Escort	7.11	5.2
Ford Capri	7.0	7.3
Vauxhall Viva	7.4	1.5
Daimler Sovereign	1.5	1.8
Rover 2000	3.7	21.3
Fiat 127	1.5	2.2
Fiat 128	1.3	3.9
Volkswagen Beetle	6.1	4.7
Volkswagen Variant	8.5	8.9
Audi 100LS	5.1	16.3

The Swedish Motor Vehicle Inspection Company has been inspecting new and used cars since 1965 and carries out about 3.5 million inspections a year. In April of 1976, their inspectors reported that in comparing the number of cars remaining in use after 15 years, Volvo outranked all others. It was followed by Mercedes-Benz, BMW, Volkswagen, and Peugeot. The Swedish government publishes these inspection reports periodically. Copies can be obtained by writing Ab Svensk Bilprovning, Fack, S-162 10 Vallingby, Sweden.

A careful comparison should also be made between the warranty coverage of domestic and foreign vehicles. Compare the wording and extent of each warranty and check with the Washington based Center for Auto Safety to see if the warranty conditions are actually followed by the dealers. Consumers Union may also be helpful.

BRITISH CARS

BRITISH LEYLAND

England's British Leyland auto manufacturer answers the important consumer question "Can an automobile manufacturer that consistently makes inferior vehicles, with a parts replacement system that moves by stagecoach, and a dealer network that is practically non-existent, survive and still be profitable?" with both a yes and a no.

BLM is in pitiful shape, as is most of the British automobile industry. British Leyland, however, has suffered the steepest decline in sales and reputation due primarily to the misjudging of the American foreign car market by its chief executive, Lord Stokes. Consequently, British Leyland is surviving, but just barely.

The Austin Marina is the English revenge against its former American colonies. It uses the same infernal combustion engine that generations of MG owners loved to hate. The Jaguar 6 cylinder is a waste of money, while the Jaguar V-12 is doubly wasteful. The remaining BLM products are also not recommended due to the high cost of servicing and parts replacement. British Leyland's warranty performance is judged to be poor by many of its hapless customers who have complained to American, British and Canadian consumer groups.

SAFETY DEFECT RECALL CAMPAIGNS

British Leyland Motors, Incorporated

Make	Model	Model Year	Brief Description of Defect (Manufacturer's Corrective Action)	No. of Pages on File	Number of Vehicles Recalled
MG	MG-Midget MGB-Roadster MGB-GT	1970	Possibility that locking bolt of steering column lock may have been ineffectively secured in assembly. Under certain circumstances, this could engage lock causing immediate loss of directional control of vehicle.	6	6,000
Rover	3500S	1970	Possibility that hood safety and main latches were misaligned. If this condition exists, could cause hood assembly to lift while in motion.	5	1,292
Austin	American Model	1968 thru 1971	Possibility that inertia valve in rear brake system may not operate correctly. If this condition exists and front brake system fails, would cause rear brake system to be less efficient. (Correct by replacing valve where necessary.)	7	41,006

Make	Model	Model Year	Brief Description of Defect (Manufacturer's Corrective Action)	No. of Pages on File	Number of Vehicles Recalled
Jaguar	XJ6	1970	Possibility that hand brake cable may become displaced from intermediate lever, causing loss of handbrake operation.	4	920
Triumph	GT-6 and GT-6 +	1968 1969 1970	Possibility that lap-type seatbelt instead of shoulder-type seatbelt was installed in vehicle. (Correct by replacing with proper belt.)	5	3,236
Austin MG	Healy/Sprite Midget	1968 thru 1971	Possibility that if front brake system fails in dual-braking systems, rear brake system may not operate at full efficiency, thereby increasing vehicle-stopping distance and possibly affecting safety in handling vehicle.	5	32,386
Triumph	GT6MK III	1971 1972	Possibility that two rear brake hoses may contact rear wheel arch flanges when rear suspension is in full "bump" position. If condition exists, hoses could chafe through and result in decreased braking efficiency.	12	3,335
Austin	Marina	1974 & 1975	Possibility that outer rubber casing of front brake hose may be subject to cracking. Cracking is due to suspension/brake hose movement which is characteristic of this model when operated under arduous conditions.	3	14,000

JAGUAR

Type of Vehicle	No. of Vehicles	Defect
1972 Jaguar V12 models	11	The seat belt warning system for models equipped with automatic transmissions were wired in accordance with requirements for manual transmissions. The warning system will activate when the hand brake is released with the automatic transmission selector in any position including "Park". The vehicles referred to therefore do not conform to the requirements of paragraph 12(b) of standard 208.

MG SPORTS CARS

1972 MG sports cars	2292	The cars have been found on inspection, to have a measurement of less than the required 24 inches between the headlamp centre to the road surface which does not conform to CMVSS 108.
1972 MGB and MGBGT vehicles	67	Glove box may open when tested in accordance with Standard 201.
Midgets from 1968 on	1,776	Defect revealed variations in reserve braking stopping distance. Brake master cylinder push rod will be replaced.

222

TRIUMPH

Type of Vehicle	No. of Vehicles	Defect
Triumph TR6	600	Seat belts manufactured by U.S. Safety Weave Corp. model USW 201 are not in compliance with Canada Motor Vehicle Safety Standard No. 209 and its cited test procedure.
Triumph Spitfire and GT6 plus vehicles	592	The defect is in the windshield washer pump mechanism.
Triumph GT6 MK III	308	Certain vehicles may not comply with CMVSS 114.

USED CAR PRICES (APPROXIMATE)
Austin

Model & Body Type	Wholesale Price	Retail Price
1975		
AUSTIN MARINA 4 Cyl. 96" W.B.		
4 Door Sedan	1400	1600
2 Door GT Coupe	1400	1600
1974		
MARINA 4 Cyl. 96" W.B.		
2 Door GT Coupe	1100	1300
4 Door Sedan	1000	1200
1973		
MARINA 4 Cyl. 96" W.B.		
2 Door GT Coupe	900	1100
4 Door Sedan	800	1000
1972		
1971		
MARINA 4 Cyl. 96" W.B.		
2 Door Coupe	700	900
4 Door Sedan	700	900
2 Door GT	800	1000
AUSTIN 4 Cyl. 93.5" W.B.		
Coach	1100	1300
Coupe	1100	1300
AUSTIN AMERICA 4 Cyl. 93.5" W.B.		
2 Door Sedan	200	500
2 Door Sedan (Auto. Trans.)	300	500
1970		
AUSTIN AMERICA 4 Cyl. 93.5" W.B.		
2 Door Sedan	200	400
2 Door Sedan (Auto.Trans.)	200	400

Model & Body Type	Wholesale Price	Retail Price
1975		
XJ6 6 Cyl. 108.8" W.B. (Cpe) 113" W.B. (Sdn)		
XJ6-6 L 4 Dr Sdn (Long W.B.)	6000	7000
XJ6-C 2 Dr Cpe (Short W.B.)	6300	7300
XJ12 12 Cyl. 108.8" W.B. (Cpe) 113" W.B. (Sdn)		
XJ12-L 4 Dr Sdn (Long W.B.)	7200	8600
XJ12-C 2 Dr Cpe (Short W.B.)	7700	9100
1974		
XKE 12 Cyl. 105" W.B.		
Convertible	6000	7000
Convertible (Auto. Trans.)	6100	7100
XJ6 Cyl. 108.8" W.B.		
Sedan (Auto. Trans.)	6500	7500
Sedan (Auto. Trans.)	6000	7000
1973		
XKE 12 Cyl. 105" W.B.		
Convertible	4100	4900
Coupe	4300	5100
Add for Auto. Trans.		
XJ6 Cyl. 108.9" W.B.		
Sedan (Automatic Trans.)	5300	5800
XJ 12 Cyl. 108.9" W.B.		
Sedan (Automatic Trans.)	5700	6200
1972		
XKE 12 Cyl. 105" W.B.		
Roadster	3500	4000
Coupe	3100	4200
Add for Auto. Trans.		
XJ 6 Cyl. 108.9" W.B.		
Sedan	3900	4400
1971		
XKE 6 Cyl. 96" W.B.		
Roadster	1900	2300
Coupe	2100	2500
XJ Sedan	3300	3700
1970		
XKE 6 Cyl. 96" W.B. (Exc. 2 + 2) 105" W.B. (2 + 2)		
Convertible Roadster	1500	1800
Coupe	1600	1900
Coupe 2 + 2	1800	2100
Coupe 2 + 2 (Auto. Trans.)	1900	2200
XJ 6 Cyl. 108.9" W.B.		
Sedan	2900	3400

Model & Body Type	Wholesale Price	Retail Price
MG		
1975		
MIDGET 4 Cyl. 80" W.B.		
Convertible	1900	2400
MGB 4 Cyl. 91.13" W.B.		
Convertible	2300	2800
1974		
MIDGET 4 Cyl. 80" W.B.		
Convertible	1600	2000
MGB 4 Cyl. 91.1" W.B.		
Convertible	2000	2400
Coupe GY	2300	2700
1973		
MIDGET 4 Cyl. 80" W.B.		
Convertible	1200	1600
MGB 4 Cyl. 91" W.B.		
Convertible	1700	2100
Hardtop	1800	2200
Coupe GT	2000	2400
1972		
MIDGET 4 Cyl. 80" W.B.		
Convertible	900	1200
MGB 4 Cyl. 91" W.B.		
Convertible	1400	1700
Hardtop	1500	1800
Coupe GT	1600	1900
1971		
MIDGET 4 Cyl. 80" W.B.		
Convertible	800	1000
MGB 4 Cyl. 91" W.B.		
Roadster	1100	1400
Coupe GT	1300	1600
1970		
MIDGET 4 Cyl. 80" W.B.		
Convertible	500	800
MGB 4 Cyl. 91" W.B.		
Roadster	900	1200
Coupe GT	1000	1300

Model & Body Type	Wholesale Price	Retail Price
Rover		
1974		
LAND ROVER 4 Cyl. 88" W.B.		
88 Hardtop Deluxe	2400	2700
1973		
LAND ROVER 4 Cyl. 88" W.B.		
88 Hardtop Deluxe	1800	2100
1972		
LAND ROVER 4 Cyl. 88" W.B.		
88 Hardtop	1400	1700
1971		
2000TC 4 Cyl. 103.4" W.B.		
4 Door Sedan	1100	1300
LAND ROVER 4 Cyl. 88" W.B.		
88 Hardtop	1000	1200
1970		
2000 4 Cyl. 103.4" W.B.		
4 Dr Sedan (Auto. Trans.)	1300	1500

Triumph

British Leyland's answer to the Ford Edsel and the Vauxhall Viva. Triumph is the ideal car to teach young sports car enthusiasts the therapeutic value of walking. It's an all-around bad car that has all the problems endemic with British Leyland automotive concoctions.

USED CAR PRICES (APPROXIMATE)
Triumph

Model & Body Type	Wholesale Price	Retail Price
1975		
SPITFIRE 4 Cyl. 83" W.B.		
1500 Convertible	2000	2500
TR-7 4 Cyl. 85" W.B. Hardtop	2500	3000
TR-6 6 Cyl. 88" W.B. Convertible	2600	3100
1974		
SPITFIRE 4 Cyl. 83" W.B. 1500 Convertible	1600	2100
TR6 6 Cyl. 88" W.B. Convertible	2300	2800

Model & Body Type	Wholesale Price	Retail Price
1973		
SPITFIRE 4 Cyl. 83" W.B. 1500 Roadster	1300	1700
GT-6 6 Cyl. 83" W.B.		
Mark III Fastback Coupe	2000	2400
TR6 6 Cyl. 88" W.B. Convertible	2200	2600
Hardtop	2300	2700
1972		
SPITFIRE 4 Cyl. 83" W.B. Mark IV Roadster	1000	1300
GT-6 6 Cyl. 83" W.B. Mark III Fastback Cpe	1400	1700
TR6 6 Cyl. 88" W.B. Convertible	1500	1800
Hardtop	1700	2000
1971		
SPITFIRE 4 Cyl. 83" W.B.		
Mark IV Softtop	500	900
Mark IV Hardtop	600	1000
TR-6 6 Cyl. 88" W.B. Convertible	1200	1500
Hardtop	1200	1500
GT-6 6 Cyl. 88" W.B. Mark III Fastback	900	1200
1970		
SPITFIRE 4 Cyl. 83" W.B. Mark III Softtop	400	800
Mark III Hardtop	500	900
TR-6 6 Cyl. 88" W.B. Convertible	1000	1300
Hardtop	1100	1400
GT-6 6 Cyl. 83" W.B. Fastback	800	900

FRENCH CARS

CITROEN

This company makes the most advanced car on the American market. Unfortunately, due to Citroen's feuding with the federal National Highway Traffic Safety Administration over its headlight and bumper design, the last Citroen imported into the United States was the 1974 SM model. The latest Canadian imports were in 1972. Therefore, the wise consumer will steer clear of any used Citroen purchases since the reported parts shortage is bound to become a chronic problem. There have been no significant recall campaigns.

Citroen

1971 & 1972 model "DS-21" Sedans and station wagons	496	Hydraulic brake lines to front and rear brakes reversed which could, under certain conditions result in irregular braking.

Citroen

Model & Body Type	Wholesale Price	Retail Price
1972		
D SPECIAL 4 Cyl. 4 Door Sedan	1000	1300
DS-21 4 Cyl. 4 Door Sedan	1500	2000
4 Dr Pallas Sdn (w/ or w/o Auto. Trans.)	1500	2000
D-21 4 Cyl. Station Wagon	1600	2000
Station Wagon (Auto. Trans.)	1800	2100
SM 6 Cyl. 2 Door Coupe	3500	4200
2 Door Coupe (Auto. Trans.)	3800	4300

PEUGEOT

In France, Peugeot is considered the poor man's Citroen. Its sophisticated engineering, and economical performance make this the perfect car for — France! In North America, the dealer body is too weak and parts supply too haphazard for the needs of most motorists. Parts prices as well as long waiting periods for repairs have also come in for strong owner criticism.

Of all the Peugeot offerings, owners report that the 304 model gave the best value for its price. Unfortunately, that model has been discontinued, so parts may be a real problem. The new Peugeot models with the diesel engine should be shunned in favor of a good second-hand Mercedes diesel which sells for the same price.

MAJOR RECALL CAMPAIGNS
Peugeot, Incorporated

Make	Model	Model Year	Brief Description of Defect (Manufacturer's Corrective Action)	No. of Pages on File	Number of Vehicles Recalled
Peugeot	504 Sedan	1970 thru 1973	Possibility that rubber windshield moldings have hardness level below design specifications.	5	13,255
Peugeot	404 504	1967 thru 1971	Possibility that seal on first piston of dual brake master cylinder may fail. If condition exists, will cause loss of rear brakes. Front braking system will be unaffected.	5	14,817
Peugeot	304, 404 & 504	Jan 1968 thru Mar 1974	Possibility that interior rear view mirror mounting stems may be defective. (Correct by inspecting and modifying mirror mounting stem.)	1	35,000

USED CAR PRICES (APPROXIMATE)
Peugeot

Model & Body Type	Wholesale Price	Retail Price
1975		
504 4 Cyl. 108" W.B. (Sdns) 114" W.B. (Wgns)		
4 Door Sedan	2500	3000
5 Door Station Wagon	1900	3400
4 Door Diesel Sedan	3200	3700
4 Door Diesel Station Wagon	3500	4000
1974		
504 4 Cyl. 108" W.B. (Sdns) 114.8" W.B. (Wgns)		
4 Door Sedan	2000	2500
5 Door Wagon	2300	2800
4 Door Diesel Sedan	2400	2900
4 Door Diesel Wagon	2700	3200
1973		
504 4 Cyl. 108" W.B.		
4 Door Sedan	1800	2200
5 Door Wagon	2000	2400
1972		
304 4 Cyl. 101.9" W.B.		
4 Door Sedan	500	700
4 Door Wagon	700	900
504 4 Cyl. 108" W.B.		
4 Door Sedan	1300	1500
4 Door Wagon	1500	1900

Model & Body Type	Wholesale Price	Retail Price
1971		
304 4 Cyl. 101.8" W.B.		
4 Door Sedan	400	600
4 Door Wagon	600	800
504 4 Cyl. 108" W.B.		
4 Door Sedan	900	1100
4 Door Sedan (Auto. Trans)	1000	1200

RENAULT

Known as the General Motors of France, Renault makes the best engineered, low-priced, economical compact and subcompact vehicles in Europe. All of its vehicles maximize both comfort and driving performance, while maintaining a solid reputation for fuel economy.

Renault's marketing experience in the United States and Canada has been marked by low sales and an inability to find a substantial number of quality dealers capable of servicing its products. As a result of these rather formidable obstacles, the French automaker practically abandoned the American market in 1965 and concentrated upon its Canadian sales. In retrospect, it was a poor marketing decision prompted by the American motorist's spurning of the defect-prone Renault Dauphine. Renault had the right idea — but the wrong car. Nevertheless, in 1959, it sold 93,000 cars and became the leader in imported car sales in the United States. This popularity was cut short, however, when other importers, such as Volkswagen, started better quality cars at lower prices. Competition got so bad that Renault's total sales in the United States for 1975 were only 7,287 vehicles.

Because of a generally weak dealer network in the United States and Canada, parts replacement has always been inadequate and has contributed to the rapid depreciation in value of Renault models throughout North America. Servicing is another problem area, according to many Renault owners interviewed. Poor diagnostic procedures, mechanical defects that are repaired and then reappear, and difficulty in getting service from independent garages were the major complaints listed. This last problem is a common complaint with many European cars.

Owners report mechanical defects affecting primarily the motor (burning oil and seizing), suspension (front suspension may wear out prematurely from road spray contaminents), and outer body shell that is prone to early rusting. Many Renault owners also report they were sold the wrong model year by both new and used car dealers. Check the manufacturer's date of manufacture plate affixed to the door on the driver's side to determine the true model year.

Although Renault has some very serious problems in servicing its cars, no other automaker either European or American, offers such inexpensive well-engineered vehicles to the North American buying public. However, because of the rapid depreciation and poor dealer servicing of new models, the only new Renault model that represents good value for the money spent is the Renault 5. This model competes favorably with the Chevrolet Chevette (An American car requiring European Metric tools), Fiat 128, and the Volkswagen Rabbit, because of its low initial cost, simplified construction, and moderate depreciation.

Anyone looking for an excellent used car buy should carefully consider the Renault 12. Although this model's best years were from 1970 through 1972 when pollution control regulations were less stringent, subsequent model years remain good used car buys because of their low retail prices caused by a devastatingly rapid depreciation rate. Plenty of spare parts are available since the Renault 12 has had few basic design changes through the years.

The worst used Renault one can buy is the Renault 16 model that has recently been discontinued. Parts are impossible to find, mechanical defects abound, and even Renault dealers have been known to refuse service on this vehicle. The Renault 16, and also to a lesser extent the Renault 12, has a front-wheel drive assembly that is failure-prone due to its defective "cardan," or rubber protector. Since these failures, which are not safety-related, occur between 24,000 and 36,000 miles, Renault France has secretly extended warranty coverage on these parts and also applied the warranty extension to second owners.

MAJOR RECALL CAMPAIGNS
Renault

Renault vehicles (1972-1973 models)	9,671	Compliance labels missing

USED CAR PRICES (APPROXIMATE)

Renault

Model & Body Type	Wholesale Price	Retail Price
1975		
4 Cyl. 96" W.B.	1500	1900
12 4 Door Sedan	1700	2100
12L 4 Door Sedan	1700	2100
12 TL 4 Door Sedan	1900	2300
12 4 Door Station Wagon	2100	2500
15TL 2 Door Coupe	2300	2700
17 Gordini 2 Door Coupe	2700	3200
17 Gordini Convertible	2900	3400
1974		
4 Cyl. 96" W.B. (Exc. Gordinis) 95.5" W.B. (Gordinis)		
12 Sedan	1100	1500
12 L Sedan	1200	1600
12 TL Sedan	1300	1700
12 Station Wagon	1400	1800
15 Coupe	1500	1900
17 TL Coupe	1700	2100
17 TL Coupe/Convertible	1800	2200
17 Gordini Coupe	1900	2300
17 Gordini Coupe/Conv.	2100	2600
1973		
4 Cyl. 96" W.B.		
12 Sedan	800	1200
12 Station Wagon	900	1300
15 Coupe	1000	1400
17 Sport Coupe	1500	2000
16 4 Door	700	900
1972		
4 Cyl. 96" W.B. (Exc. 16's) 106.6" W.B. (16's)		
12 Sedan	400	700
12 Station Wagon	500	800
Add For Auto Trans		
16 Sedan/Wagon	400	600
16 Sedan/Wagon (Auto. Trans.)	400	600
15 Coupe	800	1100
15 Coupe (Auto. Trans.)	900	1200
10 Sedan	600	700

Model & Body Type	Wholesale Price	Retail Price
1971		
4 Cyl. 89" W.B. (10) 105.8" W.B. (16)		
10 Sedan	300	500
10 Sedan (Auto. Trans.)	400	600
16 Sedan/Wagon	300	500
16 Sedan/Wagon (Auto. Trans.)	300	500
12 Sedan	600	800
12 Wagon	700	900
4 4 Door	300	500
4 Fourgonette	300	500
1970		
4 Cyl. 89" W.B. (10) 105.8" W.B. (16)		
10 Sedan	200	300
10 Sedan (Auto. Trans.)	300	400
16 Sedan/Wagon	300	400
16 Sedan/Wagon (Auto. Trans.)	300	400
8 Gordini 4 Door	500	700
4 Wagon	400	500
4 Fourgon.	300	400

GERMAN CARS

BMW (Bavarian Motor Works)

Good reliability, sophisticated engineering and a slow rate of depreciation combine to make the BMW an expensive and popular dream machine. Owners have complained of inadequate dealer service facilities and many drivers have switched over to independent garages to avoid being stuck with high repair bills. Parts are so scarce and expensive that a black market in used parts presently exists among scrapyards along the northeast coast of the United States and in the Maritimes.

BMW used car prices are inflated due to fluctuating European currency rates, the increased retail prices for new models and BMW's well-earned reputation for quality. The best used car model is the 2002 manufactured before the 1973 emission control regulations. The 530 i 6 cylinder model is not recommended because of early production problems with the fuel injection system and the impossibility of finding replacements parts.

MAJOR RECALL CAMPAIGNS

Bayerische Motoren Werke (BMW)

Make	Model	Model Year	Brief Description of Defect (Manufacturer's Corrective Action)	No. of Pages on File	Number of Vehicles Recalled
BMW	Six cylinder Model 2500 and 2600	Imptd since Jan. 1 1969	Possibility that headlights may not comply with Federal Safety Standard 108, because minimum height from ground level to center of head lights may need to be modified. (Correct by modifying head lights to meet Standard 108.)	3	1,306
BMW	6 cylinder 182 CID engines	1972	Possibility that carburetor malfunction may occur, which in certain cases could result in engine compartment fire.	3	4,000
BMW	R75/5 motor-cycle	1973	Possibility that bolts used to retain flywheel may not have been properly torqued. If condition exists, bolts could break under stress causing loss of driving power through clutch to transmission and rear wheel.	4	1,136

USED CAR PRICES (APPROXIMATE)

BMW
(West Germany)

Model & Body Type	Wholesale Price	Retail Price
1975		
2002 4 Cyl. 98.4" W.B.		
2 Door Sedan	3900	4500
2 Door Sedan Automatic	4400	4900
530 i 6 Cyl. 103.8" W.B.		
4 Door Sedan	6000	6500
5 Door Sedan Automatic	6200	6700
3.0 Si 6 Cyl. 106" W.B.		
4 Door Sedan	9700	10300
4 Door Sedan Automatic	10000	10600
1974		
2002 4 Cyl. 98.5" W.B.	3000	3500
2 Door Sedan	3000	3500
Tii 2 Door Sedan	3400	3900
3.0 6 Cyl. 106" W.B. (Sdns) 103.3" W.B. (Cpes)		
Bavaria 4 Door Sedan	5600	6100
Bavaria 4 Dr Sdn. (Auto. Trans.)	5100	6000
S 4 Door Sedan	7500	8100
S 4 Door Sedan (Auto. Trans.)	7600	8200
CS 2 Door Coupe	7700	8300
CS 2 Door Coupe (Auto. Trans.)	8000	8500
1973		
2002 4 Cyl. 98.5" W.B.		
2 Door Sedan	2400	2900
Tii 2 Door Sedan	2700	3200
3.0 6 Cyl. 106" W.B. (Exc. CS) 103.3" W.B. (CS)		
Bavaria 4 Door Sedan	3500	4000
Bavaria 4 Dr Sdn. (Auto. Trans.)	3600	4100
CS 2 Door Coupe	5000	5500
CS 2 Door Coupe (Auto. Trans.)	5200	5800
1972		
2002 4 Cyl. 98.5" W.B.		
2 Door Sedan	1700	2300
Tii 2 Door Sedan	2100	2600
BAVARIA & 3.0 6 Cyl. 106" W.B. (Bavs) 103.1" W.B. (Cpes)		
Bavaria 4 Door Sedan	3000	3500
Bavaria 4 Dr Sdn (Auto. Trans.)	3100	3600
3.0 CS 2 Door Coupe	4200	4700
3.0 CSA 2 Door Coupe	4400	4900

CAPRI

Ford's best European car. After all, with the Cortina disaster, Ford of Europe had to make some move to bolster its European import reputation in the United States. Unfortunately, the early '71 and '72 models had many quality control defects affecting the front disc brakes, windshield wipers, heater and defroster, alternator and regulator. These Capri models also had problems with an excessive shimmy in the front suspension, a high oil consumption, hood cable breakage, and door adjustments. For many of the above-noted problems, Ford has made several special secret warranty extensions.

Anyone wishing to purchase a used Capri would be prudent to stick with the post-1973 models. In that category, the 1975-1976 Capri 2 looks like the only choice around, even if it is still rather unimpressive. In overall driving performance, Ford's European Capri makes the American Ford Mustang 2 look like it contracted hoof and mouth disease. Unfortunately they both are rust-catchers.

USED CAR PRICES (APPROXIMATE)
Capri
(West Germany)

Model & Body Type	Wholesale Price	Retail Price
1975		
Capri II 4 Cyl. 100.8" W.B.		
3 Door Sport Coupe	2400	2900
Ghia 3 Door Sport Coupe	—	—
Add For Auto. Trans.	—	—
1974		
2000 4 Cyl. 100.8" W.B.		
2 Door Sport Coupe	1600	2100
2600 6 Cyl. 100.8" W.B.		
2 Door Sport Coupe	1900	2400
1973		
2000 4 Cyl. 100.8" W.B.		
2 Door Sport Coupe	1300	1800
2600 6 Cyl. 100.8" W.B.		
2 Door Sport Coupe	1500	2000
1972		
1600 & 2000 4 Cyl. 100.8" W.B.		
1600 2 Door Sport Coupe	900	1400
2000 2 Door Sport Coupe	1000	1500
2600 6 Cyl. 100.8" W.B.		
2 Door Sport Coupe	1100	1600
1971		
4 Cyl. 100.8" W.B.		
2 Door Sport Coupe	800	1000

MERCEDES-BENZ

The married man's BMW. Actually the Mercedes-Benz models are even more reliable than the BMW with a slower rate of depreciation, too. Servicing and parts supply appear adequate, probably due to the large number of models sold in North America and the demands made by some of the more affluent Mercedes owners.

The diesel models are the best buy, either new or used. Some owners have reported that the diesel fuel may jell at low temperatures, but Mercedes-Benz is working on an additive to correct the problem.

The only negative reports concerning Mercedes have been regarding the frequent replacement of the exhaust system in colder climates, and the charges for periodic maintenance work. Some customers have reported that Mercedes will pay 50 percent of the bill for the replacement of the exhaust system within the first two years of ownership. This alleged warranty extension has not been confirmed, however.

MAJOR RECALL CAMPAIGNS
Mercedes-Benz of North America, Incorporated

Make	Model	Model Year	Brief Description of Defect (Manufacturer's Corrective Action)	No. of Pages on File	Number of Vehicles Recalled
Mercedes-Benz	220/9 to 300SEL/ 8 6.3	Manfd from mid March to Sept. 30, 1970	Possibility that check valve of vacuum line from brake booster to intake manifold might develop cracks, causing booster system assist reduction and resulting in possible reduced braking capacity. (Correct by replacing line and check valve.)	9	16,107
Mercedes-Benz	280SE Convertible 3.5 280SE Coupe 3.5 300SEL 3.5 Sedan	1971	Possibility that fuel supply connecting hoses and fuel injection nozzle hose may develop leaks at connecting point creating possibility of fuel escaping which could ignite causing fire damage.	10	2,281
Mercedes-Benz	280 & 280 Coupe	1973	Possibility that brake line from master cylinder to right front wheel may rub against automatic transmission filler pipe causing line to rupture and leak.	9	6,300
Mercedes-Benz	220D, 220 250, 250c, 280, 280c	1972 & 1973	Possibility that seat belts fail to meet requirement of Federal Motor Vehicle Safety Standard No. 208. Condition exists because length of belt, when front seat is in most forward position, prevents or impedes belt usage by certain individuals who might find seat belt uncomfortably tight.	15	29,228

USED CAR PRICES (APPROXIMATE)
Mercedes-Benz

Model & Body Type	Wholesale Price	Retail Price
1975		
4 Cyl. 108.3" W.B.		
230 Sedan Automatic	8000	8600
240D Sedan	7500	8000
240D Sedan Automatic	8100	8700
5 Cyl. 108.3" W.B.		
300D Sedan Automatic	10300	11000
6 Cyl. 108.3" W.B. (Exc. S) 112.8" W.B. (S)		
280 Sedan Automatic	10500	11300
280C Coupe Automatic	10900	12000
280S Sedan Automatic	12000	13600
8 Cyl. 112.6" W.B. (SE) 116.5" W.B. (SEL)		
96.9" W.B. (SL) 111" W.B. (SLC)		
450SL Coupe Roadster Auto.	13200	14800
450SE Sedan Automatic	14100	15900
450SEL Sedan Automatic	15000	17400
450SLC Coupe Automatic	17200	19400
1974		
4 Cyl. 108.3" W.B.		
230 4 Dr Sedan (Auto. Trans.)	5700	6300
240 D 4 Dr Sedan	5800	6400
240 D 4 Dr Sdn (Auto. Trans.)	6100	6900
6 Cyl. 108.3" W.B.		
280 4 Dr Sedan (Auto. Trans.)	6900	7700
28 C 2 Door Coupe (Auto Trans.)	7300	8300
8 Cyl. 112" W.B. (SE) 116" W.B. (SEL)		
96.6" W.B. (SL) 111" W.B. (SEL)		
450 SE 4 Door Sedan (Auto. Trans.)	11900	12900
450 SEL 4 Door Sedan)Auto. Trans.)	12800	14000
450 SL Coupe/Roadster (Auto. Trans.)	11300	12500
450 SLC Coupe (Auto. Trans.)	15200	17400
1973		
4 Cyl. 108.3" W.B.		
220 4 Door Sedan (Auto. Trans.)	4200	5000
220 D 4 Door Sedan	4300	5100
220 D 4 Door Sedan (Auto. Trans.)	4400	5200
6 Cyl. 108.3" W.B.		
280 4 Door Sedan (Auto. Trans.)	5400	6100
280 C 2 Door Coupe (Auto. Trans.)	5700	6400
8 Cyl. 108.3" W.B. (SE) 112.2" W.B. (SEL)		
96.9" W.B. (SL) 111" W.B. (SLC)		
450 SE 4 Door Sedan (Auto. Trans.)	11000	12000
450 SEL 4 Door Sedan (Auto. Trans.)	11600	12600
450 SL Coupe/Roadster (Auto. Trans.)	10500	11500
450 SLC 2 Door Coupe (Auto. Trans.)	13100	14100

Model & Body Type	Wholesale Price	Retail Price
1972		
4 Cyl. 108.3" W.B.		
220 4 Door Sedan (Auto. Trans.)	3300	3900
220 D 4 Door Sedan	3400	4000
220 D 4 Door Sedan (Auto. Trans.)	3500	4100
6 Cyl. 108.3" W.B.		
250 4 Door Sedan (Auto. Trans.)	3800	4400
250 2 Door Sedan (Auto. Trans.)	4200	4800
280 SE 4 Door Sedan (Auto. Trans.)	5000	5600
8 Cyl. 108.3" W.B. (SE) 112.2" W.B. (SEL) 96.9" W.B. (SL)		
280 SE 4.5 Sedan (Auto. Trans.)	5200	6000
280 SEL 4.5 Sedan (Auto. Trans.)	5400	6200
300 SEL 4.5 Sedan (Auto. Trans.)	6300	7400
350 SL 4.5 Coupe/Roadster (Auto. Trans.)	6300	7400
600 4 Door Sedan	8500	9900
1971		
4 Cyl. 108.3" W.B.		
220 4 Door Sedan	2200	2500
220 D 4 Door Sedan	2300	2600
6 Cyl. 108.3" W.B. (Exc SE & SL's)		
112.8" W.B. (SEL) 94.5" W.B. (SL's)		
250 4 Door Sedan	2700	3200
250 2 Door Coupe	3100	3700
280 S 4 Door Sedan	3100	3700
280 SE 4 Door Sedan	3200	3900
280 SEL 4 Door Sedan	3600	4500
280 SL Roadster	**4600**	5300
280 SL 2 Door Coupe	4100	4900
280 SL Coupe/Roadster	4000	4800
1970		
4 Cyl. 108.3" W.B.		
220 4 Door Sedan	1800	2300
220 D 4 Door Sedan	1900	2400
6 Cyl. 108.3" W.B. (Exc. SEL's & SL's)		
112.8" W.B. (SEL) 95.4" W.B. (SL)		
250 4 Door Sedan	2000	2500
250 2 Door Coupe	2400	2900
280 S 4 Door Sedan	2400	2900
280 SE 4 Door Sedan	2500	3000
280 SEL 4 Door Sedan	2700	3200
280 SL 2 Door Roadster	3300	4000
280 SL 2 Door Coupe	3400	4200
280 SL 2 Door Coupe/Roadster	3500	4300
280 SE 2 Door Coupe	4800	5800
280 SE Convertible	5500	6500
300 SEL 2.8 4 Door Sedan	4700	5700

OPEL

A German import that has disappointed many North American motorists, with its reputation for mechanical failures and inadequate servicing. General Motors has never been very lucky with its European imports ever since its Vauxhall fiasco (Yes, Virginia, GM is **now** selling its Vauxhall Viva and Firenza in South Africa).

Opel owners complain of an inadequate parts supply, rapid depreciation rate, and repeated malfunctioning of the electrical system. The Opel is not recommended, new or used.

MAJOR RECALL CAMPAIGNS

General Motors Corporation-Buick Division-Opel

Make	Model	Model Year	Brief Description of Defect (Manufacturer's Corrective Action)	No. of Pages on File	Number of Vehicles Recalled
Opel	Kadetts Model 31, 31D, 36, 36D and 39-1900 Series	1970 1971 1972	Possibility that windshield may not have been mounted to conform with retention requirement of Federal Motor Vehicle Safety Standard No. 212. If condition exists and vehicle is involved in high impact frontal collision, windshield may come out. (Correct by inspecting and securing with improved adhesive where necessary.)	12	100,661

USED CAR PRICES (APPROXIMATE)

Opel

Model & Body Type	Wholesale Price	Retail Price
1972 GT4 Coupe Cyl. 95.7" W.B.	1200	1600

VOLKSWAGEN

The Beetle has always been Volkswagen's ideal city car, with a solid reputation for economy, reliability, and defective heaters that almost never worked in the Winter. Unfortunately, VW's love affair with North American motorists has come to a sad, and untimely, end. Japanese and European models are now taking an increasingly larger share of the imported car market.

Since Volkswagen abandoned the Beetle, it has repeatedly struck out with its subsequent models. The Audi, Dasher, VW 411 and 412 have all been losers, and Volkswagen appears to be intent on continuing that tradition with its new Rabbit and Scirocco.

Rabbit owners complain of chronic starting problems, inoperative door locks, defective interior trim and finish, body rattles, transmission clunks, and exhaust system thumps. Rubber dampers used to protect the exhaust system from striking the chassis also have a high failure rate. In addition to serious mechanical defects, Rabbit and Scirocco owners also report that dealer service is expensive and spare parts scarce. Fires have been reported in California and Canada, due to a defective catalytic converter system in California, and a defective rubber damper used on the non-catalytic converter equipped model in Canada. Both models have been recalled.

Because of Volkswagen's serious shortcomings with its Rabbit/Scirocco models, the company has extended the warranty on its '75 models to "upgrade the '75's to the level of the '76's," according to Josef L. Metz, vice-president in charge of corporate service, Volkswagen of America. Rabbit/Scirocco owners will receive free repairs for problems in the following areas: poor driveability, carburetor malfunctioning, exhaust system rattles, cold-starting difficulties, and plastic door trim defects. This major warranty extension program is expected to cost VW more than $5 million and could possibly affect more than 100,000 vehicles.

AUDI

The Audi is another new Volkswagen model that has tarnished the rising VW star. Owners complain of major mechanical defects such as an exhaust system that self-destructs, and premature brake wear around 10,000 miles. The motor often acts like an old fashioned oil burner and reports from Audi owners of major engine overhauls between 24,000 and 36,000 miles are not uncommon. The transmission may also malfunction because of defective internal gears. Much to its credit, Volkswagen has extended the warranty coverage on the exhaust system, motor, and transmission defects up to 36,000 miles.

246

Many Audi owners report that servicing is expensive and parts are constantly on back order. Consequently, many owners who were polled stated they would not buy another Audi.

VW 411 AND 412

Even Volkswagen dealers admit that these models were commercial duds due to the countless number of mechanical defects and poor dealer servicing. Both models have now been discontinued, so they are definitely not recommended as used car choices.

SAFETY DEFECT RECALL CAMPAIGNS

Volkswagen of America, Incorporated

Make	Model	Model Year	Brief Description of Defect (Manufacturer's Corrective Action)	No. of Pages on File	Number of Vehicles Recalled
Volkswagen	Type 1, 3, 4 and Super Beetle	1971	Possibility that guide pin in steering column lock may have been damaged in assembly. Also, ignition switch may have manufacturing defect. These conditions could result in difficulty in unlocking steering and starting engine. (Correct by replacing locks and switches where necessary.) Possibility that left front hood hinge may rub against wiring harness causing damage to wiring.	21	78,100
Volkswagen	Type I	1975	Possibility that rear axle shaft could break in vicinity of spline/thread junction due to improper heat treatment.	6	1,760
Volkswagen	Model 14 Karmann Ghia	1968 1969 1970 1971 1972	Possibility that fuel vapors or small amounts of liquid fuel may enter passenger compartment through small opening in wall which separates the car's interior from luggage compartment.	5	112,000

Audi, Incorporated

Audi	100	1973	Possibility that electrical fan motor controlling temperature of engine cooling system may develop short. If condition occurs, it could result in electrical fire in lead wire to the motor.	3	16,000

Make	Model	Model Year	Brief Description of Defect (Manufacturer's Corrective Action)	No. of Pages on File	Number of Vehicles Recalled
Audi	100, 100LS & 100GL	1973	Possibility that chemical residue from thread rolling process was not entirely removed from brake caliper bolt threads. If condition exists, residue may affect caliper bolts and cause bolt breakage.	3	12,500
Audi	80 (Fox)	1973	Possibility that mounting bolts for rear wheel backing plates were extended by lateral force applied when rig was used to hoist vehicle for loading in ship.	10	13,500
Audi	100	1975	Possibility that securing nut which holds front exhaust pipe bracket to automatic transmission housing may come loose. If condition exists, bracket may vibrate and contact return fuel line resulting in damage to line.	2	2,000

Porsche, Incorporated

Make	Model	Model Year	Brief Description of Defect (Manufacturer's Corrective Action)	No. of Pages on File	Number of Vehicles Recalled
Porsche	914 and 914/6	1970	Possibility that seat lock adjustment mechanism may, under extreme loading of seat, fail to hold seat in firm position. (Correct by replacing with improved lock mechanism.)	13	2,017
Porsche	914, 914/6	1970	Possibility that fuel line connections and fuel filter may have been improperly secured during assembly, which could cause small quantities of fuel to escape. Also, fuel lines of fuel injectors for right bank of cylinders may in some instances have become deteriorated as a result of electrolyte dripping from battery. (Correct by modifying as required.) Possibility that retaining bolt for front axle sub-frame may have been overtightened during assembly. (Correct by replacing where necessary.)	15	8,340
Porsche	911T & 911 equipped w/ CIS	1973 1974	Possibility that fuel hose inner diameter exceeds specifications. Condition prevents proper connections, resulting in fuel leaks in engine compartment of underneath vehicle. Also, O-ring gasket at rear of cold start valve may have been improperly installed and could permit gasoline leakage. If conditions exists, they could result in fire hazard.	5	6,000

USED CAR PRICES (APPROXIMATE)
Volkswagen

Model & Body Type	Wholesale Price	Retail Price
1975		
BEETLE 4 Cyl. 94.5" W.B.		
2 Door Sedan	1700	2200
2 Door Super Beetle	1900	2400
2 Door Sedan Le Grande	2200	2700
Convertible	2600	3200
RABBIT 4 Cyl. 94.5" W.B.		
2 Door Hatchback Sedan	1900	2400
4 Door Hatchback Sedan w/ Perf. Pkg.	2400	2900
DASHER 4 Cyl. 97.2" W.B.		
2 Door Sedan	2400	2900
4 Door Sedan	2500	3000
4 Door Station Wagon	2600	3100
SCIROCCO 4 Cyl. 94.5" W.B.		
2 Door Sedan	2600	3100
TRANSPORTERS 4 Cyl. 94.5" W.B.		
Campmobile Basic	2900	3400
Kombi	2900	3400
7 Seat Station Wagon	3000	3500
9 Seat Station Wagon	3000	3500
Panel Delivery	3000	3500
Add For Auto. Trans.		
1974		
VOLKSWAGEN 4 Cyl. 94.5" W.B. (Exc. Super) 95.3" W.B. (Super)		
2 Door Beetle Sedan	1400	1700
2 Door Super Beetle Sedan	1500	1600
Super Beetle Convertible	1900	2400
Karmann Ghia Coupe	1900	2400
Karmann Ghia Convertible	2000	2500
DASHER 4 Cyl. 97.2" W.B.		
2 Door Sedan	2000	2500
4 Door Sedan	2100	2600
4 Door Wagon	2200	2700
412 4 Cyl. 98.4" W.B.		
2 Door Sedan	2000	2500
4 Door Sedan (Auto. Trans).	2200	2700
Station Wagon (Auto. Trans.)	2300	2800
STATION WAGONS 4 Cyl. 94.5" W.B.		
Panel Delivery	2200	2700
7 Passenger Wagon	2200	2700
9 Passenger Wagon	2200	2700
Kombi Wagon	2000	2500
Campmobile w/ Equipment	2900	3400

249

Model & Body Type	Wholesale Price	Retail Price
1973		
VOLKSWAGEN 4 Cyl. 94.5" W.B. (Exc.Super) 95.3"W.B. (Super)		
2 Door Beetle Sedan	1000	1500
2 Door Super Beetle Sedan	1100	1600
Super Beetle Convertible	1300	1800
Karmann Ghia Coupe	1300	1800
Karmann Ghia Convertible	1400	1900
2 Door Squareback Sedan	1400	1900
Type 3 Fastback Sedan	1300	1800
'The Thing'	1300	1800
412 4 Cyl. 98.4" W.B.		
2 Door Sedan	1000	1200
4 Door Sedan (Auto. Trans.)	1100	1300
Station Wagon (Auto. Trans.)	1200	1400
STATION WAGONS 4 Cyl. 94.5" W.B.		
Panel Delivery	2000	2500
7 Passenger Wagon	1900	2400
9 Passenger Wagon	2000	2500
Kombi Wagon	1700	2200
Campmobile	1700	2200
1972		
VOLKSWAGEN 4 Cyl. 94.5"W.B. (Exc.Super) 95.3"W.B. (Super)		
2 Door Beetle Sedan	800	1100
2 Door Super Beetle Sedan	1000	1200
Super Beetle Convertible	1200	1400
Karmann Ghia Coupe	1000	1300
Karmann Ghia Convertible	1100	1400
2 Door Fastback Sedan	900	1200
2 Door Squareback Sedan	1000	1300
Type 3 2 Door Sedan	1000	1300
411 4 Cyl. 98.4" W.B.		
4 Door Sedan	900	1100
3 Door Sedan	900	1100
STATION WAGONS 4 Cyl. 94.5" W.B.		
Panel Delivery	1200	1700
7 Passenger Wagon	1200	1700
9 Passenger Wagon	1200	1700
Wagon	1100	1600
Campmobile	1100	1600

Model & Body Type	Wholesale Price	Retail Price
1971		
VOLKSWAGEN 4 Cyl. 95.3" W.B. (Beetle) 94.5"W.B. (Others)		
2 Door Beetle Sedan	500	800
2 Door Super Beetle Sedan	600	900
Super Beetle Convertible	800	1100
Karmann Ghia Coupe	800	1100
Karmann Ghia Convertible	800	1100
2 Door Squareback Sedan	800	1100
Type 3 2 Door Sedan	900	1200
411 4 Cyl. 98.3" W.B.		
3 Door Sedan	600	800
4 Door Sedan	600	800
STATION WAGONS 4 Cyl. 94.5" W.B.		
Panel Delivery	1000	1300
Station Wagon	1000	1300
Kombi Wagon	900	1200
Campmobile	900	1200
1970		
VOLKSWAGEN 4 Cyl. 94.5" W.B.		
2 Door Beetle Sedan	500	800
Beetle Convertible	700	1000
Karmann Ghia Coupe	700	1000
Karmann Ghia Convertible	600	900
2 Door Fastback	600	900
2 Door Squareback	800	1100
STATION WAGONS 4 Cyl. 94.5" W.B.		
Wagon	800	1100
7 Passenger Wagon	900	1200
9 Passenger Wagon	1000	1300

Audi

Model & Body Type	Wholesale Price	Retail Price
1975		
FOX 4 Cyl. 105.3" W.B.		
2 Door Sedan	2600	3000
4 Door Sedan	2700	3100
4 Door Wagon	2700	3100
100 LS 4 Cyl. 97.2" W.B.		
2 Door Sedan	3000	3400
4 Door Sedan	3000	3400
1974		
100 LS 4 Cyl. 105.3" W.B.		
2 Door Sedan	2200	2600
4 Door Sedan	2300	2700
FOX 4 Cyl. 97.2" W.B.		
2 Door Sedan	2000	2400
4 Door Sedan	2200	2600

Model & Body Type	Wholesale Price	Retail Price
1973		
FOX 4 Cyl. 105.3" W.B.		
2 Door Sedan	1600	2100
4 Door Sedan	1700	2300
100 LS 4 Cyl. 105.3" W.B.		
2 Door Sedan	1900	2400
100 GL 4 Cyl. 105.3" W.B.		
2 Door Sedan (Auto. Trans.)	2300	2800
4 Door Sedan (Auto. Trans.)	2400	2900

PORSCHE

The ideal medium-priced sports car. While giving excellent overall driving performance and fuel economy. Porsche also brings with it a strong dealer network and a good supply of replacement parts. Depreciation is less than average, helping to offset the initial high retail sales price.

Porsche owners hve complained that dealer servicing is expensive, so it may be a good idea to cut loose from the dealer servicing as soon as the warranty period is terminated.

The mid-engined 914 is a much better buy as a used car investment than the rear-engined 911 because the 914 can be bought used for almost half the price of a used 911. The 914 is also a more forgiving car on the highway and does not require as much of the expert handling as the 911. Don't look for used car bargains, though, Porsche owners are usually well informed about their car's value and will not sell below list price unless there are some costly mechanical repairs on the horizon.

USED CAR PRICES (APPROXIMATE)

Porsche

Model & Body Type	Wholesale Price	Retail Price
1975		
914 4 Cyl. 96.8" W.B.		
1.8 5 Speed Roadster	5000	5700
1.8 5 Speed Roadster w/App. Group	5200	5900
2.0 5 Speed Roadster	5400	6100
2.0 5 Speed Roadster w/App. Group	5600	6300
911 6 Cyl. 89.4" W.B.		
S 4 Speed Coupe (Anniv. Ed.)	9500	10400
S 4 Speed Coupe	10500	11400

Model & Body Type	Wholesale Price	Retail Price
S 4 Speed Targa Coupe (Anniv. Ed.)	13400	14800
S 4 Speed Targa Coupe	11500	12500
Carrera 5 Speed Coupe	12500	13600
Carrera 5 Speed Targa Coupe	13500	14700
1974		
914 4 Cyl. 96.8" W.B.		
1.8 Roadster	3300	3700
1.8 Roadster w/App. Group	3400	3800
2.0 Roadster	3500	3900
2.0 Roadster w/App. Group	3800	4400
911 6 Cyl. 89.4" W.B.		
4 Speed Coupe	7000	8000
Targa 4 Speed Roadster	7200	8200
S 4 Speed Coupe	8200	9200
S Targa 4 Speed Roadster	9200	10200
Carrera 4 Speed Coupe	9900	10800
Carrera Targa 4 Speed Roadster	10900	11900
1973		
914 4 Cyl. 96.5" W.B.		
1.7 5 Speed Roadster	2800	3400
1.7 5 Speed Roadster w/App. Group	2900	3500
2.0 5 Speed Roadster	3100	3700
2.0 5 Speed Roadster w/App. Group	3200	3800
911 6 Cyl. 89.5" W.B.		
T 4 Speed Coupe	5700	6400
T Targa 4 Speed Roadster	6200	6900
E 4 Speed Coupe	6200	6900
E Targa 4 Speed Roadster	6400	7200
S 4 Speed Coupe	6500	7200
S Targa 4 Speed Roadster	6900	7900
1972		
914 4 Cyl. 96.5" W.B.		
2 Door 5 Speed Roadster	2000	2500
2 Door 5 Speed Roadster	2000	2500
2 Door 5 Speed Roadster w/App. Group	2100	2600
911 6 Cyl. 89.5" W.B.		
T 4 Speed Coupe	4400	5100
T Targa 4 Speed Roadster	5000	5800
E 4 Speed Coupe	5100	5900
E Targa 4 Speed Roadster	5400	6200
S 4 Speed Coupe	5500	6300
S Targa 4 Speed Roadster	6000	6900

Model & Body Type	Wholesale Price	Retail Price
1971		
911 6 Cyl. 89.5" W.B.		
T 4 Speed Coupe	3500	4200
T Targa 4 Speed Roadster	4000	4700
Add for 5 Speed		
Add for Auto. Trans.		
E 5 Speed Coupe	4100	4800
E Targa 5 Speed Roadster	4500	5200
S 5 Speed Coupe	4500	5200
S Special Ratio Coupe	4600	5300
S Targa 5 Speed Roadster	5100	5800
1970		
911 6 Cyl. 89.3" W.B.		
T 4 Speed Coupe	2500	3000
T Targa 4 Speed Roadster	2900	3400
E 5 Speed Coupe	3000	3500
E Targa 5 Speed Roadster	3400	3900
S 5 Speed Coupe	3500	4000
S Special Ratio Coupe	3600	4100
S Targa 5 Speed Roadster	3900	4400

ITALIAN CARS

ALFA ROMEO

A fair weather sports car. Highly recommended for mild weather zones like California, Florida and other areas south of lattitude 40. The initial retail price is high and depreciation is low despite a small dealer network. The Berlina Sedan, Spider Veloce and GTV 2plus2 Coupe are excellent used car buys.

When buying a used Alfa, verify the true model year by checking the date of manufacture production plate affixed to the driver's side inside door frame. Alfas also have a tendency to fall quickly into disrepair if periodic maintenance has not been done competently. Naturally, a complete mechanical examination, preferably by an Alfa specialist, is a prerequisite to the purchase of any used Alfa Romeo. With fuel injection, dual overhead cam, a 2 litre engine, 5-speed transmission and four wheel disc brakes, the Alfa needs few options. A well-maintained Alfa Romeo is one used car offer that not even Don Corleone could refuse.

The 1971-1973 Berlina models have had severe starting problems which have been corrected by a free carburator kit supplied by the manufacturer to Berlina owners requesting the kit.

MAJOR RECALL CAMPAIGNS

Alfa Romeo, Incorporated

Make	Model	Model Year	Brief Description of Defect (Manufacturer's Corrective Action)	No. of Pages on File	Number of Vehicles Recalled
Alfa-Romeo	105.62— 1750 Spider Veloce 105.51—1750 G.T. Veloce 105.71—1750 Berlina	1970	Possibility that brake master cylinder may contain defective seal.	4	2,405
Alfa-Romeo	Spider 105.62 G.T.V. 105.51 Berlina 105.71	1971	Possibility that during assembly of fuse holder spring cup, which is secured to fusebox by a hollow rivet, rivet was incorrectly installed. If condition exists, could result in total loss of electric power.	8	2,552

USED CAR PRICES (APPROXIMATE)

Alfa Romeo

Model & Body Type	Wholesale Price	Retail Price
1975		
4 Cyl. 88.6" W.B. (Spid) 98.8"W.B. (Ber) 94.5"W.B. (GT)		
2000 Spider Veloce Convertible	4200	4700
Alfetta Berlina Sedan	4000	4500
GT Coupe	5000	5500
1974		
2000 4 Cyl. 101.1" W.B. (Ber) 88.6"W.B. (Spid) 92.5"W.B. (GT)		
4 Door Berlina	3000	3500
Spider Veloce	4000	4500
GT Veloce 2 + 2	3800	4300
1973		
2000 4 Cyl. 92.5" W.B. (Exc. Ber) 101.1" W.B. (Ber)		
4 Door Berlina	2200	2700
Spider Veloce	2700	3200
GT Veloce 2 + 2	2500	3000
1972		
2000 4 Cyl. 92.5"W.B. (Exc. Ber) 101.1"W.B. (Ber)		
4 Door Berlina	1600	2100
Spider Veloce	2100	2500
GT Veloce 2 + 2	1900	2400
1971		
2000 4 Cyl. 92.5"W.B. (Exc. Ber) 101.1"W.B. (Ber)		
4 Door Berlina	1200	1500
Spider Veloce	1600	2100
GT Veloce 2 + 2		

FIAT

Fiats are freaky. They are well-built machines that have given millions of European motorists excellent fuel economy while providing sports car performance on the highway. North American motorists should expect the same, but, according to the hundreds of complaint letters pouring into North American auto consumer groups, such as the Washington Center For Auto Safety and the Canadian Automobile Protection Association, Fiat imports take on a classic Dr. Jekyl and Mr. Hyde disposition as they cross the Atlantic.

Owners are most concerned over what they call inadequate servicing. Complaints regarding the high cost of parts replacement and periodic maintenance (some owners call it the "Italian Connection") abound. And because of the poor after sales service by Fiat's weak dealer body, many Fiat owners state they would never buy another one. One disgruntled Fiat owner's frank evaluation of Fiat's North American service was, "It's not worth a +&##/".

Reliability is another problem area reported by Fiat owners that could be traced back to poor service procedures. Although owners reported that their cars gave excellent gas mileage, many complained of frequent stalling or surging that was difficult to correct at the dealer level. Cold weather performance north of the 40th parallel also was said to be unacceptable.

By far the most angry responses from Fiat owners came from owners that were asked about Fiat's warranty performance. Owners complained that Fiat dealers would often overcharge for periodic inspections, charge for warranty work that was supposed to be free, or stall warranty work until the warranty period elapsed and then "discover" that the work was urgent. Just so Fiat will not feel this criticism is unfair, they are invited to read the numerous small claims court decisions on file which back up each of the owner allegations published above. In fact, Fiat's warranty performance is so bad in Canada, one Superior Court judge was forced to conclude in his written Judgment that Fiat's warranty promises were nothing more than "promises thrown into the wind". **(Fleury vs. Fiat,** Montreal, Quebec, 1975). Fiat officials in the United States have promised to reform their warranty procedures. However judging by the complaints still being received, this promise is not very convincing.

The major mechanical defects complained of by Fiat owners run the gamut of possible trouble spots. Nevertheless, most owners complained of defective motors, clutch assembly, and suspension system. One of the main reasons why Fiat cannot be considered a good buy, either as a new or used car, is because of the severe corrosion reported by many owners of the 1971-1974 models. The premature corrosion affects particularly the 128 model, but complaints have been numerous on other models as well.

MAJOR RECALL CAMPAIGNS

Fiat Motor Company, Incorporated

Make	Model	Model Year	Brief Description of Defect (Manufacturer's Corrective Action)	No. of Pages on File	Number of Vehicles Recalled
Fiat	Spider 850 Spider 124	1970	Possibility that seat belts may not fit properly in all seat positions. (Correct by replacing fixed segment of belt with one of proper length, where necessary.)	7	15,104

Make	Model	Model Year	Brief Description of Defect (Manufacturer's Corrective Action)	No. of Pages on File	Number of Vehicles Recalled
Fiat	850 Spider 850 Racer	1970	Possibility that emission control hose may interfere with bracket which could cause hose to wear. Also, possibility that alternator fuse wire may interfere with hose clamp.	7	12,550
Fiat	All models	1974	Possibility that small metal shield was omitted during production. Shield is located between exhaust pipe and floor panel to prevent possible overheating of anti-rust protective substance sprayed under floor panel. If condition exists, anti-rust protective substance may overheat and cause fire.	3	NR
Fiat	128 Sedan, station wagon & coupe	1971 1972 1973	Possibility that under carriage, particularly cross member where front suspension is attached, might become corroded from winter weather conditions where salt and/or sand are used to melt snow and ice. Corrosion can result in bending of frame where suspension control arm is attached. Condition could impair handling of vehicle.	7	40,831
Fiat	X1/9	1974 1975	Possibility that accelerator cable was installed in manner which would cause accelerator assembly to function abnormally, causing breakage of accelerator cable. If condition exists, engine will idle and car will decelerate and danger of vehicle crash will exist.	7	25,000

USED CAR PRICES (APPROXIMATE)

Fiat

Model & Body Type	Wholesale Price	Retail Price
1975		
128 4 Cyl. 96.4" W.B. (Sdn & Wgn)		
87.5" W.B. (Cpe) 86.7" W.B. (X1/9)		
2 Door Sedan	1300	1800
4 Door Sedan	1400	1900
Station Wagon	1500	2000
SL Coupe	1600	2100
X 1/9 Coupe	2300	2800
131 4 Cyl. 98" W.B.		
2 Door Sedan	1900	2400
4 Door Sedan	2000	2500

Model & Body Type	Wholesale Price	Retail Price
Station Wagon	2200	2700
124 4 Cyl. 95.3" W.B. (Cpe) 89.7" W.B. (Spid)		
Sport Coupe	2300	2800
Spider	2800	3100
1974		
128 4 Cyl. 96.4" W.B.(Exc.Cpe) 87.5"W.B. (Cpe)		
2 Door Sedan	1100	1600
4 Door Sedan	1200	1700
3 Door Wagon	1300	1800
SL 2 Door Sport Coupe	1600	2100
124 4 Cyl. 95.3" W.B. (Exc. Rdstr) 89.8"W.B. (Rdstr)		
4 Door Sedan	1300	1800
4 Door Wagon	1400	1900
2 Door Sport Coupe	1700	2100
Sport Spider Roadster	1900	2400
1973		
128 4 Cyl. 96.4"W.B. (Exc.Cpe) 87.5"W.B. (Cpe)		
2 Door Sedan	700	1200
4 Door Sedan	750	1250
3 Door Wagon	1000	1500
SL 2 Door Sport Coupe	1200	1700
124 4 Cyl. 95.3"W.B. (Exc. Rdstr) 89.9"W.B. (Rdstr)		
4 Door Sedan	800	1300
4 Door Wagon	900	1400
2 Door Coupe	1500	2000
2 Door Spider Roadster	1700	2200
1972		
850 4 Cyl. 79" W.B.		
2 Door Spider Roadster	600	900
128 4 Cyl. 96.4" W.B.		
2 Door Sedan	400	600
4 Door Sedan	500	700
3 Door Wagon	600	900
124 4 Cyl. 95.3"W.B. (Exc. Rdstr) 89.8"W.B. (Rdstr)		
4 Door Special Sedan	600	800
4 Door Wagon	700	900
2 Door Sport Coupe	1200	1500
Spider Roadster	1300	1800
1971		
850 4 Cyl. 79" W.B.		
2 Door Sedan	200	400
2 Door Sport Coupe	400	600
Spider Roadster	500	700
Spider Hardtop	600	800
Racer Coupe	700	1000
124 4 Cyl. 95.3"W.B. (Sdn & Wgn) 89.8"W.B. (Cpe & Spids)		

Model & Body Type	Wholesale Price	Retail Price
4 Door Special Sedan	500	700
Station Wagon	700	900
2 Door Sport Coupe	1000	1300
Spider Roadster	1100	1400
Spider Hardtop	1200	1500
1970		
850 4 Cyl. 79" W.B.		
2 Door Sedan	100	300
2 Door Sport Coupe	300	400
Spider Roadster	400	600
Racer Coupe	500	700
124 4 Cyl. 95.3"W.B. (Sdn & Wgn) 89.5"W.B. (Cpe&Spids)		
4 Door Special Sedan	300	500
Station Wagon	400	600
2 Door Sport Coupe	600	900
Spider Roadster	800	1100
Spider Hardtop	900	1300

JAPANESE CARS

COLT

Other Japanese automakers could take lessons from the Colt's marketing staff on selling an economical "foreign" car to the American motoring public. (Chrysler markets the Colt, while Mitsubishi, Japan, manufactures the car, thank goodness.) Now with a 5-speed overdrive transmission option and a 2000cc engine, this import is the best new or used subcompact buy. There are some negative reports from Colt owners concerning inadequate servicing by some Chrysler dealers dissatisfied with the low profit margin they receive from selling and servicing Chrysler's Japanese import. Remember, the Colt's name has been changed to the Arrow for the 1976-1977 model year.

MAJOR RECALL CAMPAIGNS

Dodge Colt

Dodge Colt wagon models	345	If the plug which covers the spare tire release nut and seals the access hole in the floor is removed and is not reinstalled, and if that action is coupled with a deteriorated exhaust system, it could be possible under some conditions for exhaust gases to enter the passenger compartment.

USED CAR PRICES (APPROXIMATE)
Colt

Model & Body Type	Wholesale Price	Retail Price
1975		
COLT 4 Cyl. 95.3" W.B.		
2 Door Coupe	1700	2200
4 Door Sedan	1700	2200
2 Seat Wagon	1800	2300
2 Door Hardtop	1800	2300
'GT' 2 Door Hardtop	1800	2300
Add for Auto. Trans. (GT)		
Add for Auto. Trans. (All Others)		
1974		
4 Cyl. 95.3" W.B.		
2 Door Coupe	1200	1400
2 Door Hardtop	1400	1600
4 Door Sedan	1400	1600
2 Door GT Hardtop	1500	1700
4 Door Wagon	1600	1800
4 Door Custom Wagon	1700	1900

Model & Body Type	Wholesale Price	Retail Price
1973		
4 Cyl. 95.3" W.B.		
2 Door Coupe	800	1000
4 Door Sedan	1000	1200
2 Door Hardtop	1000	1200
2 Door GT Hardtop	1100	1300
4 Door Wagon	1100	1300
Add for Auto. Trans. (All Models)		
1972		
4 Cyl. 95.3" W.B.		
2 Door Coupe	600	900
4 Door Sedan	700	1000
2 Door Hardtop	700	1000
4 Door Wagon	800	1100

DATSUN

After making its reputation with very economical and efficient small cars like the 510, Datsun has now contracted "Detroit fever" by adding on a lot of unnecessary gimmick options that price its cars out of many economy-minded motorists' reach. All of Datsun's 510 models, especially the 2 door 1973 model, are highly recommended, despite electrical and tire defects. Datsun's other models would be better left in Japan.

The 1971 and 1972 Datsun 240Z had very serious brake defects, for which the vehicle was never officially recalled but, as can be seen from the following confidential memorandum, these cars should have been recalled by the Department of Transport.

Rusting has been so bad on the 240Z and the 510 that Datsun has bought back, through its dealers, some vehicles where it was alleged that the premature rusting weakened the frame and suspension components, possibly making the car unsafe. So, Datsun has extended its warranty. Datsun's new F10 is unimpressive.

DATSUN CONFIDENTIAL BRAKE REPORT

SERVICE DEPARTMENT FRIDAY'S REPORT
WEEK ENDING MAY 5, 1972
PAGE 2

The 240Z front brake situation is starting to get out of proportion, the customers are refusing to pay the expense for freeing-up the pads or the replacement of the pads (as well as disc re-finishing in some cases).

The brake failures are occuring at mileage as low as 2,000 miles. In some cases, dealers absorbed the expenses when customer definitely refused to pay, but now dealers cannot anymore due to the quantity of 240Z needing brake repairs.

We have to decide as soon as possible a solution before it gets in the hands of A.P.A. and consumers affairs. Since the installation of the new modified caliper could definitely improve the situation the complaints will probably drop with newly equipped model.

But for the previous one, those already on the road and probably that still in inventory situation will remain, if we decide to accept on warranty the repairs of the brake system providing it happened within the 12,000 miles, at that moment suggesting to dealers to remove a slight amount of material on the pad sides, we are aware that very little should be removed not to create any other problem, it is my opinion that the situation would be corrected, and would be quite less expensive than replacing the caliper ass. because being a security item of the first importance the D.O.T. people if they start to investigate could probably insist on the replacement of calipers on all units.

MAJOR RECALL CAMPAIGNS
Nissan Motor Corporation in U.S.A.

Make	Model	Model Year	Brief Description of Defect (Manufacturer's Corrective Action)	No. of Pages On File	Number of Vehicles Recalled
Datsun	PL510, WPL510 and HLS30	1968 1969 1970	Possibility that salts used in winter on highways will form mixture of salt water and mud which will accumulate on backs of sealed beam headlight units. When wet, the electrical circuit grounds through these deposits may set up an electrical corrosive action which could result in air entering sealed beam unit, causing failure. (Correct by installing rubber protectors.)	14	118,976
Datsun	WPL 510 Station Wagon PL 521 Pickup Truck	1968 1969	Possibility that under extremely high temperatures, brake fluid may form chemical deposits on wheel cylinder wall. These deposits may slightly deform piston cup lip when it rides over them, resulting in leakage from loss of sealing. This condition could cause gradual loss of braking power and consequently is a driving hazard.	12	37,196
Datsun	PL510 Sedan WPL510 Station Wagon	Mnfd 8-9 1971 thru 3-15 1972	Possibility that under extreme cold weather and severe driving conditions, front brake hose, which is clamped to shock strut in a manner restricting its free movement, can crack at clamp, due to repeated bending of hose. Should crack occur, could result in loss of brake fluid, and loss of front brake function.	1	61,434
Datsun	LB110 Sedan KL110 Coupe	1971	Possibility of misalignment of secondary hood latch between hood and body, which could result in complete disengagement of hood latch, if primary hood latch has not been properly engaged and if vehicle is subject to strong wind pressure at high speeds.	2	86,429
Datsun	L520 & L521	Manfd 4-65 thru 5-69	Possibility that accelerator pedal pad could lock under travel stop bolt head. If condition exists, depressed accelerator pedal would not return to closed position when released. (Correct by inspecting and installing bolt with larger head to preclude pedal pad from locking up.)	1	62,000
Datsun	240-Z	1973	Possibility that under some driving conditions, driver may experience difficulties in restarting engine when hot or engine may stall when making sharp right hand turn.	1	16,274

USED CAR PRICES

Datsun

Model & Body Type	Wholesale Price	Retail Price
1975		
210 4 Cyl. 92.1" W.B.		
2 Door Sedan	1600	1900
4 Door Sedan	1300	1900
2 Door Coupe	1700	2000
620 LI'L HUSTLER 4 Cyl. 100.1"W.B.(PU) 110"W.B.(PU 7)		
Pickup	1700	2100
Add for Auto. Trans.		
710 4 Cyl. 96.5" W.B.		
2 Door Sedan	1600	2000
4 Door Sedan	1600	2000
2 Door Hardtop	1700	2100
4 Door Station Wagon	1800	2200
610 4 Cyl. 98.4" W.B.		
4 Door Sedan	1800	2200
2 Door Hardtop	1900	2300
4 Door Station Wagon	2000	2400
280-Z 6 Cyl. 90.7" W.B.(Cpe) 102.6"W.B.(2+2)		
2 Door Coupe	3800	4400
2+2 Coupe	4100	4700
1974		
B210 4 Cyl. 92.1" W.B.		
2 Door Sedan	1200	1500
4 Door Sedan	1300	1600
2 Door Hatchback	1300	1600
610 4 Cyl. 98.4" W.B.		
4 Door Sedan	1400	1800
2 Door Hardtop	1500	1900
4 Door Wagon	1500	1900
710 4 Cyl. 96.5" W.B.		
2 Door Sedan	1200	1500
4 Door Sedan	1300	1600
2 Door Hardtop	1400	1700
260Z 6 Cyl. 90.7" W.B.		
2 Door Coupe	3000	3500
2 Door 2+2 Coupe	3300	3800
LI'L HUSTLER 4 Cyl. 100.2" W.B.		
2 Door Pickup	1400	1700

Model & Body Type	Wholesale Price	Retail Price
1973		
1200 4 Cyl. 90.6" W.B.		
2 Door Sedan	900	1100
2 Door Coupe	1000	1200
510 4 Cyl. 95.3" W.B.		
2 Door Sedan	1100	1300
610 4 Cyl. 98.4" W.B.		
2 Door Hardtop	1200	1400
4 Door Sedan	1300	1500
4 Door Wagon	1200	1400
240Z 6 Cyl. 90.7" W.B.		
2 Door Coupe	1500	3000
LI'L HUSTLER 4 Cyl. 100.1" W.B.		
2 Door Pickup	1100	1300
1972		
1200 4 Cyl. 90.6" W.B.		
2 Door Sedan	600	800
2 Door Coupe	700	900
510 û Cyl. 95.3" W.B.		
2 Door Sedan	700	900
4 Door Sedan	800	1100
4 Door Wagon	1100	1400
240Z 6 Cyl. 90.7" W.B.		
2 Door Coupe	2000	2500
521 4 Cyl. 99.6" W.B.		
2 Door ½ Ton Pickup	1200	1500
1971		
1200 4 Cyl. 90.6" W.B.		
2 Door Sedan	500	700
2 Door Coupe	600	800
510 4 Cyl. 95.3" W.B.		
2 Door Sedan	400	600
4 Door Sedan	500	700
4 Door Wagon	800	1100
240Z 6 Cyl. 90.7" W.B.		
2 Door Coupe	1600	2100
1970		
PL-510 4 Cyl. 95.3" W.B.		
2 Door Sedan	200	400
4 Door Sedan	300	500
4 Door Wagon	500	700
SPL-311 4 Cyl. 89.8" W.B.		
1600 Sport Roadster	700	1000
240Z 6 Cyl. 90.7" W.B.		
Sport Roadster	1400	1800

HONDA

The best Japanese import sold in North America. Parts supply is excellent, depreciation is slow, and Honda's initial retail sales prices for its new models are very reasonable. The secret of Honda's success rests with its solid dealer network. Many of its dealers were first chosen when Honda penetrated the North American market with its popular motorcycles and then given the automobile franchise after submitting proof of their honesty, financial stability, and competency with the motorcycle trade.

Some Honda owners have complained of paint fading and excessive oil burning with some engines, however, Honda's customer relations people have been very liberal in applying extended warranty coverage to these problems even after the initial warranty period has elapsed. As with all subcompact cars, the Honda is principally an urban vehicle and should be used for city travel. Travel on fast expressways or rural highways can be dangerous because of the subcompact's small size. In fact, the Washington-based Insurance Institute for Highway Safety has determined that subcompact passengers have a mortality rate two and one-half times greater in collisions than passengers in intermediate-sized cars.

MAJOR RECALL CAMPAIGNS
American Honda Motor Company, Incorporated

Make	Model	Model Year	Brief Description of Defect (Manufacturer's Corrective Action)	No. of Pages on File	Number of Vehicles Recalled
Honda	CL360	1974	Possibility that main wire harness may become chafed by forward edge of left front fuel tank mounting bracket. If condition exists, chafing may short circuit or sever wires within harness and cause electrical fuses to burn out. (Correct by inspecting and installing holder to prevent chafing of wire harness.)	3	66,856
Honda	Civic automobile	1974	Possibility that front seat left assemblies do not conform to requirements of Federal Motor Vehicle Safety Standard No. 209. (Correct by inspecting and modifying plastic boot to remove material which may cover buckle push-button release mechanism.)	2	66,109
Honda	CB360 & CB360G, CL360, CB360T, CL360K1	1974 1975	Possibility that if adjustment of cam chain tensioner is not properly maintained, or if cam chain tensioner slipper is broken, it is possible for chain to contact tensioner holder. If cam chain breakage occurs, there is possibility of engine and rear wheel lockup.	2	131,817

USED CAR PRICES (APPROXIMATE)
Honda

Model & Body Type	Wholesale Price	Retail Price
1975		
CIVIC 4 Cyl. 86.6" W.B.		
2 Door Sedan	1600	2000
Hatchback Sedan	1700	2100
Special 5 Spd Hatchback Sedan	1800	2200
4 Door Station Wagon	1800	2200
1974		
CIVIC 4 Cyl. 86.6" W.B.		
2 Door Sedan	1200	1500
Hatchback Sedan	1200	1500

MAZDA

Mazda is the worst Japanese import found in North America. Parts are difficult to obtain, depreciation is rapid, the dealer network is constantly changing franchisers, after sales service is atrocious, and many of its vehicles have been fraudulently misrepresented as the wrong model year.

Mazda owners complain of defects affecting the motor (both conventional and rotary models), clutch, and braking performance. Mazda has extended the warranty to cover mechanical defects with the "o" rings of its rotary engines that cause an excessive burning of oil due to improper internal sealing, however, many Mazda owners have complained that this warranty extension is not applied equitably to all rotary Mazda owners.

1972 and earlier Mazdas were particularly susceptible to failure of the rotor housing water "o" rings and accompanying overheating. First symptoms are usually hard starting, rough idle for 10-20 seconds after start, white smoke in the exhaust, and coolant loss. In the latter stages, it may also lead to overheating. Should these symptoms occur, visit your local dealer to confirm the diagnosis. If confirmed, contact the Mazda Branch Service Representative for your area for information concerning Mazda's engine rebuild/exchange program. All factory rebuilt engines are equipped with an improved, Teflon-backed water "o" ring to reduce the chance of a second failure.

Mazda has recently been sued by the California Department of Consumer Affairs for allegedly not respecting the extended warranty on its rotary motors as it advertised it would.

MAJOR RECALL CAMPAIGNS
Mazda

Make	Model	Model Year	Brief Description of Defect (Manufacturer's Corrective Action)	No. of Pages on File	Number of Vehicles Recalled
Mazda	RX-4 sedan, hard top & wagon	1974	Possibility that when engine is started, steering wheel will turn by itself, forcefully, in either direction due to improper tolerance within reaction sensing system. This could be caused by turning steering wheel without power steering pump in operation. (Correct by inspecting and replacing complete gear box assembly.)	12	2,218
Mazda	Pick-up trucks	1974	Possibility that exhaust pipe protector may be deformed, resulting from hitting projection on ground in vehicle off-road use. Should protector be crushed into exhaust pipe, shield surface temperature could rise to point where dry grass could smolder. This could occur only if vehicle is parked in tall dry grass and grass is in contact with protector. (Correct by installing additional protector underneath existing protector.)	9	8,422

USED CAR PRICES (APPROXIMATE)
Mazda

Model & Body Type	Wholesale Price	Retail Price
1975		
1800 4 Cyl. 104" W.B.		
2 Door Pickup	1300	1700
808 4 Cyl. 91" W.B.		
4 Door Sedan	1300	1700
2 Door Coupe	1300	1700
4 Door Wagon	1400	1800
ROTARY PICKUP Rotary 104" W.B.		
2 Door Pickup	1600	1900
RX3 Rotary 91" W.B.		
2 Door Coupe	1700	2000
4 Door Wagon	1800	2100
Add for Auto. Trans.		
RX4 Rotary 99" W.B.		
4 Door Sedan	2100	2400
2 Door Hardtop	2100	2400
4 Door Wagon	2200	2500

Model & Body Type	Wholesale Price	Retail Price
1974		
808 4 Cyl. 91" W.B.		
Coupe	1000	1300
RX-3 Rotary 91" W.B.		
2 Door Coupe	1400	1700
4 Door Wagon	1500	1800
Add for Auto. Trans. (RX3 & RX2)		
RX-4 Rotary 99" W.B.		
4 Door Sedan	1700	2000
2 Door Coupe	1700	2000
4 Door Wagon	1800	2100
1973		
RX-3 Rotary 91" W.B.		
2 Door Coupe	1000	1200
4 Door Sedan	1000	1200
4 Door Wagon	1200	1400
RX-2 Rotary 97" W.B.		
Sport Coupe	1300	1500
4 Door Sedan	1200	1400
808 4 Cyl. 91" W.B.		
2 Door Coupe	700	900
4 Door Sedan	700	900
4 Door Wagon	900	1100
Add for Auto. Trans.		
1800 4 Cyl. 104" W.B.		
Truck	1000	1200
1972		
RX-2 Rotary 91" W.B.		
2 Door Coupe	700	900
4 Door Sedan	700	900
4 Door Wagon	900	1100
RX-2 Rotary 97" W.B.		
Sport Coupe	1000	1200
4 Door Sedan	1000	1200
618 4 Cyl. 97" W.B.		
2 Door Coupe	600	700
4 Door Sedan	600	700
808 4 Cyl. 91" W.B.		
2 Door Coupe	300	400
4 Door Sedan	300	400
4 Door Wagon	500	600
Add for Auto. Trans. (618 & 808)		
1600 4 Cyl. 104" W.B.		
Truck	600	800

TOYOTA

Datsun's bigger twin brother, Toyota has very few differences with Datsun except for a more liberal warranty, larger dealer network, and better qualified dealership staff. For these reasons, Toyota only trails Honda and the Mitsubishi (Chrysler) Colt in overall product quality and driving performance. Toyota's rate of depreciation is average, though, its new cars are priced a bit higher than competitive subcompacts.

The major mechanical defects reported by Toyota over the past 5 years concern primarily the motor, carburetor, brakes, air conditioner, and chassis construction. Hundreds of consumers have reported that the engine heads on their 1971-1973 Corolla 1600 have cracked as a result of faulty manufacture. Toyota also admitted liability for this mechanical defect by secretly extending the warranty up to 5 years for Corolla owners affected by this defect. This warranty extension was never announced publicly. Copies of this secret warranty extension, as well as others, have been obtained and are published in the Chapter on Secret Warranty Extension, Chapter V.

MAJOR RECALL CAMPAIGNS
Toyota Motor Company, Limited

Make	Model	Model Year	Brief Description of Defect (Manufacturer's Corrective Action)	No. of Pages on File	Number of Vehicles Recalled
Toyota	Mark II	Produced for U.S.A. June 1969 to June 1970	Possibility that during cold weather brake fluid may not adequately flow between reservoir tank and master cylinder. This condition would permit gradual accumulation of air into master cylinder system, resulting in soft pedal during application of brakes. (Correct by installing improved master cylinder components.)	20	47,879
Toyota	Corona	1965 thru 1970	Possibility that items placed in package tray under the right dash panel may inadvertently fall over protective partition and cause possible malfunction of accelerator linkage. (Correct by installing new partition.)	11	190,000
	Corolla	1970 1971			
	Corolla-1200 Sedan Coupe Station Wagon	1971	Possibility that engine stall or engine hesitation may occur due to malfunctions in evaporative emission control system. Engine hesitation or stall may be hazardous in road driving due to lack of fuel or loss of power after prolonged high speed driving. (Correct by inspecting and modifying emission control system.)	13	110,614
	Corolla 1600 Sedan Coupe Station Wagon	1971			

USED CAR PRICES (APPROXIMATE)
Toyota

Model & Body Type	Wholesale Price	Retail Price
1975		
COROLLA 4 Cyl. 93.3" W.B.		
2 Door Sedan	1500	1900
2 Door Deluxe Sedan	1500	1900
4 Door Deluxe Sedan	1600	2000
2 Door Hardtop	1700	2100
4 Door Station Wagon	1800	2200
SR-5 2 Dr HT (5 Spd Trans.)	1900	2300
Add for Auto. Trans		
Add for 5 Spd Trans.		
CORONA 4 Cyl. 98.4" W.B.		
2 Door Deluxe KD Sedan	1800	2200
4 Door Sedan	1300	2200
4 Door Station Wagon	1900	2300
2 Door Hardtop Automatic	2000	2400
SR-5 2 Door HT (5 Spd Trans.)	2000	2400
Add for Auto. Trans.		
Add for 5 Spd Trans.		
CELICA 4 Cyl. 95.5" W.B.		
2 Door Coupe	1800	2200
ST Hardtop	1900	2300
GT Hardtop (5 Spd Trans.)	2000	2400
Add for Auto. Trans.		
Mark II 6 Cyl. 101.7" W.B.		
4 Door Sedan Automatic	2500	3000
2 Door Hardtop Automatic	2500	3000
4 Door Station Wagon Automatic	2700	3200
PICKUPS 4 Cyl. 101.6" W.B. (Exc. Longbed) 110"W.B. (Longbed)		
2 Door Pickup	1800	2100
2 Door Long-Bed Pickup	1900	2300
SR-5 Spt Truck (5 Spd Trans.)	2000	2400
Add for Auto. Trans.		
LAND CRUISER 6 Cyl. 90"W.B. (Exc. Wgn) 106.3"W.B.(Wgn)		
Softtop	2300	2700
Hardtop	2400	2800
Station Wagon	2800	3300
1974		
COROLLA 4 Cyl. 91.9" W.B.		
1200 2 Door Sedan	1300	1600
1600 2 Door Sedan	1500	1800
1600 4 Door Sedan	1600	1900
1600 2 Door Coupe	1700	2000
1600 2 Door Wagon	1700	2000

Model & Body Type	Wholesale Price	Retail Price
CORONA 4 Cyl. 98.4"W.B.(Exc.Mark II) 101.8"W.B.(Mark II)		
2 Door Sedan	1600	1900
4 Door Sedan	1200	2000
2 Door Hardtop (Auto. Trans.)	1700	2000
4 Door Wagon	1800	2100
Mark II 4 Door Sedan	1800	2100
Mark II 2 Door Hardtop	2000	2300
Mark II 4 Door Wagon	2100	2400
CELICA 4 Cyl. 95.5" W.B.		
ST 2 Door Coupe	2000	2300
GT 2 Door Coupe	2100	2400
HI-LUX 4 Cyl. 101.7"W.B.		
2 Door Pickup Truck	1700	2000
LAND CRUISER 6 Cyl. 90" W.B.(Exc.Wgn) 106.3"W.B.(Wgn)		
2 Door Softtop	2200	2500
2 Door Hardtop	2500	2800
4 Door Wagon	2800	3100
1973		
COROLLA 4 Cyl. 91.9" W.B.		
1200 2 Door Sedan	900	1200
1600 2 Door Sedan	1100	1400
1600 4 Door Sedan	1100	1400
1600 2 Door Coupe	1200	1500
1600 2 Door Wagon	1200	1500
CORONA 4 Cyl. 95.7"W.B.(Sedn&Hdtp) 101.8"W.B.(Mark II)		
4 Door Sedan	1200	1500
2 Door Hardtop	1300	1600
4 Door Wagon	1400	1700
Mark II 4 Door Sedan	1400	1700
Mark II 2 Door Hardtop	1500	1800
Mark II 4 Door Wagon	1600	1900
CELICA ST 4 Cyl. 95.5"W.B.		
2 Door Sport Coupe	1500	1800
Add for Auto. Trans. (Car & Cel)		
HI-LUX 4 Cyl. 101.8"W.B.		
2 Door Pickup Truck	1300	1600
LAND CRUISER 6 Cyl. 90" W.B.(Exc.Wgn) 106.3"W.B.(Wgn)		
2 Door Softtop	2100	2600
2 Door Hardtop	2200	2800
4 Door Wagon	1600	3200
1972		
COROLLA 4 Cyl. 91.9"W.B.		
1200 2 Door Sedan	700	800
1600 2 Door Sedan	700	800
1600 4 Door Sedan	800	900
1600 2 Door Coupe	800	900
1600 2 Door Wagon	900	1200

Model & Body Type	Wholesale Price	Retail Price
CORONA 4 Cyl. 195.7" W.B. (Exc. Mark II) 98.8" W.B. (Mark II)		
4 Door Sedan	900	1000
2 Door Hardtop	1000	1100
Mark II 4 Door Sedan	1100	1200
Mark II 2 Door Hardtop	1100	1200
Mark II 4 Door Wagon	1200	1300
CELICA ST 4 Cyl. 95.5" W.B.		
2 Door Sport Coupe	1200	1500
HI-LUX 4 Cyl. 99.8" W.B.		
2 Door Pickup Truck	1200	1500
Add for Auto. Trans. (All Modela)		
LAND CRUISER 6 Cyl. 90" W.B.(Exc.Wgn) 106.3"W.B. (Wgn)		
2 Door Softtop	1600	2100
2 Door Hardtop	1800	2300
4 Door Wagon	2200	2700
1971		
COROLLA 4 Cyl. 91.9"W.B.		
2 Door Sedan	500	700
Sprinter Coupe	600	800
2 Door Wagon	600	800
1600 2 Door Sedan	600	800
1600 4 Door Sedan	600	800
1600 2 Door Coupe	600	800
1600 2 Door Wagon	700	900
CORONA 4 Cyl. 95.7"W.B.(Exc.Mark II) 98.8"W.B. (Mark II)		
4 Door Sedan	700	900
2 Door Hardtop	800	1000
Mark II 4 Door Sedan	700	900
Mark II 2 Door Hardtop	800	1000
Mark II 4 Door Wagon	900	1100
CROWN 6 Cyl. 105.9" W.B.		
4 Door Sedan	1000	1200
4 Door Wagon	1200	1400
Add for Auto. Trans.		
HI-LUX 4 Cyl. 98.8"W.B.		
2 Door Pickup	900	1100
LAND CRUISER 6 Cyl.90"W.B.(Exc.Wgn) 106.3"W.B.(Wgn)		
2 Door Softtop	1200	1500
2 Door Hardtop	1500	1800
4 Door Wagon	1800	2100
1970		
COROLLA 4 Cyl. 90" W.B.		
2 Door Sedan	300	500
Sprinter Coupe	400	600
2 Door Wagon	400	600

Model & Body Type	Wholesale Price	Retail Price
CORONA 4 Cyl. 95.3" W.B. (Exc. Mark II) 98.8" W.B. (Mark II)		
4 Door Sedan	500	700
2 Door Hardtop	600	800
Mark II 4 Door Sedan	600	800
Mark II 2 Door Hardtop	700	900
Mark II 4 Door Wagon	800	1000
LAND CRUISER 6 Cyl. 90"W.B.(Exc. Wgn.) 106.3"W.B. (Wgn)		
2 Door Softtop	1100	1500
2 Door Hardtop	1300	1700
4 Door Wagon	1500	1900

SWEDISH CARS

SAAB

Since 1961, Saab has been selling its Swedish economy car in the United States (in Canada, since 1975) as a direct competitor to the highly publicized Volvo. Despite its early start, however, Saab has never been recognized by the North American motoring public as a credible alternative to the Volvo. In fact, some motoring magazines have characterized the early Saab owners as "intellectuals" and "misfits."

Actually Saab is a much better car than the Volvo, especially in view of the rapid decline in Volvo quality since 1972. Gas mileage is excellent, and driving performance is everything one would expect in a European car. As with the Volvo, Saab has a rapid depreciation rate, but due to Saab's lower initial cost, the total financial loss is minimized.

Servicing is one major deficiency reported by Saab owners. Because of its small franchised dealer network, Saab of Sweden and their North American importers have been criticized by Saab owners for concentrating on the sale of new vehicles while used vehicle servicing is neglected. The Washington-based Center For Auto Safety has been petitioned by one group of irate Saab owners for help in resolving what the owners group collectively calls their "Saab story".

Saab has many of the same quality control defects with its malfunctioning carburetor and electrical system as the Volvo. Owners report, though, that the manufacturere is very liberal in applying the warranty even if the mileage or period of ownership warranty limitations have been exceeded.

The Saab has been criticized in this report by using the Volvo as a benchmark for comparison. This is unfair because the Saab must succeed or fail on its own merits. The Volvo comparison was unavoidable, though, because many motorists compare the two companies as a result of their common origin.

The Saab is a recommended new car buy only for those motorists who plan to keep their vehicles 5 years or more. Anything less than that would be a losing proposition with Saab and most other European makes.

USED CAR PRICES (APPROXIMATE)
Saab

Model & Body Type	Wholesale Price	Retail Price
1975		
99 4 Cyl. 97.75" W.B.		
LE 2 Door Sedan	2800	3300
LE 4 Door Sedan	1900	3400
LE 3 Door Wagonback	3000	3500
EMS 2 Door Sedan	3000	3500

VOLVO

By directing much of its advertising to what it calls the "leisure" class and arrogantly boasting of its engineering refinements, Volvo provides potential customers with a preview of its attitude that has turned many Volvo owners sour on Volvo.

Owners complain of repeated mechanical failures involving the carburetor (hard starting and excessive fuel consumption), electrical system (tune-ups are often a monthly affair), and a fuel injection system by Bosch that leaks gasoline to such an extent that the National Highway Traffic Safety Administration has ordered that the problem be investigated to determine if a safety-related defect exists.

Until 1971, Volvo had one of the best reputations in North America for providing its customers with well-built cars, and providing a strong warranty to cover what small defects might have cropped up. But time marches on, and Volvo's customer relations policies and reputation have since changed dramatically. Owners complain that Volvo's warranty is no longer as liberal in practice as it once was, and what free warranty service that is provided is handed out like food stamps to indigents.

Because of quality control problems, Volvo has extended the guarantee on the fuel injection assembly and carburetor for 36,000 miles without restriction to first owners. Lowell Dodge, former Director of the Washington Center for Auto Safety, has informed the President of Volvo U.S.A., Bjorn Ahlstrom, that hundreds of American Volvo owners are still discontented with Volvo's motor defects. On January 28, 1974, Volvo's President wrote the following reply:

"...In 1972 Volvo also extended the warranty period on spare parts from six to twelve months. The public has also been informed about this extension.

In your letter you referred to some 300 customer letters received since 1971. There are now well over 350,000 Volvo owners in the United States. It is evident that we, in spite of our efforts to meet their expectations, may in single cases fail in achieving the full satisfaction of the customer. We are determined to do our best to give every single customer fair treatment, and would, therefore, appreciate your forwarding the customer letters to us so that we may look into each individual case."

Because of its frequent mechanical failures and high cost of servicing, Volvo cannot be recommended as a wise choice for a new car. Some used Volvos, like the 140 series may make excellent used car buys as long as the pre-1971 models are chosen. Later models have serious problems with the brakes, clutch, chronic stalling, and a general lack of power according to the Center for Auto Safety.

MAJOR RECALL CAMPAIGNS
Volvo of America Corporation

Make	Model	Model Year	Brief Description of Defect (Manufacturer's Corrective Action)	No. of Pages on File	Number of Vehicles Recalled
Volvo	142,144,145 - Fitted with evaporation	1970	Possibility that paper covered hot air hose used for evaporation system may catch on fire.	9	17,000
Volvo	142, 144 145, 164 182, 183	1968 thru 1972	Possibility that throttle control cable inner wire may become frayed and possibly cause throttle to become stuck in partially-open position. If condition exists, vehicle would become difficult to control.	7	39,943
Volvo	142, 144, 145	1973 1974	Possibility that accelerator pedal lever could be of such design that rubber accessory floor mat or vehicle carpet could retard pedal's normal return to idle position.	11	17,523
Volvo	242 244 245	1975	Possibility that insufficient torque was applied during assembly which could allow bolt to become separated from steering shaft coupling. Condition would result in reduction of steering precision and ultimately in loss of steering control.	5	10,000
Volvo	142, 144 & 145	1973	Possibility that fuel supply hose connecting fuel supply pipe to cold start valve (injector) on certain fuel injected models could have incorrect inside diameter which in turn could result in eventual fatigue and possible fuel leakage. If fuel leakage does occur, there is danger of fire starting in engine compartment.	2	12,000

USED CAR PRICES (APPROXIMATE)

Volvo

Model & Body Type	Wholesale Price	Retail Price
1975		
242 4 Cyl. 104" W.B.		
242 2 Door Sedan	2600	3100
244 4 Door Sedan	2700	3200
245 4 Door Station Wagon	2800	3300
164 6 Cyl. 107" W.B.		
4 Door Sedan	3800	4300
1974		
142 SERIES 4 Cyl. 103" W.B.		
142 2 Door Sedan	2000	2400
144 4 Door Sedan	2200	2600
145 5 Door Wagon	2200	2600
164E SERIES 6 Cyl. 107" W.B.		
5 Door Wagon	2900	3400
1973		
142 & 1800 SERIES 4 Cyl. 103"W.B.(Exc. 1800) 96.5"W.B.(1800)		
142E 2 Door Sedan	1500	1800
144E 4 Door Sedan	1600	1900
145 4 Door Wagon	1700	2000
1800 ES Coupe (Auto. Trans.)	2500	3000
164E SERIES 6 Cyl. 107" W.B.		
4 Door Sedan (Auto. Trans.)	2400	2700
1972		
142 & 1800 SERIES 4 Cyl. 103.2"W.B.(Exc.1800) 96.5"W.B.(1800)		
142 2 Door Coupe	1200	1400
142E 2 Door Coupe	1300	1500
144 4 Door Sedan	1200	1400
145 4 Door Wagon	1400	1600
180E Coupe	2000	2300
1800ES Wagon	2200	2500
164 SERIES 6 Cyl. 107.1" W.B.		
4 Door Sedan	1900	2100
164E 4 Door Sedan	2100	2300
1971		
142 & 1800 SERIES 4 Cyl.102.4"W.B.(Exc.1800) 103.1"W.B.(1800)		
142 2 Door Sedan	900	1100
142E 2 Door Sedan	1000	1200
144 4 Door Sedan	900	1100
145 4 Door Wagon	1100	1300
1800 E Coupe	1600	2000
164 SERIES 6 Cyl. 106.3" W.B.		
164 4 Door Sedan	1500	1800

1970

142 & 1800 SERIES 4 Cyl.102.4"W.B.(Exc.1800-96.5"W.B.(1800)

142 2 Door Sedan	500	600
144 4 Door Sedan	500	600
145 4 Door Wagon	700	800
1800 E Coupe	1300	1700
122S 2 Door Sedan	500	700
164 SERIES 6 Cyl. 106.3" W.B.		
164 4 Door Sedan	1000	1300

Other books
By the same author

●

Automobilistes Défendez-vous/
Justice for the Exploited Motorist

●

Roulez sans vous faire rouler, Edition 75

●

Roulez sans vous faire rouler, Edition 76

●

Lemon-Aid, Edition 76

Les Editions Edmonston
1440 St-Catherine West,
Suite 426, Mtl., P.Q.